Speaker's Desk Book of

Quips

Quotes

& Anecdotes

SPEAKER'S

DESK BOOK of

Quips

and ANECDOTES
Quotes

✔ Jacob M. Braude

Prentice-Hall, Inc. ✔ Englewood Cliffs, N. J.

Speaker's Desk Book of Quips, Quotes and Anecdotes, by Jacob M. Braude,
© 1963 by Prentice-Hall, Inc., Englewood Cliffs, N. J.

Library of Congress Catalog Card Number: 63–11784

PRINTED IN THE UNITED STATES OF AMERICA
82402—B & P

I affectionately dedicate this volume
to my three loves:
Adele—my wife
Ann and *Deedy*—my daughters

By the Same Author
and the Same Publisher

SPEAKER'S ENCYCLOPEDIA OF STORIES,
QUOTATIONS AND ANECDOTES

BRAUDE'S SECOND ENCYCLOPEDIA OF STORIES,
QUOTATIONS AND ANECDOTES

BRAUDE'S HANDBOOK OF HUMOR
FOR ALL OCCASIONS

NEW TREASURY OF STORIES
FOR EVERY SPEAKING AND WRITING OCCASION

SPEAKER'S ENCYCLOPEDIA OF HUMOR

LIFETIME SPEAKER'S ENCYCLOPEDIA

EXECUTIVE SPEAKING COURSE

Every man who knows how to read
has it in his power to magnify
himself, to multiply the ways in
which he exists, to make his life
full, significant and interesting.
—ALDOUS HUXLEY

Introduction

The "pre-jump jitters" of the postprandial parachutist have always afflicted even professional speakers. That these qualms alert the speaker and get him on his toes does not abate the misery for me despite a quarter century of experience on such occasions; they must simply be endured. But long ago I learned that an immediate *and appropriate* anecdote could relieve my own tension and the audience's, and get me off to a running start. So I began the years of gathering, sorting, compiling—and filing!—which have resulted in my own desk reference which is presented in this book.

Following a few brief pages of established tips on speech-making, *which I offer partly in self-defense since I listen as well as speak(!),* you will find a copious supply of quotes, quips, and "facts about whales," not only to enhance your own introductions but to refresh the desert passages of public addresses with frequent oases of bright, sharp, and *pertinent* jests and anecdotes. These are the choicest items winnowed from thousands and thousands used during many years of speaking and lecturing. They have been carefully arranged and indexed both by subject and source for your easy and constant use and enjoyment as a basic aid in preparing speeches and addresses.

For, make no mistake, good speeches, even "impromptus," must be carefully planned. In your planning, the *proper* use of this material will really augment your effectiveness.

I do not offer the contents of this book as a substitute for either a thought-provoking topic or a stimulating delivery. These you must develop on your own. But I do offer them as a collection of appropriate illustrations, stories and anecdotes which you might well work judiciously into any talk you choose to give. And I offer them to you with the assurance that they should add immeasurably to the flavor and impact of that talk.

Since the items themselves are all here for you to use, let's first address ourselves for a moment to the basic fundamentals of good speech-making. Let's do this so you may use the items to a maximum advantage.

Here, then, are some suggestions I think you will find extremely useful in putting together for public utterance at almost any sort of gathering—local PTA or Boy Scout meeting or national business or professional group.

Before the Speech

1. *Have something to say.* It is remarkable how many speakers actually steal the time of the audience when they have nothing to say. Unless you know in advance clearly and specifically *why* you are talking and what end you hope to achieve (and a talk given for pure entertainment in itself could well be a justifiable end), you have no business getting up on your feet in the first place. If all speechmakers would adhere strictly to this rule, it probably would cut the number of public speeches in half almost overnight.

2. *Know what you are talking about.* Another large swatch could be cut from the fabric of public speeches were we to eliminate those speakers who simply don't know what they are talking about. Unless one can speak authoritatively on the subject assigned or with adequate advance study and preparation, he has no business speaking at all.

3. *Be prepared.* Usually one receives adequate advance notice that he is expected to speak. When he accepts the invitation, he also accepts the implied obligation to come prepared; there is little excuse for the speaker who bungles his way through a talk only because he didn't take the time to prepare. Actually his audience has a right to take this lack of preparation as an out-and-out insult. If he has not been given sufficient time within which to adequately prepare himself, he should decline the invitation.

4. *Be organized.* It is well to remember that a group of people who have probably overeaten, and who quite possibly wish they were somewhere else, will be trying to follow you through your speech. If you permit your thoughts to wander, theirs will wander too, and you will find it extremely difficult to get them back onto the track that carries your train of thought. It is well, therefore, to keep the organization of the speech as simple and direct as possible. One of the best ways of achieving this end is to work from an outline, carefully conceived and planned in advance. This helps one think logically, and enables an audience to follow the speaker along the route of the speech. I highly recommend this practice. It is a useful, and indeed almost indispensable, tool in constructing a well-organized and effective speech.

5. *Avoid too intimate contact with the audience before speaking.* Many good speakers lose their audience simply because they talk away their speech at the luncheon table or during a chit-chat gathering before

the meeting. It is well to fraternize *after* the talk, but not much in advance. There's always a subconscious holding back later because of the feeling that one has already said the very same things to some who are in the audience.

6. *Check and re-check your schedule—the time and place where you are to appear.* I offer this bit of advice from bitter personal experience: I once arrived in a town in the early morning prepared to speak at a luncheon meeting and to my utter consternation, picked up the local newspaper and read on the front page that I had disappointed an unhappy and (I hope) large audience the day before. That was the day I was due to be there. It takes but a few moments to double-check arrangements a day or two before the talk, and this may save many hours of acute embarrassment. By all means be sure of your schedule and be sure you get to the right place at the right time.

7. *Don't fret.* A good stout case of jitters before a speech is nothing unusual. Most professionals experience a certain amount of stomach-churning before facing an audience, and consider this a good thing because it keeps the speaker on his toes. After a while you learn to live with it! I have, and so can you.

During the Speech

1. *Wake them up—and often.* The speaker who captures audience attention at the start has a better chance of holding it than the one whose approach is from the flank. Thus, a shocking or electrifying start can be a considerable asset to a speaker. This does not necessarily mean one has to start out with a funny story. Audiences have so grown to expect this that unless it is unusually funny and highly appropriate, the result achieved might be exactly the opposite of that sought. What I mean to say here is that what is needed is a vigorous or positive statement or an appropriate anecdote geared directly to winning over the audience right from the start.

2. *Keep it close to home.* Too often a visiting or out-of-town speaker makes no advance effort to acquaint himself with local conditions which he can weave into the body of his talk. It takes but a few minutes to glance at a local newspaper or to pick up a few tidbits of local conversational gossip which, worked into the beginning of a speech, immediately and dramatically bring the audience into intimate relationship with the speaker. This small investment in time will bring large dividends in attention and rapport. Try it; you'll find it pays.

3. *Avoid preachment.* Talk *with* and not *at* your audience. People are preached *at* from the time they are small children and most of us have developed a built-in master control that automatically switches to

"off" when preachment starts. Once again, try to avoid preaching to your audience—unless you are the minister and your audience is your congregation!

4. *Modulate your voice.* Don't blast. The electronic age has given us the public address system, so learn how to use it. Bellowing into it, you're apt to produce an effect that sounds like an air raid warning. The cautious speaker makes sure that he tests the system beforehand. Then when you are reasonably certain that it is under control, try to speak in an easy, conversational manner with a vocal volume that will be adequate to reach the remote corners of the lecture hall. Should you chance to observe people straining to hear you, or conversing in some back row, that should be your cue to increase your volume. If you are speaking without the benefit of a microphone or public address system, then adjust your volume accordingly, but do *not* change your style of delivery. The high school declamation style of delivery may be all right for an interscholastic contest, but day-to-day occasions do not call for the obvious gesture and voice inflection. If you are natural and conversational, you will have a better grip on your audience.

5. *Communicate with your eyes.* Next to your voice, your most effective means of communication is by the use of your eyes. *See* your audience—don't just look at them. See *individuals* and take notice of how they are reacting. Individual members of the audience will know whether or not you are looking *at* them or *through* them, and they will react accordingly.

6. *Take charge from the start—and try to stay in the saddle.* The moment a speaker allows himself to be distracted, he loses his audience and frequently has to fight against heavy odds to regain it. Naturally, in some groups there are bound to be distractions. Children will cry. People may drop things on the floor. There will be late-comers, and others may have to leave before you finish. When these things happen, you are thrown into competition with your audience for attention and it will certainly call for a little more effort on your part to maintain your position of importance.

Don't permit yourself to become flustered or irritated; if you do, your chances of success deteriorate. Extreme irritation produced by hecklers, while rare, cannot be entirely ignored. Try to train yourself to think on your feet fast enough to turn these interruptions to your advantage. This can best be accomplished through good humor, or if circumstances justify, by biting sarcasm. Then again, you may be annoyed by sleepers in your audience. When this situation arises, it is well to take a look at yourself to make sure that either the content of your message or the method of your delivery is responsible for putting these folks to sleep. It may be an indication that already you have talked too long—or if not too long, too uninterestingly; if the former, look for a convenient breaking-off point; if the latter, then inject some thought or story which may dissipate boredom and recapture the attention of the audience.

7. *Speak—don't read.* Nothing is more disconcerting to a speaker than to sense the despair that pervades the atmosphere when an audience realizes that it is being read to by a speaker who really ought to know his subject well enough to be able to speak without a manuscript. The use of notes does not fall into this category and their use is to be encouraged. But if you *must* read from a script, then for heaven's sake don't stick your head into it and read it from beginning to end without even raising your eyes. Throw a glance at the audience every now and then. Try occasional improvisation by throwing in some asides. Tell a story or anecdote *if* it is appropriate. And even if you have it in the manuscript, try to tell it without reading it; that is, if you know it well enough.

8. *Use aids—not distractions.* All sorts of visual aids are now available to help the speaker, but these are distinctly mixed blessings. Although visual aids can be most useful in putting across a talk, care must be taken that they are not allowed to dominate the speech to the point where the spirit is completely lost in the letter. Not all addresses lend themselves to visual aids. Hence you must first ask yourself, "Would the use of visual aids really be of benefit? Would they enhance the talk? Would they make it easier for the audience to understand?" If you conclude that they would, then you must be careful to use the aids only at those points where they make an actual contribution. And even then, one must be careful not to be carried away by gimmicks for the sake of gimmicks. While it is true that visual aids will almost always wake up an audience and guarantee high attention, it is also true that if the attention is to the device itself, the aid becomes a distraction and its usefulness is lost. So, to repeat—use the latest device available but use it knowingly and sparingly and only when you know it will *add* to the talk and not detract.

9. *Talk up—not down.* One of the worst sins a speaker can commit is to underrate or underestimate his audience. People are talked down to so much these days—in advertising, television and books, which frequently cater to the lowest common mental denominator—that they feel flattered to be treated as persons of reasonable intelligence, as thinking human beings—which most of them are. Give them the benefit of the doubt in this respect and avoid the mistake of insulting their intelligence. This will pay large dividends whether your audience is composed of children, society women, or junior or senior executives.

After the Speech

1. *Be careful in answering questions.* A question-and-answer period at the close of a speech usually adds spice to the entire presentation and if the speaker is sufficiently informed on his subject, he should be both willing and anxious to answer questions. If it is known in advance that there will be a Q&A period, the presiding officer should be alerted to keep questions from degenerating into speechmaking by members of the audience. It is well for the speaker to stop a moment and think before undertaking to answer a question, and then proceed to answer it tersely and to the point.

And . . .

finally

before, during and after the speech:

Use pertinent anecdotes and illustrations. There is an art to delivering a story well and to fitting an anecdote or an illustration into the pattern of a speech. You will find it extremely useful:

1. *Not to deliver a story unless first you are sure you enjoy it yourself.* It is too much to expect to arouse enthusiasm in others without oneself being enthusiastic. The first and most exacting test of an illustrative anecdote is this: Does the speaker think it's good? If he doesn't, then it should not be inflicted on the audience.

2. *Tell the story clearly and concisely and keep it simple.* Nothing kills a good story as quickly as overcomplicating it to the point where the audience finds it difficult, if not impossible, to follow. Characters should be held to the minimum and every detail which is not pertinent or essential should be omitted. Simplicity of both style and content is a remarkable virtue in storytelling.

3. *Conclude the story with a strong punch line.* Whatever the story— be it humorous, semi-humorous or serious—punch the point home with a climactic word or phrase, and then, for heaven's sake, *quit.* The speaker should not stumble all over himself with an anticlimactic conclusion. A conclusion there must be; but it should be sharp, cogent and punchy.

4. *Be sure that the story that is being delivered is pertinent to the talk.* Don't tell a story just for the sake of telling one. While it is commendable to have a change of pace, which telling a story affords, the real purpose is to relax the audience and win them over to the speaker's side. But this, too, of itself is not enough. The story to be effective must at all times be pertinent to the thesis of the speech.

5. *Use meaningful material.* This point is a corollary of the previous one: Meaningful material is that which is close enough to the experience of the majority of the audience so that the illustration will make sense to them. Making use of Greek mythology before a meeting of steamfitters or a football analogy to the Ladies Aid Society would both be ineffective ways of conveying an idea. But this does not mean that one must talk down to his audience; rather he should talk to them within their own sphere of knowledge and experience.

One further thought before closing: One learns rules only that he may violate them intelligently. I may have been guilty of preaching to you in this introduction. But my reasons for doing so are the same that may lead you down a similar track: and it is only because of my earnest desire that this material, which I have been collecting the greater part of my life, be used properly that I have permitted myself to be carried away in suggesting how you go about using this volume. I am sure you will enjoy it and that you will get at least a small portion of the pleasure that I have had in compiling it.

Table of Contents

Speaker's Desk Book of

Quips

Quotes

& Anecdotes

Ability

1. Behind an able man there are always other able men.

—*Chinese Proverb*

2. Natural abilities are like natural plants; they need pruning by study.

—Francis Bacon

3. It is a fine thing to have ability, but the ability to discover ability in others is the true test.

—Elbert Hubbard

4. Ever notice that ability is often inversely proportional to the size of the briefcase?

—Don McKechnie

Absence

5. Absence makes the heart go wander.

—C. Harold Crump

6. The absent are always in the wrong.

—*English Proverb*

7. Is not absence death to those who love?

—Alexander Pope

Abuse

8. Use, do not abuse; neither abstinence nor excess renders man happy.

—Voltaire

9. Abuse, if you slight it, will gradually die away; but if you show yourself irritated you will be thought to have deserved it.

—Tacitus

Accomplishment

10. The world expects results. Don't tell others about the labor pains. Show them the baby.

—Arnold Glasow

11. The surest way to get a job done is to give it to a busy man. He'll have his secretary do it.

12. Every really able man, if you talk sincerely with him, considers his work, however much admired, as far short of what it should be. What is this Better, this flying Ideal, but the perpetual promise of his Creator!
—RALPH WALDO EMERSON

Accord

13. You can always tell when a man's well-informed. His views are pretty much like your own.
—LOUIE MORRIS

14. When a man and wife say they always see eye to eye, they are probably the same height.

Achievement

15. No one hates a job well done.

16. Nothing is done. Everything in the world remains to be done or done over.
—LINCOLN STEFFENS

17. Young people tell what they are doing, old people what they have done and fools what they wish to do.
—*French Proverb*

18. Hit the ball over the fence and you can take your time going around the bases.
—JOHN W. RAPER

19. Few things are so embarrassing as watching your boss do what you just said couldn't be done.

20. The penalty of one achievement is the need to achieve again, or the fate of being forgotten or of having your one achievement disparaged.
—F. D. VAN AMBURGH

21. You can't make a place for yourself under the sun if you keep sitting in the shade of the family tree.

22. In the final analysis you should not measure your success by what you *have* accomplished, but by what you *should* have accomplished with your ability.

23. The only people who achieve much are those who want knowledge so badly that they seek it while the conditions are still unfavorable. Favorable conditions never come.

—Clive Staples Lewis

24. The greatest achievements of mankind have been accomplished by two types of men—those who were smart enough to know it could be done, and those too dumb to know it couldn't.

25. Life affords no higher pleasure than that of surmounting difficulties, passing from one step of success to another, forming new wishes and seeing them gratified. He that labors in any great or laudable undertaking has his fatigues first supported by hope and afterward rewarded by joy.

—Dr. Samuel Johnson

Action

26. The best way out is always through.

—Robert Frost

27. One who thinks only in terms of silver cannot act in terms of gold.

28. Keep in mind that even if you're on the right track, you'll get run over if you just sit there.

29. No statue was ever erected to the memory of a man or woman who thought it was best to let well enough alone.

30. Every time a man puts a new idea across, he finds ten men who thought of it before he did—but they only thought of it.

31. Between the great things we cannot do and the small things we will not do . . . the danger is that we shall do nothing.

—Henry G. Weaver

32. To *look* is one thing. To *see* what you look at is another. To *understand* what you see is a third. To *learn* from what you understand is still something else. But to *act* on what you learn is all that really matters, isn't it?

33. Suppose a half dozen of us are seated around the walls of a very dark room. We are told that somewhere in the open middle space is a chair. Who would find it? Not those of us who sat still and philosophized about where chairs are placed in rooms. The fellow who would locate it is the one who'd get up, then walk and stumble around until he discovered it. Nobody ever found anything while sitting down. So, Q.E.D., *don't be afraid to stumble.*

—CHARLES F. KETTERING

Actor–Actors

34. Actors are the only honest hypocrites.

—WILLIAM HAZLITT

35. An actor is a sculptor who carves in snow.

—LAWRENCE BARRETT

36. When a hand comes out and wipes away a tear, that's my reward. The rest goes to the Government.

—VICTOR BORGE

37. Every playwright ought to try acting, just as every public prosecutor should spend some weeks in jail—to find out what he is meting out to others.

—ERICH MARIA REMARQUE

Adaptability

38. A wise man adapts himself to circumstances as water shapes itself to the vessel that contains it.

—*Chinese Proverb*

39. The survival of the fittest is the ageless law of nature, but the fittest are rarely the strong. The fittest are those endowed with the qualifications for adaptation, the ability to accept the inevitable and conform to the unavoidable, to harmonize the existing or changing conditions.

—DANE E. SMALLEY

Admiration

40. Admiration begins where acquaintance ceases.

—DR. SAMUEL JOHNSON

41. None knew thee but to love thee, nor named thee but to praise.

—FITZ-GREENE HALLECK

42. To love is to admire with the heart; to admire is to love with the mind.

—T. GAUTIER

43. In some respects it is better to be admired by those with whom you live than to be loved by them, because admiration is more tolerant than love.

—*Ancient Proverb*

Adversity

44. Adversity makes men, and prosperity makes monsters.

—Victor Hugo

45. When things get rough, remember: it's the rubbing that brings out the shine.

46. Little minds are tamed and subdued by misfortune; but great minds rise above them.

—Washington Irving

47. When you are at the end of your rope, it's a good idea to keep your feet on the ground.

—D. O. Flynn

48. Prosperity is too apt to prevent us from examining our conduct; but adversity leads us to think properly of our state, and so is most beneficial to us.

—Dr. Samuel Johnson

49. Extraordinary afflictions are not always the punishment of extraordinary sins, but sometimes the trial of extraordinary graces.

—Matthew Henry

50. Remember that there is nothing stable in human affairs; therefore avoid undue elation in prosperity, or undue depression in adversity.

—Socrates

51. When the patient Chinese wish to bring their jade ornaments to a fine polish, they place the crude shapes in a leather pouch and shake them together until the rough edges are rounded off. The friction of one against the other smooths an otherwise unsightly mineral.

It takes the hard knocks, the abrasives of daily living, to remove the unsightly bumps in our character in order for us to have a beauty and a life that will never wear out.

Advertising

52. Advertising is like a bombardment; its effectiveness depends upon keeping it up.

53. The business which does not advertise is paying for the space used by its competitor.

54. The man who stops advertising to save money is like the man who stops the clock to save time.

55. A farmer who sent for a book on *How to Grow Tomatoes* wrote the publisher: "The man who writ the ad shoulda writ the book."

56. Advertising came into the world when men became too impatient to wait for Mrs. Jones to tell Mrs. Smith that Brown's pickles were good.

—Roy Durstine

57. If you think advertising doesn't pay—we understand there are twenty-five mountains in Colorado higher than Pike's Peak. Can you name *one?*

58. If a man builds a better mousetrap, the world may beat a path to his door. If he tells the world about it, there will be a four-lane highway.

59. Not one person in a thousand knows a good thing when he sees it, and, without salesmanship and advertising, we would still be a nation of bicyclists.

60. Advertising is the fine art of making you think you have longed for something all your life that you never heard of before.

61. The businessman who does not advertise because somebody said it did not pay, should not believe the world is round because the Ancients said it was flat.

62. Intelligent, effective advertising is not an expense—it is insurance against the loss of business that the other fellow is fighting for.

—F. D. Van Amburgh

63. Robert Q. Lewis used to tell of a friend who had to delay opening his new store on 42nd street in Manhattan.

His "Going Out of Business" signs didn't arrive in time.

64. Two Philadelphia stores which make keys are separated by only a few doors, but they're miles apart in their ability to lure customers. The sign in one reads, "Keys made while you wait"; the other, "Keys made while you watch."

65. By cleverly composed advertisements one may persuade others to think that they want what one wants to sell, but one must be sure that he has not made the double mistake of paying for the advertisement and paying the price of a lost customer.

66. The force of the printed word was feared by P. T. Barnum, the noted circus man, who said: "If you have $10 to put to good use, put one for the article and the other nine for advertising. I can out-talk any man on earth but a printer. The man who can stick type and the next morning talk to a thousand people while I am talking to one is the man I am afraid of—I want him for a friend."

67. An alert businessman advertised in the paper that he would give away 250 shovels to the owners of coal furnaces; as there were no strings attached, the supply was gone in short order.

When the receiver of the shovel used it he found printed on the handle where he couldn't miss seeing it: If you owned one of our modern oil furnaces, you'd be upstairs now instead of shoveling coal.

—ANNA HERBERT

68. America is still young enough for us to wonder what our culture will be like when it reaches full maturity. Someone has suggested that hundreds of years from now the museums will be filled with examples of American package designs of our time, with comic strips as examples of our art, and with advertisements as reflections of our way of living. The advertising business may be contributing more to current American culture—as future historians will see it—than we think.

—ELDRIGE PETERSON,
Publisher, *Printers' Ink*

69. Nearly two hundred years ago, the famous Dr. Samuel Johnson looked about him and concluded: "The trade of advertising is now so near to perfection that it is not easy to propose any improvement. But as every art ought to be exercised in due subordination to the public good, I cannot but propose it as a moral question, whether they do not sometimes play too wantonly with our passions." If Dr. Johnson could only know it, thoughtful people today still ask that same question about the work of some of our modern "hidden persuaders."

Advice

70. The worst men often give the best advice.

—PHILIP J. BAILEY

71. Ask advice of your equals, help of your superiors.

—*Danish Proverb*

72. Advice after an evil is done is like medicine after death.

—*Danish Proverb*

73. Write down the advice of him who loves you, though you like it not at present.

—Ancient Proverb

74. Advice is cheap when it's cheap advice, and cheap advice is dear at any price.

75. Don't be troubled if the temptation to give advice is irresistible; the ability to ignore it is universal.

76. It is peculiar that Presidents don't do better. Heaven knows they receive plenty of advice from the newspapers.

77. The best counsel I can give is the advice a friend wrote to a young man who had just been promoted: "Keep on doing what it took to get started."

—John L. McCaffrey

78. There is sometimes as much ability in knowing how to profit by good advice as in arriving at a correct opinion ourselves.

—François de la Rochefoucauld

Age

79. The best 10 years of a woman's life are between 35 and 36.

80. A woman is as old as she looks to a man who likes to look at her.

—Finley Peter Dunne

81. The young don't know what age is, and the old forget what youth was.

—Seumas MacManus

82. A new broom sweeps well, but an old one is best for the corners.

—*Old Saying*

83. The three ages of man—school tablet, aspirin tablet and stone tablet.

84. Any man who guesses a woman's age correctly ought to be ashamed of himself.

85. When women are asked their age, they usually are shy in more ways than one.

86. It's paradoxical, but when some people begin to show their age they try to hide it.

87. Every girl looks forward to the day when she will be old enough to start getting younger.

88. A girl and an automobile are much alike. A good paint job conceals the years, but the lines tell the story.

89. The beauty of marrying a girl your own age is that she'll always be younger than you are.

—A. A. SCHILLING

90. The woman who tells her age is either too young to have anything to lose or too old to have anything to gain.

—*Chinese Proverb*

91. You'll always stay young if you live honestly, eat slowly, sleep sufficiently, work industriously, worship faithfully—and lie about your age.

92. The people who will always seem young are those who never reveal their rage.

93. When a United States Senator met a prominent ball player, the newspapers referred to the 38-year-old ball player as "aging" and the 42-year-old Senator as "boyish."

94. When friends told John Quincy Adams that a young congressman was ridiculing him on account of his age, which then was approaching eighty, the venerable old politician remarked slyly: "Tell that young man that an ass is older at thirty than a man at eighty years."

—*If Elected, I promise*, by
JOHN F. PARKER (Doubleday & Company, Inc.)

95. Middle age is not the beginning of the end; it is the end of the beginning. . . . In China a person is not accepted as a mature adult until he is 40. Before that time, he is not permitted to speak his mind in the presence of the wise. To the Chinese, the passing of one's 40th year has an exciting meaning rather than a fearsome one.

—ERIC BUTTERWORTH,
"How to Avoid Middle-Age Letdown," *Good Business*

Aging

96. It is magnificent to grow old, if one keeps young.
—HARRY EMERSON
FOSDICK

97. It is foolish to resent growing old. Many are denied the privilege.

98. You don't grow old. When you cease to grow, you *are* old.

99. Everybody wants to live longer but nobody wants to grow old.
—JULES ROSTAND

100. Growing old is no more than a bad habit which a busy man has no time to form.

101. The one great advantage to growing older is that you can stand for more and fall for less.

102. A man is getting old when he doesn't care what the new stenographer looks like—just as long as she can spell.

103. To forget is the secret of eternal youth. One grows old through memory. There's too little forgetting.
—ERICH MARIA REMARQUE

104. The easiest thing for our friends to discover in us, and the hardest thing for us to discover in ourselves, is that we are growing old.
—H. W. SHAW

105. Having a purpose distinguishes those persons who grow old from those who get old. Those who get old suffer from the tragic but preventable disease of boredom. Those who grow old, don't.
—From *The Second Forty Years*, by EDWARD J. STIEGLITZ, M.D. (Published by J. B. Lippincott Company)

106. SEVEN STAGES OF MAN

 1. Milk
 2. Milk, vegetables
 3. Milk, ice cream sodas, candy

4. Steak, Coke, French fries, ham and eggs
5. Frogs' legs, caviar, Crepe Suzettes, champagne
6. Milk and crackers
7. Milk

107. Thoughtless youth sometimes speaks of growing old as if it were a kind of imbecility. But normal aging is not deterioration, which comes of some abuse of living. Normal age is maturity, healthy adjustment, integrity. Years that bring experience establish clear vision, sound judgment, wisdom and charity. These are the elements of happiness.

—GARDNER HUNTING,
"Fruits of Success,"
Weekly Unity

108. Victor Hugo, titan of French literature, was once called upon to comfort a friend who had arrived at his 50th birthday and was depressed at the idea of growing old.

"You should rejoice, my friend," Hugo told him, "that you have escaped your forties, which are the old age of youth, and have at last arrived at the age of fifty, which is the youth of old age."

109. The misfortune is, that body and mind, like man and wife, do not always agree to die together. It is bad when the mind survives the body, and worse still when the body survives the mind; but when both these survive our spirits, our hopes, and our health, this is worst of all.

—CHARLES C. COLTON

110. Nobody grows old by merely living a number of years. People grow old only by deserting their ideals. Years may wrinkle the skin, but to give up interest wrinkles the soul. Worry, doubt, self-distrust, fear and despair . . . these are the long, long years that bow the head and turn the growing spirit back to dust.

Whatever your years, there is in every being's heart the love of wonder, the undaunted challenge of events, the unfailing, childlike appetite for "what next," and the joy and the game of life.

You are as young as your faith, as old as your doubt; as young as your self-confidence, as old as your fear; as young as your hope, as old as your despair. In the central place of your heart, there is a recording chamber; so long as it receives messages of beauty, hope, cheer, and courage, so long you are young. When the wires are all down, and your heart is covered with the snow of pessimism and the ice of cynicism, then—and then only—are you grown old.

—GENERAL DOUGLAS
MACARTHUR

Agnosticism

111. I do not consider it an insult, but rather a compliment to be called an agnostic. I do not pretend to know where many ignorant men are sure—that is all that agnosticism means.

—CLARENCE DARROW, at
Scopes trial, Dayton,
Tennessee, July 13, 1925

112. Robert G. Ingersoll, a notorious agnostic, was noticed by some of his friends when he attended the sermons of a famous Lutheran minister. "What does that mean, Bob," inquired the friends, "you, a convinced agnostic, attend the sermons of an orthodox Christian?"

"You don't understand," replied the lawyer, with a grin. "Yes, I am an agnostic, but once in a while I like to listen to a man who actually believes in what he says!"

Agreeability

113. Complaisance renders a superior amiable, and an inferior acceptable.

—*Old Proverb*

114. If you wish to appear agreeable in society, you must consent to be taught many things which you know already.

—JOHANN KASPAR
LAVATER

115. The person who agrees with everything you say will bear watching in other matters too.

Alertness

116. The day dawns only to those who are awake.

117. Folks who are wide awake during the day can afford to sleep during the night.

118. If you lean back and close your eyes you can see things that happened years ago. But if you want anything to happen now, you'd better keep them open.

—AGNES GUILFOYLE

Alimony

119. Alimony: merely a contraction of "all his money."

120. Alimony is like paying the installments on the car after the wreck.

121. Paying alimony is like pumping gasoline into another man's car.

122. Alimony is a system by which, when two people make a mistake, one of them continues to pay for it.

Altruism

123. The very core of peace and love is imagination. All altruism springs from putting yourself in the other person's place.
—HARRY EMERSON
FOSDICK

124. Money spent on ourselves may be a millstone about the neck; spent on others it may give us wings like eagles.
—RAYMOND HITCHCOCK

125. To see without envy the glory of a rival shows a worthy man; to rejoice at it, a good heart; but to contribute to it, a noble soul.

Ambition

126. The road is always better than the inn.
—MIGUEL DE CERVANTES

127. Where ambition ends happiness begins.
—*Hungarian Proverb*

128. Ambition: a boy's future; a man's past.

129. Reaching high keeps a man on his toes.

130. There is no point high enough that one can say, "This is the peak."
—JASCHA HEIFETZ

131. Ten people hurry to catch up where one hurries to get ahead.

132. The ambitious do not belong to themselves: they are the slaves of the world.

133. A man who is contented with what he has done will never become famous for what he will do.

134. Ambition is a lust that is never quenched, but grows more inflamed and madder by enjoyment.

—Thomas Otway

135. If you aspire to the highest place it is no disgrace to stop at the second, or even third.

—Cicero, *De Oratore*,
80 B.C.

136. Many imagine that the higher you go, the easier the climbing. Don't be governed by that theory unless you have a soft place to fall back into.

—J. L. Boggus

137. A definite ambition is a source of power and promotes achievement. An indefinite ambition causes only restlessness and discontent.

138. Ambition, as you know, can cut two ways: It was ambition and its fueling force, perseverance, which gave us the electric light, the telephone, and all the other servants of our mechanized state. On the other hand, it was ambition which produced Mussolini and Hitler and Khrushchev, without dipping deeper into history for horrendous examples. May we not conclude, therefore, that ambition needs some sort of checkrein to keep it from getting out of hand.

—T. Harry Thompson

America–American

139. This will remain the land of the free only so long as it is the home of the brave.

—Elmer Davis

140. This country, with its institutions, belongs to the people who inhabit it.

—Abraham Lincoln

141. You Americans are strange people. You devote one day out of the year to your mothers and an entire week to pickles.

—*Author Unknown*

142. The real mission of America is to continue to demonstrate that a great people spread over a great country is capable of self-government, and to demonstrate that a republic is the best form of government for people of intelligence and character.

—William W. Cook

143. America does not consist of groups. A man who thinks of himself as belonging to a particular national group in America has not yet become an American.

—WOODROW WILSON

144. America used to be owned by the Indian who hunted and fished so much that he didn't have time to work and worry. Then it was taken over by the superior white man who works and worries so much that he doesn't have time to hunt and fish.

145. Give me your tired, your poor,
   Your huddled masses, yearning to breathe free,
The wretched refuse of your teeming shores,
   Send these, the homeless, tempest-tossed, to me;
I lift my lamp beside the golden door.

—EMMA LAZARUS (Inscription on the Statue of Liberty)

146. Six things we individual Americans can never afford are: Intolerance, indolence, injustice, indifference, intemperance and ingratitude. Whenever any of these enter, they lead to deterioration, defeat, and disaster. Any nation given to them inevitably falls.

—DR. J. RICHARD SNEED

147. Someone once summed up the American character by speculating that if two Americans woke up one day to discover that the earth had been laid waste and that they alone, among all human inhabitants and institutions, had survived, they would respond to the situation by starting a business and then organizing an association.

148. You who have been born in America, I wish I could make you understand what it is like not to be an American—not to have been an American all your life—and then suddenly . . . to be one, for that moment, and forever after. Think of it. One moment you are a citizen of Armenia, a brave and tiny state out of sight beneath the red tide of Russia. The next, you are an American. One moment, you belong with your fathers to a million dead yesterdays. The next, you belong with America to a million unborn tomorrows.

—GEORGE MARDIKIAN

American History

149. Careless students of history sometimes gain an impression the Civil War actually was fought "to free the slaves." It might be well to recall the opening sentence of a letter written by President Lincoln to Horace Greeley, August 22, 1862:

"My paramount purpose in this struggle is to save the Union, and is not either to save or destroy slavery."

150. When the Star-Spangled Banner was first flown at the head of the Continental Army, General Washington described its symbolism as follows:

"We take the stars from heaven, the red from our mother country, separating it by white stripes, thus showing that we have separated from her, and the white stripes shall go down to posterity representing liberty."

Americanism

151. To be a good American means to understand the simple principles on which our nation was founded, to observe them in our daily life and to fight for them. It makes no difference when we came here, whether we landed at Plymouth Rock, streamed through the gates at Ellis Island or landed last week at Idlewild Airport. What counts is what we did for America when we got here.

—NEWBOLD MORRIS

152. Three things constitute Americanism, the recognition of rights, the guarantee of those rights by law, and a system to apply that law. When people are taught by education the value of those three principles of Americanism, our work will be largely accomplished.

—DAVID JAYNE HILL

153. If this Republic is to remain the land of the free and continue to grow in strength and usefulness, both the native and foreign born, who exercise the right of suffrage, must one and all be thoroughly schooled in the meaning of democracy and in the duties and obligations of the citizen.

The Republic cannot endure permanently half American and half hyphenated.

—GEN. JOHN J. PERSHING

Ancestors—Ancestry

154. They brag most of their ancestors who are unworthy of them.
—*Danish Proverb*

155. He who serves his country well has no need of ancestors.
—VOLTAIRE

156. Conceal not the meanness of thy family, nor think it disgraceful to be descended from peasants; for when it is seen that thou art not thyself ashamed, none will endeavor to make thee so.

—Miguel de Cervantes

157. Of all the vanities and fopperies, the vanity of high birth is the greatest. True nobility is derived from virtue, not from birth. Titles, indeed, may be purchased, but virtue is the only coin that makes the bargain valid.

—Robert Burton

Anecdote–Anecdotes

158. One personal anecdote of a man is worth a volume of biography.

—*Ancient Proverb*

159. An anecdote is like a shoe, it must fit; otherwise it pinches.

160. Anecdotes are windows which let light into the topic upon which you are speaking. They are hooks upon which you can hang your thoughts.

161. A well-chosen anecdote frequently reveals a character more happily than an elaborate delineation; as a glance of lightning will sometimes discover what had escaped us in full light.

—Benjamin Disraeli

162. For most public speakers, anecdotes are the plums in the oratorical pudding; without them, the average audience goes away nourished, perhaps, but not exhilarated.

—In Foreword of *Louder
and Funnier,* compiled
by Allan M. Laing
(George Allen & Unwin)

163. A famous author was presented with a copy of a book containing several anecdotes about himself. When acknowledging the gift he wrote: "I enjoyed immensely the stories about myself . . . especially those I hadn't heard before."

Anger

164. Keep cool; anger is not an argument.

—Daniel Webster

165. The best answer to anger is silence.

—*German Proverb*

166. Anger is only one letter short of danger.

167. Steel loses much of its value when it loses its temper.

168. An angry man is again angry with himself when he returns to reason.

—PUBLILIUS SYRUS

169. A man should study ever to keep cool. He makes his inferiors his superiors by heat.

—RALPH WALDO EMERSON

170. When one mistakes the fire of anger for the light of argument, the flame of logic goes out.

—F. D. VAN AMBURGH

171. It wouldn't hurt so much to become angry, except that, for some reason, anger makes your mouth work faster than your mind.

172. Anybody can become angry—that is easy; but to be angry with the right person, and to the right degree, and at the right time, and for the right purpose, and in the right way—that is not within everybody's power and is not easy.

—ARISTOTLE

173. Sister Elizabeth Kenny, the famed Irish-Australian nurse, was once asked by a friend how she managed to stay so constantly cheerful, no matter what the provocation was.

Said a friend: "I suppose you were just born calm and smiling."

"Oh, no," laughed Sister Kenny. "As a girl my temper often got out of bounds. But one day when I became angry at a friend over some trivial matter, my mother gave me advice that I stored in my mind and have called upon for guidance ever since.

"Mother told me, 'Elizabeth, anyone who angers you conquers you.'"

Animal–Animals

174. Brutality to an animal is cruelty to mankind—it is only the difference in the victim.

—ALPHONSE DE
LAMARTINE

175. No civilization is complete which does not include the dumb and defenseless creatures within the sphere of charity and mercy.

—QUEEN VICTORIA

176. I think I could turn and live with animals, they are so placid and self-contained; I stand and look at them long and long. They do not sweat and whine about their condition; they do not lie awake in the dark and weep for their sins; not one is dissatisfied; not one is demented with the mania of owning things.

—WALT WHITMAN

Anthology

177. Originality is not required of an anthologist, but a sense of selection is.

178. He who compiles a book of helpful philosophy out of the material provided by other minds does the world a greater service than he who creates an epic of despair.

—ELLA WHEELER WILCOX

Anticipation

179. A danger foreseen is half avoided.

—*Ancient Proverb*

180. Nothing is so good as it seems beforehand.

—GEORGE ELIOT

181. A man's delight in looking forward to and hoping for some particular satisfaction is a part of the pleasure flowing out of it, enjoyed in advance. But this is afterward deducted, for the more we look forward to anything the less we enjoy it when it comes.

—ARTHUR SCHOPENHAUER

Antique—Antiques

182. The trouble with antique shops is that their prices are so modern.

183. An antique in your home is proof that your ancestors had very well-behaved children.

184. Judging from the amount of furniture brought over on the *Mayflower,* the boat was slightly more than three miles long.

—WILL CRESSY

185. Two kinds of families are likely to have a house full of antique furniture: the kind with money and the kind with kids.

186. About the smartest thing the pioneers of this country did was to stuff their covered wagons full of many things their descendants could wire up for lamps.

Anxiety

187. Anxiety can actually be beneficial. It has a definite effect upon our bodies. It releases the natural store of adrenalin, which, in turn, stimulates us into activity—both mental and physical.

It spurs us on when we must work particularly hard. It keeps us alert when a crisis is threatened. It enables us to fight—or run—in times of danger. If we were not capable of experiencing anxiety—that is, *normal* anxiety—we should be in a sorry state.

188. Freedom from anxiety is not the most important goal in life. . . . The ideas, inventions and techniques that make for social progress, usually have their origin in the minds of anxious or discontented persons. The advances and improvements in the social complex generally come from those who are dissatisfied with its status, can see its shortcomings and have the inclination and ability to devise better methods, materials and equipment. These are the individuals who are alert and anxious about the status quo and who undertake to improve it. . . . Anxiety is necessary for progress.

—CHARLES SELLERS, M.D.

Apology

189. Apology is only egotism wrong side out.

—OLIVER WENDELL HOLMES

190. Eating words has never given me indigestion.

—WINSTON CHURCHILL

191. Apologies only account for that which they do not alter.

—BENJAMIN DISRAELI,
Speech in the House of
Commons, July 28, 1871

192. It's a good idea to keep your words soft and sweet—you never know when you may have to eat them.

193. I detest an apology. The world is full of people who are always making trouble and apologizing for it. If a man respects me, he will not give himself occasion for apology. An offense cannot be wiped out in that way. If it could, we would substitute apologies for hangings. I hope you will never apologize to me; I should regard it as evidence that you had wronged me.

—E. W. HOWE

Appearances

194. If the beard were all, goats could preach.

—*Danish Proverb*

195. A red-nosed man may be a teetotaller, but will find no one to believe it.

—*Chinese Proverb*

196. The world more often rewards the appearances of merit more than it does merit itself.

—François de la
Rochefoucauld

197. A man should never judge by appearances. The woman who looks like a dumb blonde, may really be a bright brunette.

198. We should gain more by letting ourselves be seen such as we are, than by attempting to appear what we are not.

—François de la
Rochefoucauld

Applause

199. A slowness to applaud betrays a cold temper or an envious spirit.

—Hannah More

200. When most the world applauds you, most beware;
'Tis often less a blessing than a snare.

—Edward Young, *Love
of Fame*

Appreciation

201. Next to excellence is the appreciation of it.

—William Makepeace
Thackeray

202. We like those to whom we do good better than those who do us good.

—César Vichard de
Saint Réal

203. It is a matter of the simplest demonstration that no man can be really appreciated but by his equal or superior.

—John Ruskin

204. A greater poverty than that caused by lack of money is the poverty of unawareness. Men and women go about the world unaware of the beauty, the goodness, the glories in it. Their souls are poor. It is better to have a poor pocketbook than to suffer from a poor soul.

—Thomas Dreier

205. As a simple, unpretentious admirer of fine art, Elbert Hubbard derived much pleasure from visiting the great art galleries. One day he was admiring a priceless painting in a New York gallery when a friend chidingly remarked, "Elbert, why do you allow yourself to become so enthused over things you can never afford to own?"

"Harry," replied the sage of East Aurora, "I would rather be able to appreciate things I cannot have than to have things I am not able to appreciate."

206. "If I should die, John, I suppose you would spend a great deal of money for flowers."

"Why, yes, Anna; but whatever put that into your head?"

"Oh, nothing, only I thought that ten-dollar wreaths and fifty-dollar anchors wouldn't make any difference to me when I'm dead, and just a little flower now and then when I'm living would mean so much to me."

"Just a little flower, now and then, while I'm living." The reply of the young wife is eloquent of the heart-hunger of thousands.

Why do we withhold the appreciative word, the loving look, the fervent hand-clasp until the pulses are stilled, the eyes closed, the ears unheeding? Why wait until flowers can no longer give pleasure to shower them upon our near and dear ones?

207. In his autobiography, *Take My Life,* Eddie Cantor tells about the time when Florenz Ziegfeld said to him, "I was just thinking, Eddie, how lucky you are. You have a family, you have money. You're the biggest hit in New York, working for the biggest producer in the world. You've got everything."

Eddie told him he didn't have everything. "I haven't a Rolls-Royce."

He then told Ziegfeld that thirteen years before when he was playing on the New Amsterdam Roof, he used to watch the rich people arrive in Rolls-Royces. He'd dream how it felt to own one. He never had found out.

That was Tuesday. After Saturday matinee, Zieggy said, "Let's have dinner at Dinty Moore's. I'll meet you out front."

Eddie washed the black off his face, met Zieggy, and started down the street. At 46th, against the curb, was a brand-new Rolls-Royce, gray, convertible. An orchid was tied to the handle of the door, and a card.

"Read the card," Flo said. The card said, "Eddie, now you have everything."

After the 1929 crash Ziegfeld was broke. There were no rich angels to provide money for his shows. Eddie went to his office one afternoon and found him with his head in his arms. He said he was broke. He had a show in production but needed $84,000 for scenery, costumes, and expenses.

Eddie rushed to the telephone and called his wife.

"Ida," he said, "don't ask me why. Go to the Bank of Manhattan, take your safe deposit key with you. You'll find a hundred thousand-dollar bills. Bring them to the theatre."

That's how Eddie paid interest on Flo's Rolls-Royce investment.

The show was put on the road. Flo paid back $5,000 a week for 20 weeks. But if he hadn't, Eddie and Ida would not have wept. The relationship that expressed itself in trust, in helpfulness, was the essential element.

Architecture

208. The physician can bury his mistakes, but the architect can only advise his clients to plant vines.

—FRANK LLOYD WRIGHT

209. Architecture is a handmaid of devotion. A beautiful church is a sermon in stone, and its spire a finger pointing to heaven.

—PHILIP SCHAFF

210. In 1875, President Ulysses S. Grant officially opened the bizarre old State Department building with its gingerbread exterior and weird interior decor. A guide, having proudly given Grant a full tour of the building, said, "One thing more, Mr. President. The building is fireproof."

"What a pity," said the President.

Argument–Arguments

211. Fools, for arguments, use wagers.

—*Old Proverb*

212. It takes *you* to make an argument.

213. Arguments out of a pretty mouth are unanswerable.

—JOSEPH ADDISON

214. People generally quarrel because they cannot argue.

—GILBERT K. CHESTERTON

215. A long dispute means both parties are wrong.

—VOLTAIRE

216. Argument seldom convinces anyone against his inclination.
—*Ancient Proverb*

217. Nothing is ever gained by winning an argument and losing a customer.
—C. F. Norton

218. Discussion is an exchange of intelligence. Argument is an exchange of ignorance.
—Bill Gold

219. The only thing worse than being on the wrong side of an argument is being in the middle.
—Pat Kraft

220. Drop the subject when you cannot agree; there is no need to be bitter because you know you are right.
—*Thoughts* (Dodge)

221. In any argument the man with the greater intelligence is always wrong, because he did not use his intelligence to avoid the argument in the first place.

222. Whoever fears to submit any question to the test of free discussion, loves his own opinion more than the truth.
—*Ancient Proverb*

Arrogance

223. Those who are surly and imperious to their inferiors are generally humble, flattering and cringing to their superiors.
—Thomas Fuller

224. Early in life I had to choose between honest arrogance and hypocritical humility. I chose honest arrogance, and have seen no occasion to change, even now.
—Frank Lloyd Wright

Art

225. When art is understood by everybody it will cease to be art.
—Arsène Houssaye

226. Art is more godlike than science. Science discovers; but art creates.
—John Opie

227. There's nothing wrong with a surrealist painting that a good paint remover can't remedy.

228. Opinion on abstract art is divided. Some people think it's a waste of time. Others think it's a waste of paint.

229. Art is a jealous mistress, and if a man has a genius for painting, poetry, music, architecture or philosophy, he makes a bad husband and an ill provider.

—Ralph Waldo Emerson

230. Art is the universal diplomat. We seek French painting, and love the French; we read Russian novels, and love the Russians; we hear German music, and love the Germans. If races and nations communicated with each other solely through the medium of their art, would there be any national prejudice?

—Forbes Watson

231. A miser engaged Hogarth to paint for half price, for his staircase, a representation of the *Destruction of Pharaoh's Host in the Red Sea.* Hogarth painted the canvas red all over, and when the astonished purchaser asked, "Where are the Israelites?" he answered, "They are all gone over." "Where are the Egyptians?" "They are all drowned."

Art, Modern

232. If you don't understand modern art, and it frightens you— just think what it must do to those who do understand it.

233. By mechanical means, in modern times, an image is now fixed on a photographic plate in a few seconds—an image more precise and exact than it is humanly possible to draw—and so with the advent of photography disappeared the necessity for exact reproduction in art.

—Henri Matisse

Artifice

234. Treacheries and acts of artifice only originate in a want of ability.

—François de la
Rochefoucauld

235. The ordinary employment of artifice is the mark of a petty mind; and it almost always happens that he who uses it to cover himself in one place, uncovers himself in another.

—François de la
Rochefoucauld

Artist–Artists

236. The great artists of the world are never Puritans, and seldom even ordinarily respectable.

—HENRY L. MENCKEN

237. Every portrait that is painted with feeling is a portrait of the artist, not of the sitter.

—OSCAR WILDE

238. The artist and the scientist have much in common. They are profoundly interdependent. They share the creative mind, the irresistible undying need to explore and to know. Perhaps the artist goes one step further. For him the need is also to understand, and understanding, to explain mankind, even to itself.

—PEARL S. BUCK

239. The value of the artist lies in the fact that he asserts a sense of order, of the power of the human spirit, into the sordid conflict of our everyday lives. He sees all life as a battle between chaos and order. It is the vision of order, of conquest of the obstacles and complications of living, that inspires men with new energy and purpose. Life is inconceivable without this vision of purpose.

—COLIN WILSON

240. The artist is one who is urged on by instinctive needs which are too clamorous; he longs to attain to honor, power, riches, fame and the love of woman; but he lacks the means of achieving these gratifications. So, like any other with an unsatisfied longing, he turns away from reality, and transfers all his interest, and all his libido too, on to the creation of his wishes in the life of phantasy.

—SIGMUND FREUD

241. A great musician one day visited the painter Matisse at his home on the shores of the Mediterranean. He asked Matisse: "What is your inspiration?"

"I grow artichokes," replied Matisse. "Every morning I go into the garden and watch these plants. I see the play of light and shade on the leaves and I discover new combinations of colors and fantastic patterns. They inspire me. Then I go back into the studio and paint."

Surely, if artichokes can provide inspiration for a great artist, the common things of life that we so often overlook must hold much of inspiration for us.

—JOHN H. CROWE, *You Can Master Life*

Assistance

242. I not only use all the brains I have but all I can borrow.

—WOODROW WILSON

243. Facts are worthless to a man if he has to keep running to somebody else for advice on how to use them.

—SVEN HALLA

244. When General Lee heard of Stonewall Jackson's wound, he said, "He is better off than I am. He has lost his *left* arm, but I have lost my *right* one."

—ALBERT FREDERICK
POLLARD

245. The truest help we can render an afflicted man is not to take his burden from him, but to call out his best energy, that he may be able to bear the burden.

—PHILLIPS BROOKS

Associate—Associates

246. When a dove begins to associate with crows its feathers remain white but its heart grows black.

—*German Proverb*

247. In business, as most of it is constituted today, a man becomes valuable only as he recognizes the relation of his work to that of all his associates.

248. Associate yourself with men of good quality if you esteem your own reputation; for 'tis better to be alone than in bad company.

—GEORGE WASHINGTON

Atheism

249. An atheist is one who hopes the Lord will do nothing to disturb his disbelief.

—FRANKLIN P. JONES

250. Nobody talks so constantly about God as those who insist that there is no God.

—HEYWOOD BROUN

251. A good question for an atheist is to serve him a fine dinner, and then ask him if he believes there is a cook.

252. Heinrich Heine, brilliant German-Jewish poet of the last century, has left us this quip exposing the silliness of atheism: "In Frankfurt I met a watch that did not believe in the existence of watchmakers."

—RABBI ELY E. PILCHIK,
Jeshurun Sermons
(Bloch)

253. When William Quayle, the gifted Methodist bishop, heard that his friend, John Burroughs, famous naturalist who thought himself an unbeliever, had died, he said, "Poor John, he loved the garden, but he never met the Gardener."

—From "Priming the
Preacher's Pump,"
by DAVID A. MAC-
LENNAN in *Church
Management*

Atomic Age

254. The world started with Adam and may end with *atom.*

—JACK HERBERT

255. One of the most likely uses of atomic energy seems to be the cooking of the world's goose.

—D. O. FLYNN

256. Atomic era advice: Men who are smart enough to destroy the world shouldn't be dumb enough to do it.

—DAN KIDNEY, *Scripps-
Howard Newspapers*

257. One of the tragedies of our day is that we've succeeded in splitting the atom before acquiring the wisdom to unite humanity.

258. Our atomic age is like a knife: in the hands of a surgeon it can save a life; in the hands of an assassin it can take one. But to blame the knife is ridiculous.

—DAVID SARNOFF in
Guideposts

259. Our problem, now, is not to make thermo-nuclear bombs. Our problem is to create a moral and intellectual atmosphere that will prevent their use. The first task is scientific; the second is definitely humanistic.

—BURT GARNETT

260. Asked by a Congressional Committee if there was any defense against the weapon, Dr. Robert Oppenheimer, who supervised the creation of the first atomic bomb, answered "Certainly," and added softly, "the defense is peace."

261. If we are to survive the Atomic Age, we must have something to live by, to live on, and to live for. We must stand aside from the world's conspiracy of fear and hate and grasp once more the great monosyllables of life: faith, hope, and love. Men must live by these if they live at all under the crushing weight of history.

—O. P. KRETZMANN, D.D.

262. When people accuse science of irresponsibility, for fooling with machines too frightening to live with, they forget that it's the other side of the equation that is really at fault. It is ignorance and indifference that are dangerous, not knowledge and dedication. In the atomic age these incompatible bedfellows can no longer sleep side by side. "Wise up or blow up" is the crude formula by which we must live.

—Reprinted by permission of Dodd, Mead & Company from *Atoms for Peace*, by DAVID O. WOODBURY. Copyright, 1955, by David O. Woodbury

Attire

263. Always dress to please the man—even if you haven't met him yet.

264. Most women dress on the theory that a man can't think while he's looking.

—DAN BENNETT

265. The way the modern girl dresses, she's obviously a firm believer in "never leave off tomorrow what you can leave off today."

266. Those who make their dress a principal part of themselves, will, in general, become of no more value than their dress.

—WILLIAM HAZLITT, *Political Essays*

Attitude–Attitudes

267. Success or failure in business is caused more by mental attitudes than by mental capacities.

—WALTER DILL SCOTT

268. No condition or set of circumstances is in itself a calamity to be feared. It is our reaction to it that makes it a "waterloo" or a field of triumph.

Auction–Auctions

269. It is only an auctioneer who can equally and impartially admire all schools of art.

—Oscar Wilde

270. Auctioneers, before they begin, hang out red flags, and that should be sufficient warning to anyone that "danger's ahead!"

271. My wish is that my drawings, my prints, my curiosities, my books—in a word, those things of art which have been the joy of my life—shall not be consigned to the cold tomb of a museum, and subjected to the stupid glance of the careless passer-by; but I require that they shall be dispersed under the hammer of the auctioneer, so that the pleasure which the acquiring of each one of them has given me shall be given again, in each case, to some inheritor of my own tastes.

—Will of Edmond de
Goncourt, 1896

Authority

272. Who holds a power but newly gained is ever stern of mood.

—Aeschylus

273. Authority without wisdom is like a heavy ax without an edge, fitter to bruise than polish.

—Anne Bradstreet

274. Authority and responsibility are like the bow and arrow, the hammer and the anvil, rain and sunshine, man and woman—each useless without the other.

Authorship

275. The worst miser is the learned man that will not write.

—Austin O'Malley

276. If you want to know who your friends are, try writing a book.

277. The ink of the scholar is more sacred than the blood of the martyr.

—Mohammed

278. Every good journalist has a novel in him—which is a good place for it.

—Russell Lynes

279. An autobiography usually reveals nothing bad about its writer except his memory.

280. The art of writing is the art of applying the seat of the pants to the seat of the chair.

—MARY HEATON VORSE

281. A woman who writes commits two sins: she increases the number of books, and decreases the number of women.

—ALPHONSE KARR

282. He who has published an injurious book sins in his very grave, corrupts others while he is rotting himself.

—ROBERT SOUTH

283. Your manuscript is both good and original; but the part that is good is not original, and the part that is original is not good.

—DR. SAMUEL JOHNSON

284. Many books require no thought from those who read them, and for a very simple reason:—they made no such demand upon those who wrote them.

—CHARLES C. COLTON

285. The most original authors are not so because they advance what is new, but because they put what they have to say as if it had never been said before.

—JOHANN WOLFGANG VON GOETHE

286. The most discourging thing about writing TV gags is to spend hours perfecting one, only to find out that some wise guy stole it from you 100 years ago.

287. He came from a family of writers. His sister wrote books that no one would read. His brother wrote songs that no one would sing. His mother wrote plays no one would see. His father wrote checks no one would cash.

288. Hosts of people say, "I'd just love to be a writer." Would they? No! They mean they would like to see their names in print. Hardly one person in a thousand wants to do the work of a writer—a life of hard study and exhausting application.

—ALBERT EDWARD WIGGAM

289. Carl Sandburg, asked to confirm the rumor that he had been commissioned by a magazine to write another Chicago poem: "Ordering a man to write a poem is like commanding a pregnant woman to give birth to a red-headed child. You can't do it—it's an act of God!"

290. I do not know a better training for a writer than to spend some years in the medical profession.

I suppose that you can learn a good deal about human nature in a solicitor's office; but there on the whole you have to deal with men in full control of themselves. They lie perhaps as much as they lie to the doctor, but they lie more consistently, and it may be that for the solicitor it is not so necessary to know the truth.

—W. Somerset Maugham

Automation

291. Automation will not be really complete until the machine that makes the product also makes money to buy it.

292. Automation is bringing a new kind of fringe benefit. Workers in an automated British oil refinery see so few human beings that they have demanded "lonely money."

293. Don't be too worried about these mechanical brains making man obsolete. Like all other great inventions—from the cigarette machine to TV—they still need somebody standing by to kick them when they refuse to work.

294.
Within her automatic home
The housewife lolls and lingers;
No longer plagued by dishpan hands;
Instead push-button fingers.

295. Automation has many advantages over human labor, but management experts tell us that automation costs may equal or exceed the direct labor bill. The big cost, and one that cannot be avoided, is depreciation. Actually, a million dollar machine installed this month may be completely outmoded by a new machine a year hence.

296. Mental tension is supplanting muscular fatigue as the chief complaint of workers in newly automated factories, according to a recent study by Yale University. New machines have eliminated drudgery but the strain of watching and controlling them is said to make workers "jumpy."

Jobs are physically easier, but the worker now takes home worries instead of an aching back.

—HOMER BIGART, *New York Times*

297. Complicated machines have a habit of frightening men. Inventors have been persecuted, progressive managements have been criticized, and the machines themselves have been blamed for all manner of evils. Laws have been proposed which would outlaw machines because they would throw men out of work. This is ridiculous, for statistics show that the higher the degree of mechanization the higher the total labor force.

—R. BOWLING BARNES

298. Perhaps you have heard that automation will some day put an end to most human labor. Yet engineer John Diebold, who coined the word, thinks the result will be "an enormous demand for trained personnel to maintain the complex machines." A McGraw-Hill survey indicated that 40% of companies with automation require more skilled maintenance men than before. General Mills named 23 skilled jobs created by automation. A college degree wasn't required for any of them. Special training was. In the world of automation there may be almost no place left for unskilled labor.

—JERRY KLEIN and BILL FISHER, JR., *You Didn't Go to College?*

Automobile–Automobiles

299. Two ways of getting a lasting finish for motor cars: lacquer or liquor.

300. Even though the automobile has replaced the horse, it is a good thing for the driver to stay on the wagon.

301. The trouble is that the car of tomorrow is being driven on the highway of yesterday by the driver of today.

302. An automobile is a machine with four wheels, a motor, and not quite enough seats, which enables people to get about with great rapidity and ease to places they never bothered going to before and where they'd just as soon not be now, because now that they're there, there's no place to park.

—ELINOR GOULDING SMITH

Avarice. See *also* Greed

303. Avarice is always poor.

—Dr. Samuel Johnson

304. Avarice is the vice of declining years.

—George Bancroft

305. It is sheer madness to live in want in order to be wealthy when you die.

—Juvenal

Aviation

306. New planes are so fast you don't have time to get acquainted with the hostess.

307. A man soon will be able to get clear around the world in two hours—one hour for flying and the other to get out to the airport.

Bachelor—Bachelorhood

308. A man who's lucky in love is called a bachelor.

309. A bachelor with money to burn soon meets his match.

310. A bachelor is one who enjoys the chase but does not eat the game.

311. The problem many bachelors face is whether to stay single or knot.

—Hal Chadwick

312. Bachelor: A fellow who usually wants one single thing in life —himself.

313. He never knew what happiness was until he got married— and then it was too late.

314. Don't pity the unmarried man—he can keep his bachelor quarters until they become dollars.

—Leo Sanford

315. A bachelor is a souvenir of some woman who found a better one at the last minute.

316. A bachelor has been defined as a man who will get married as soon as he can find a girl who will love him as much as he does.

317. It is admitted that married men have better halves, but it is claimed that bachelors have better quarters.

318. A man doesn't know how to live until a woman has taught him, and then it often happens he prefers to live alone.

319. Rich bachelors should be heavily taxed. It is not fair that some men should be happier than others.

—OSCAR WILDE, *In Conversation*

320. WHY WOMEN LIKE BACHELORS

A married man looks comfortable and settled and finished; he looks at a woman as if he knew all about her.

A bachelor looks unsettled and funny and he always wants to be running around seeing things.

He looks at a woman sharply and then looks away and then looks back again, so she knows he is thinking about her and wondering what she is thinking about him.

Bachelors are always strange, and that's why women like them.

—JAMES STEPHENS

321. Among famous bachelors was Horace Walpole, who satirized women for more than half a century (although it is said he fell in love during his later years but could not find courage to ask the burning question). Beethoven was also a bachelor, while Hans Andersen, Voltaire, Macaulay and Michelangelo had their own reasons for remaining single.

There were others, too, who would have married, but circumstances would not allow them. Charles Lamb never married because of an ailing sister, while Pope was too much devoted to his mother.

Obesity was the reason why Gibbon remained a bachelor; so fat was he that on one occasion when he fell down on his knees to propose, he could not rise and had to be helped up by two attendants!

Baldness

322. A bald head is no disgrace if the baldness is confined to the outside.

323. Experience is a comb which nature gives to men when they are bald.

324. There is nothing more contemptible than a bald man who pretends to have hair.

—MARTIAL, *Epigrams*

325. It still is being claimed only "he-men" get bald; that bald-headed men are far more virile than those who have plenty of hair. Also that bald-headed men are the best lovers. That is strictly the bunk. It is all propaganda which has been circulated for centuries but never proved. It was started by Hippocrates, the father of medicine. Hippocrates was bald-headed. Fellows with plenty of hair always were stealing his girl friends. Especially the fellows with curly hair. So Hippocrates began to circulate the claim that bald-headed men were the real "he-men," greatest lovers, etc.

—E. V. DURLING, King
Features Syndicate

Bank–Banks–Banking

326. Bankers never die; they just lose interest.

327. His wife's use of a joint bank account may cause a man to lose his balance.

328. Joint checking account: a device to allow the wife to beat her husband to the draw.

329. The retired general obtained a seat on the board of a bank. Every day the chief cashier brought him a statement of the bank's financial position. The soldier would glance at it, open a drawer in his desk, examine a document in the drawer, refer to the statement again, and then dismiss the chief cashier with a brisk nod.

This procedure was repeated daily for ten years. Then the general died. Consumed by curiosity, the chief cashier hurried to the general's desk, opened the drawer and read the document which it contained. It was short and to the point. It merely said: "The column nearest the window is the credit one."

Beauty

330. Rare is the union of beauty and modesty.

—JUVENAL

331. When the woman won't take time, time takes the woman.

—MINNA THOMAS ANTRIM

332. Concealing beauty is the cleverest way of revealing it.

333. Beauty without modesty is like a flower broken from its stem.

334. Beauty is worse than wine; it intoxicates both the holder and the beholder.

—ZIMMERMAN

335. People who say that you cannot fool nature, have never watched a beauty shop operator at work.

336. Beauty is the first gift Nature gives to woman, and the first she takes from her.

—MÉRÉ

337. There are no ugly women; there are only women who do not know how to look pretty.

—A. P. BERRYER

338. Dean Swift proposed to tax beauty, and to leave every lady to rate her own charms; he said the tax would be cheerfully paid and very productive.

—FREDERIC SAUNDERS

339. There are two kinds of beauty—loveliness and dignity. We ought to regard loveliness as the quality of woman, dignity that of man.

—CICERO, *De officiis*

340. Beauty depends a lot on geography. For example, we admire white, flashing teeth, whether they be Nature's own or selected out of a catalog. East Indian tribesmen prefer theirs black. Some of them have tooth blackeners which are passed around as they are needed.

341. When they hanged Helen of Troy the executioners were blindfolded because, on two previous occasions when threatened with death the famed woman's marvelous beauty had caused her enemies to falter and rebel at the deed.

Begging

342. It is a beggar's pride that he is not a thief.

—*Japanese Proverb*

343. Never stand begging for that which you have the power to earn.

—MIGUEL DE CERVANTES

344. Beggars should be abolished. It annoys one to give to them, and it annoys one not to give to them.

—FRIEDRICH WILHELM NIETZSCHE, *Thus Spake Zarathustra*

Beginning–Beginnings

345. He that climbs a ladder must begin at the first round.
—WALTER SCOTT, *Kenilworth*

346. Always begin somewhere. You can't build a reputation on what you are going to do.

347. The world knows well that whoever takes one step will take more: it is important, then, to take the first step well.
—BERNARD LE BOVIER DE FONTENELLE

Behavior

348. Always live as if you expected to live always.

349. Let us endeavor so to live that when we come to die even the undertaker will be sorry.
—MARK TWAIN

350. Man may not live by bread alone, but many try to get along on crust.

351. Live with men as if God saw you; converse with God as if men heard you.
—SENECA

352. It pays a girl to remember that although one swallow never makes a summer, one lark often makes a fall.
—CY N. PEACE

353. When a man forgets himself he usually does something that everyone else remembers.

354. Statistics show that there are three ages when man misbehaves—young, old and middle.

355. Maybe there is "no such thing as a bad boy," but there are a lot of bad things some of the "good" boys are doing.

356. The only trouble with being able to read a woman like a book is you're liable to forget your place.

357. The means some people use in getting ahead in this world probably means they are getting behind in the next.

358. If just knowing the difference between right and wrong were enough, every jail in the country would be empty.

359. No one knows about your integrity, your sincerity, your talent or your goodness unless you give out samples in action.

360. It is worth remembering that you cannot whitewash yourself by blackening others; that success comes in cans, failure in can'ts; that a day of worry is more exhausting than a week of work; that cheerfulness is what greases the axles of the world; that luck needs a "P" on it to make it worthwhile.

361. Your greatness is measured by your kindness—your education and intellect by your modesty—your ignorance is betrayed by your suspicions and prejudices—your real caliber is measured by the consideration and tolerance you have for others.

—WM. J. H. BOETCKER

362. During the London blitz I remarked to newspaper friends on the superb behavior of the British people. They told me, "They did not, initially, behave so well. There was a great deal of panic, and egotism, as each sought to save himself."

"What changed this?" I inquired.

"We helped a lot," I was told. "We made it a policy to report only acts of courage and helpfulness. When people thought everybody but themselves was behaving well, they behaved well too."

—DOROTHY THOMPSON, "Is
Morality 'Normal'?"
Ladies' Home Journal

Belief

363. To believe with certainty we must begin by doubting.

—KING STANISLAS I of
Poland

364. What can be more foolish than to think that all this rare fabric of heaven and earth could come by chance, when all the skill of science is not able to make an oyster.

—JEREMY TAYLOR

365. A thing that you sincerely believe in, cannot be wrong. Because belief does not come at will. It comes only from the Holy Ghost within. Therefore a thing you really believe in cannot be wrong.

—D. H. LAWRENCE, *Studies in Classical American Literature*

Betting

366. The less you bet, the more you lose when you win.

367. Betting is a fool's argument, but it's very convincing when you win.

—*Ancient Proverb*

368. It may be that the race is not always to the swift nor the battle to the strong—but that's the way to bet.

—DAMON RUNYON

Bible, The

369. *Little girl:* "Why does your Granny read her Bible so much?" *Little boy:* "I dunno—I think she's cramming for her finals."

370. In Denver, the members of a Sunday-school class were asked to set down their favorite Biblical truths. One youngster laboriously printed: "Do one to others as others do one to you."

—LEE OLSON in the Denver *Post*

371. I thoroughly believe in a university education for both men and women, but I believe a knowledge of the Bible without a college course is more valuable than a college course without the Bible.

—WILLIAM LYON PHELPS

372. I am of the opinion that the Bible contains more true sublimity, more exquisite beauty, more pure morality, more important history, and purer strains of poetry and eloquence, than can be collected from all other books, in whatsoever age or language.

—SIR WILLIAM JONES

373. In the Bible there is more that finds me than I have experienced in all other books put together; the words of the Bible find me at greater depths of my being; and whatever finds me brings with it an irresistible evidence of its having proceeded from the Holy Spirit.

—SAMUEL T. COLERIDGE

374. The Bible is a library. We do not enter a library and start reading every book on every shelf. Books are not all of equal importance. We read with a purpose and select accordingly. We have certain well-defined aims in mind before we begin. So with the Bible.

—HARRIS FRANKLIN RALL,
Professor Emeritus, Garrett Biblical Institute,
Together

375. The Bible has been the *Magna Charta* of the poor and of the oppressed. Down to modern times, no state has had a constitution in which the interests of the people are so largely taken into account; in which the duties, so much more than the privileges, of rulers are insisted upon, as that drawn up for Israel in Deuteronomy and Leviticus. Nowhere is the fundamental truth, that the welfare of the state, in the long run, depends upon the righteousness of the citizen, so strongly laid down. The Bible is the most democratic book in the world.

—THOMAS H. HUXLEY

376. When John Wanamaker was eleven years old he purchased a Bible. In later years he said of this purchase: "I have, of course, made large purchases of property in my time, involving millions of dollars, but it was as a boy in the country, at the age of eleven years, that I made my greatest purchase. In the little mission Sunday School I bought a small red leather Bible for $2.75, which I paid for in small installments. Looking back over my life I see that that little red Book was the foundation on which my life has been built, and the thing which has made possible all that has counted in my life. I know now that it was the greatest investment and the most important and far-reaching purchase I ever made."

377. The Swedish Nightingale, Jenny Lind, made a great success as an operatic singer, and money poured into her purse. Yet she left the stage when singing her best and never went back to it. She must have missed the money, the fame, and the applause of thousands, but she was content to live in privacy.

Once an English friend found her sitting on the steps of a bathing machine on the sea sands, with a Lutheran Bible on her knee, looking out into the glory of a sunset.

They talked, and the conversation drew near to the inevitable question: "Oh, Madame Goldschmidt, how is it that you ever came to abandon the stage at the very height of your success?"

"When, every day," was the quiet answer, "it made me think less of this (laying a finger on the Bible) and nothing at all of that (pointing to the sunset), what else could I do?"

Bigness

378. A business is too big when it takes a week for gossip to go from one end of the office to the other.

379. The dinosaur's eloquent lesson is that if some bigness is good, an over-abundance of bigness is not necessarily better. If our trend to bigness continues unrestrained, American society as we know it may be infinitely damaged. For we will move inevitably from free-enterprise to *socialized capitalism.* And our political and personal freedoms will suffer as well. We are already moving down a road toward security rather than risk, toward belonging rather than beginning, toward adjustment rather than enterprise. The road may seem broad and pleasant. . . . But what will we find at the end . . . a society that is static rather than dynamic? . . . a people who are led, rather than leading? . . . a nation grown safe and sterile and feeble at its source?

—Eric Johnston, address-
ing National Defense
Transport Association

Blame

380. A bad workman quarrels with his tools.

—*Old Proverb*

381. Who allows oppression shares the crime.

—Charles Darwin, *Loves
of the Plants*

382. He is foolish to blame the sea who is shipwrecked twice.

—Publilius Syrus

383. If something goes wrong, it is more important to talk about who is going to fix it than who is to blame.

—Francis J. Gable,
quoted in *Forbes*

Bluff—Bluffing

384. Many people reach the heights by putting up a big bluff.

385. A couple of men made an automobile trip to the Pacific Coast and camped out along the way. In Arizona they arrived late on a moonlit night at a clearing where there were several other tourist parties camped in tents—all of whom had already retired.

As the two men put up their own tent, they noticed a pair of large, rugged hob-nailed boots sticking out conspicuously from under the flaps of one of the tents. They wondered what kind of man could fill boots of that size, so they got up early to find out.

From the tent from which the boots protruded, two comely young women came out and busied themselves taking down the tent and loading their luggage. There was no sign of any giant man. The last thing the girls loaded was the formidable pair of oversized men's boots.

If you haven't real strength yourself, it may be wise to put up a bluff.

Boastfulness

386. When you start crowing you stop growing.

—Albert B. Lord

387. Don't brag; it isn't the whistle that pulls the train.

—T. Harry Thompson

388. He that boasts of his own knowledge proclaims his ignorance.

—Old Proverb

389. They who boast most, generally fail most, for deeds are silent.

—Old Proverb

390. He who prides himself upon wealth and honor hastens his own downfall.

—Lao Tzu

391. When a man boasts about what he'll do tomorrow we like to find out what he did yesterday.

392. The man who boasts that he never made a mistake has a wife who did.

393. It is harder to be poor without complaining than to be rich without boasting.

—Chinese Proverb

394. A man with unusual knowledge is like a woman with a fancy petticoat, it's hard to forego the temptation of displaying some of it.

395. To brag little—to show well—to crow gently, if in luck— to pay up, to own up, and to shut up, if beaten, are the virtues of a sporting man.

—Dr. Oliver Wendell Holmes, *The Autocrat*

Book–Books

396. A wicked book cannot repent.

—*Old Proverb*

397. A room without books is like a body without a soul.

—Cicero

398. The newest books are those that never grow old.

—Holbrook Jackson

399. Some novels you just can't put down. Others you don't dare to if the children are around.

400. Seems like all you need for a best seller is a beautiful girl on the cover and no cover on the beautiful girl.

401. A book is a mirror: If an ass peers into it, you can't expect an apostle to look out.

—G. C. Lichtenberg

402. People seldom read a book which is given to them. The way to spread a work is to sell it at a low price.

—Dr. Samuel Johnson

403. "You certainly have a fine collection of books, but they're a bit crowded. You ought to get more shelves."
"How do you borrow shelves?"

404. It is just those books which a man possesses, but does not read, which constitute the most suspicious evidence against him.

—Victor Hugo, *Toilers of the Sea*

405. It is one of the misfortunes of life that one must read thousands of books only to discover that one need not have read them.

—Thomas De Quincey

406. To desire to have many books, and never to use them, is like a child that will have a candle burning by him all the while he is asleep.

—Henry Peacham, *The Compleat Gentleman,* 1622

407. Truly, each book is as a ship that bears us away from the fixity of our limitations into the movement and splendor of life's infinite ocean.

—Helen Keller

408. There is no such thing as a worthless book, though there are some far worse than worthless; no book that is not worth preserving, if its existence may be tolerated; as there may be some men whom it may be proper to hang, but none who should be suffered to starve.

—SAMUEL T. COLERIDGE

409. One would imagine that books were like women, the worse for being old; that they have a pleasure in being read for the first time; that they open their leaves more cordially; that the spirit of enjoyment wears out with the spirit of novelty; and that, after a certain age, it is high time to put them on the shelf.

—WILLIAM HAZLITT

410. The lover of books is a miner, searching for gold all his life long. He finds his nuggets, his heart leaps in his breast; he cannot believe in his good fortune.

Traversing a slow page, to come upon a lode of the pure shining metal is to exult inwardly for greedy hours. It belongs to no one else; it is not interchangeable.

—KATHLEEN NORRIS

411. A prominent author is quoted as saying, "I like pocket books that sell for 25 cents as opposed to hardcover books that sell for $3. Hardcover books break up friendships. You loan a hardcover book to a friend and, when he doesn't return it, you get mad at him. It makes you mean and petty. But 25-cent books are different. Nobody minds giving them away. They make people generous, kind and friendly. Paperback books bring people together; hardcover books break up happy relationships."

412. A young lady was at a loss to know what to select for her vacation reading. The bookstore salesman came to her relief with the suggestion: "Here's something just out and very entertaining, the *Kentucky Cardinal.*"

"No," said the customer with a shake of her head, "I don't care for religious subjects."

"But," protested the salesman, "this *Kentucky Cardinal* is a bird."

"I don't care anything about his private life either," persisted the young lady.

413. There is a sad tale told of a diffident young man who was much worried because he did not seem able to get on with the opposite sex, and thought he must try to educate himself in this important regard.

He went to a bookshop, but did not like to tell the superior young lady what he wanted, and asked whether he could look around, and perhaps find the sort of book he was after. Eventually he spied, on a high shelf, the book he thought would help him: a big volume called *How to Hug*. He paid a stiff price, carried it home, and, after his evening meal, settled himself in his armchair, all agog to learn.

It was then he discovered that what he had bought was part of an encyclopedia.

Boredom

414. Sometimes the best way to liven up the party is to leave.

415. One way a girl can stop a man from making love to her is to marry him.

416. Boredom is a vital problem for the moralist, since at least half of the sins of mankind are caused by the fear of it.
—BERTRAND RUSSELL

417. People always get tired of one another. I grow tired of myself whenever I am left alone for ten minutes, and I am certain that I am fonder of myself than anyone can be of another person.
—GEORGE BERNARD SHAW

Borrowing

418. He who borrows sells his freedom.
—*German Proverb*

419. Close friends are sometimes difficult to touch.

420. It is a fraud to borrow what we are unable to repay.
—PUBLILIUS SYRUS

421. One trouble with the chronic borrower is that he keeps everything but his word.

422. "I'm sorry, George, but I make it a rule never to lend money. It ruins a friendship."

"Don't worry about that; we never were what you would call very good friends."

Bravery

423. Valor grows by daring, fear by holding back.
—PUBLILIUS SYRUS

424. People glorify all sorts of bravery except the bravery they might show on behalf of their nearest neighbors.

—GEORGE ELIOT

Brevity

425. The more ideas a man has the fewer words he takes to express them. Wise men do not talk to kill time, they talk to save it.

426. A canon, invited to preach at St. Paul's Cathedral in Dean Inge's day, told the Dean that he was going to give the congregation "a dose of the milk of human kindness."

"Condensed, I trust," said Inge.

427. It was Joseph Pulitzer who offered the following advice on writing to editorial writers, columnists and reporters: "Put it before them briefly so they will read it, clearly so they will appreciate it, picturesquely so they will remember it and, above all, accurately so they will be guided by its light."

428. There is too much speaking in the world, and almost all of it is too long. The Lord's Prayer, the Twenty-third Psalm, Lincoln's Gettysburg Address, are three great literary treasures that will last forever; no one of them is as long as 300 words. With such striking illustrations of the power of brevity it is amazing that speakers never learn to be brief.

—BRUCE BARTON

429. The Amherst College graduates in Spain once invited Calvin Coolidge, Class of '95, to send a nice long message to be read at a big reunion of Amherst men in Madrid.

To make sure that Mr. Coolidge understood that the boys wanted him to know that he could go as far as he liked, the dinner chairman cabled him there would be no cable charges on the message.

From all over Europe the alumni gathered. The Coolidge message from Northampton was saved until the last. When the applause at mention of the ex-president's name subsided, the chairman read the cablegram. It was:

"GREETINGS.—*Calvin Coolidge.*"

—*Coolidge Wit and Wisdom,* by J. H. McKEE (Frederick A. Stokes Company)

Broad-mindedness

430. Broad-mindedness is the result of flattening high-mindedness out.

—GEORGE SAINTSBURY

431. The man who sees both sides of an issue is very likely on the fence—or up a tree.

432. The broad-minded see the truth in different religions; the narrow-minded see only the differences.

—*Chinese Proverb*

433. A man of a right spirit is not a man of narrow and private views, but is greatly interested and concerned for the good of the community to which he belongs, and particularly of the city or village in which he resides, and for the true welfare of the society of which he is a member.

—JONATHAN EDWARDS

Brotherhood

434. Christians may not see eye to eye but they can walk arm in arm.

435. Brotherhood is the very price and condition of man's survival.

—CARLOS P. ROMULO

436. We are all children of one Father and the sooner we stop calling each other names the better.

—GEORGE BERNARD SHAW

437. We do not want the men of another color for our brothers-in-law, but we do want them for our brothers.

—BOOKER T. WASHINGTON

438. The cry of the age is more for fraternity than for charity. If one exists, the other will follow, or better still, will not be needed.

—DR. HENRY D. CHAPIN in
Thoughts (Dodge)

439. Some one labeled this "the century of the common man," but how much better if we could truthfully label it "the century of the brotherhood of man."

—WALTER KIERNAN

440. A man to love and live with God, must love his neighbor as himself. And the way of deepening love of God is the way of brotherly affection.

441. Science offers us wonderful tools for helping to create the Brotherhood of Man on earth. But the mortar of Brotherhood does not come from any laboratory. It must come from the heart and mind.

—DAVID SARNOFF, President, R.C.A. "Living in a Fast Moving World," *Wisdom,* 22nd issue

442. A preacher called at the home of a very poor family that lived in a dilapidated shack. When he came out, he found one of the family's two sons admiring his new car, so the minister explained that he had received it as a gift from his brother. Now, most lads would say, "I wish I had a brother like that."

But this one said, "Mister, I wish I could *be* a brother like that."

—OREN ARNOLD, "Family Man," *Presbyterian Life*

443. Brotherhood doesn't come in a package. It is not a commodity to be taken down from the shelf with one hand—it is an accomplishment of soul-searching, prayer, and perseverance. . . . Like or dislike a person for his own intrinsic qualities, and refuse to tinge that judgment by the irrelevant fact that he belongs to a different race or religion from your own. The spontaneous feeling of brotherhood is a mark of human maturity.

—OVETA CULP HOBBY

444. To have courage with pugnacity,
To have conviction without bigotry,
To have charity without condescension,
To have faith without credulity,
To have love of humanity without mere sentimentality
To have meekness without power
And emotion with sanity—
That is brotherhood.

—CHARLES E. HUGHES

445. One day, Turgenev, the Russian writer, met a beggar who besought him for alms. "I felt in all my pockets," he said, "but there was nothing there. The beggar waited, and his outstretched hand twitched and trembled slightly. Embarrassed and confused, I seized his dirty hand and pressed it. 'Do not be angry with me, brother,' I said, 'I have nothing with me.' The beggar raised his bloodshot eyes and smiled. 'You called me brother,' he said, 'that was indeed a gift.'"

—ARCHER WALLACE

446. There is a legend in the *Talmud* of a traveler coming at twilight to a camping-place. As he looked off in the distance he saw a strange object. Through the gathering dusk it seemed to take the shape of a terrible monster. He resolved to go closer and see, if possible, what it was. Drawing nearer, he saw that it was a man. Much of his fear vanished then. Thereupon he ventured still closer and found that the object was not only a man like himself, but that it was his own brother!

—GEORGE LE ROY WILLETS

447. A troop of Boy Scouts, hiking in the country, found to their delight a stretch of unused and rusted railroad tracks. Each Scout tried his skill in walking on the rails. Most of the boys balanced precariously for a few moments and then tried again. But two boys had no such difficulty. They stood opposite each other on the rails, each extending a hand to the other. They balanced without faltering as they walked briskly along the track. That day's lesson will long linger in my mind, for one boy was white and the other colored. I realized that, as we extend a hand to another person, we shall walk more steadily along the road of life.

—W. A. KUNTZLEMAN

448. On February 3, 1943 the troop ship *Dorchester* went down in the icy Atlantic off the tip of Greenland with heavy loss of life. It was not the worst disaster of a long war, but we have good reason to remember it.

There were four men aboard, chaplains dedicated to the services of God and their fellowman. George L. Fox and Clark V. Poling were Protestant ministers, Alexander D. Goode was a Jewish rabbi, and John P. Washington was a Catholic priest.

When the torpedoes struck around one o'clock in the morning many of the inexperienced GI's were caught sleeping without their lifejackets, although that was contrary to orders. In the fright and confusion some were still without them even after all the surplus stocks had been distributed.

Each of the four chaplains wore a life jacket when he began working among the men to comfort the wounded, to calm the shocked, to help distribute lifejackets, to guide men toward the lifeboats. Places in the boats were declined by the chaplains. When last seen in the light of flares just before the ship went down, not one of the chaplains still wore a lifejacket. Theirs had been forced on unwilling soldiers taught to obey the orders of their superiors. These four dedicated men, symbolic of religious freedom in America, stood together arm-in-arm praying for those young men of America for whom now only prayers were left.

Budget

449. The trouble with the average budget is that it's hard to fill up one hole without digging another.

—DAN BENNETT

450. Living on a budget is the same as living beyond your means except that you have a record of it.

Business

451. Business is a combination of war and sport.

—ANDRÉ MAUROIS

452. One of the hardest things about business is minding your own.

453. It isn't the business you *get.* It's the business you *hold* that counts.

—BRUCE CROWELL

454. All business proceeds on beliefs, or judgments of probabilities, and not on certainties.

—CHARLES W. ELIOT

455. The trouble with women in business, according to one Detroit businessman, is that if you treat 'em like men, they cry; and if you treat 'em like women, darned if they don't get the best of you.

—BARBARA WILLIAMS,
Detroit News

456. Call on a businessman only at business times, and on business; transact your business, and go about your business, in order to give him time to finish his business.

—DUKE OF WELLINGTON

457. The more people who own little businesses of their own, the safer our country will be, and the better off its cities and towns; for the people who have a stake in their country and their community are its best citizens.

—JOHN HANCOCK

458. Whoever admits he is too busy to improve his methods has acknowledged himself to be at the end of his rope. And that is always the saddest predicament which anyone can get into.

—J. Ogden Armour

459. Those who believe we have reached the limit of business progress and employment opportunity in this country are like the farmer who had two windmills and pulled one down because he was afraid there was not enough wind for both.

—Morris S. Tremaine

460. There was a time when it was commonly assumed that the American public was opposed to bigness in business. Nothing could be further from the current truth. The average American admires bigness and he particularly likes bigness in business, if there are present two all-important ingredients—genuine competition and a feeling that there is "full disclosure." What the public is really fearful of is not bigness itself, but the potential misuse of the power that bigness makes possible.

—Elmo Roper

Calmness

461. One cool judgment is worth a thousand hasty councils. The thing to do is to supply light and not heat.

—Woodrow Wilson

462. When somebody asked Marshal Foch how he managed to "win" World War I, he is reported to have said: "By smoking my pipe, not getting excited, and reserving all my strength for the task at hand."

463. The Speech Research Unit of Kenyon College proved through tests that when a person is shouted at, he simply cannot help but shout back. . . . You can use this scientific knowledge to keep another person from becoming angry; control the other person's tone of voice by your own voice. Psychology has proved that if you keep your voice soft you will not become angry. Psychology has accepted as scientific the old Biblical injunction, *A soft answer turneth away wrath.*

—Les Giblin, *How to Have Confidence & Power in Dealing with People* (Prentice-Hall, Inc.)

Capacity

464. Little pots soon run over.

—*Dutch Proverb*

465. A pint can't hold a quart; but if it holds a pint it is doing all that can be expected of it.

—Margaret Deland

466. One can no more develop capacity by resting on his job than he can learn to spell by sitting on a dictionary.

—Arthur Dean

467. It is literally true that no man has ever used more than a small fragment of his brain power. . . . Almost from birth we are continuously blocked by conflicts among internal factions. Each man grows up to resemble a pair of moose with horns locked in battle. He dies of a struggle which he wages with himself.

—Dr. Lawrence S. Kubie

Capital

468. Capital is to the progress of society what gas is to a car.

—James Truslow Adams

469. The highest use of capital is not to make more money, but to make money do more for the betterment of life.

—Henry Ford

470. Thought, not money, is the real business capital, and if you know absolutely that what you are doing is right, then you are bound to accomplish it in due season.

—Harvey S. Firestone

Capitalism

471. Capitalism is the unequal distribution of blessings. Socialism is the equal distribution of misery.

—Winston Churchill

472. There can be no freedom of the individual, no democracy, without the capital system, the profit system, the private enterprise system. These are, in the end, inseparable. Those who would destroy freedom have only first to destroy the hope of gain, the profit of enterprise and risk-taking, the hope of accumulating capital, the hope to save something for one's old age and for one's children. For a community of men without property, and without the hope of getting it by honest effort, is a community of slaves of a despotic State.

—Russell C. Leffingwell

473. Capitalism emerged as a natural and beneficial product of evolution. Man's chief urge is to improve his lot and capitalism is the only system by which this urge can be realized.

Communists, Socialists, and other Collectivists do not agree that anyone should progress ahead of his fellows. History proves, however, that where individual thrift and initiative are unrewarded, a low and declining standard of living and culture is inevitable.

Under Socialism and Communism, sooner or later the real workers rebel against having to support those who shirk their responsibilities and then the structure becomes paralyzed and collapses. Natural law asserts itself.

Capital–Labor

474. Capital and labor both realize time is money, but they can't agree on how much.

—MAURICE SEITTER

475. The money the other fellow has is Capital. Getting it away from him is Labor.

476. It sometimes looks as if the only way to get Capital and Labor together is to keep them from meeting.

477. Capital is condensed labor. It is nothing until labor takes hold of it. The living laborer sets free the condensed labor and makes it assume some form of utility or beauty. Capital and labor are one, and they will draw nearer to each other as the world advances in intellect and goodness.

—DAVID SWING

478. Business and labor are different sides of the same problem. It is impossible wisely to treat either without reference to the interests and duties of the other—and without reference to the fact that the interests of the general public, the commonwealth, are paramount to both.

—THEODORE ROOSEVELT

Card-Playing

479. The worst kind of shindigs are those you get under the bridge table.

—KENNETH J. SHIVELY

480. I am sorry I have not learned to play at cards. It is very useful in life; it generates kindness and consolidates society.

—DR. SAMUEL JOHNSON

481. A thousand years ago, the wives of a Chinese emperor diverted themselves with delicate little ivory tiles, which were the great-great-great grandparents of our present-day playing cards.

482. Card-playing has become so much a part of our every-day life that it has added colorful expressions to our language. "Pass the buck," "blue chip," "ante up" and "stand pat" are four popular expressions the game of Poker has given us.

Faro, the most popular card game on the western frontier a century ago, is responsible for such well-known expressions as "whipsaw," "calling the turn," "sleeper," and "playing both ends against the middle."

Cause—Causes

483. The worst enemy to any cause is the friend who lies in its favor.

484. Those who lead causes and those who endure the consequences are not always the same people.

485. We are all ready to be savage in some cause. The difference between a good man and a bad one is the choice of the cause.

—WILLIAM JAMES

486. What we need for perfect happiness is a cause so important to us that we will willingly give up all we possess, even our lives, to help bring about the accomplishment of our unselfish purpose. "If you want to be an orator," said Wendell Phillips, "first get your great cause."

Cause and Effect

487. The sea is deep because it never rejects the tiniest rivulet.

488. "How come you beautiful redheads marry men who are feeble, bald, nervous and weak?"

"We don't. They get that way."

489. Perpetual motion: Rags make paper, paper makes money, money makes banks, banks make loans, loans make poverty, poverty makes rags.

Caution

490. When the cup is full, carry it even.

—*Scotch Proverb*

491. It is when we all play safe that we create a world of utmost insecurity.

—DAG HAMMARSKJÖLD

492. Don't play for safety. It's the most dangerous thing in the world.

—HUGH WALPOLE

493. Find a man smart enough to beat the other fellow's game, and he's too smart to play it.

494. Beware of ignorance when in motion; look out for inexperience when in action, and beware of the majority when mentally poisoned with misinformation, for collective ignorance does not become wisdom.

—WILLIAM J. H. BOETCKER

495. We should go through life as the traveler goes through the Swiss mountains. A hasty word may bring down an avalanche; a misstep may plunge us over a precipice.

496. A farmer whose corn crop hadn't done well decided to "borrow" from his prosperous neighbor's field. With a large sack tucked under his arm, and his small son dogging his footsteps, he hurried to a distant corner of the field.

On arrival, he peered cautiously to the left, to the right, ahead and behind, to make sure he was not observed.

Just as he reached out a hand to pluck the first ear of corn, the lad spoke: "Daddy," he reminded, "you didn't look up!"

—RUTH A. PRAY

Censorship

497. Censorship is like an appendix. When inert it is useless; when active it is extremely dangerous.

—MAURICE EDELMAN

498. I don't approve of censorship. I like the French theatre idea. Put on the play, and if the audience doesn't care for it, or feels offended by it, they rip up the seats.

—JOHN HUSTON

499. So many new ideas are at first strange and horrible though ultimately valuable that a very heavy responsibility rests upon those who would prevent their dissemination.

—J. B. S. HALDANE

500. One California librarian firmly asserted that she is so utterly opposed to censorship that "when someone complains about a book in our library, I just put the book aside in a locked room. Right now, we have two thousand books locked away like that."

Censure

501. They have a right to censure that have a heart to help.

—WILLIAM PENN, *Fruits of Solitude*, 1693

502. Let your pride pardon what your nature needs, the salutary censure of a friend.

—*Old Proverb*

503. Before we censure a man for seeming what he is *not*, we should be sure that we know what he *is*.

—THOMAS CARLYLE

504. I find that the pain of a little censure, even when it is unfounded, is more acute than the pleasure of much praise.

—THOMAS JEFFERSON

505. It is a folly for an eminent man to think of escaping censure, and a weakness to be affected with it. All the illustrious persons of antiquity, and indeed of every age in the world, have passed through this fiery persecution.

—JOSEPH ADDISON

Certainty

506. "Hello, is this Wasserman?"
"Yes."
"Are you positive?"

507. If you forsake a certainty and depend on an uncertainty, you will lose both the certainty and the uncertainty.

—*Sanskrit Proverb*

508. When a member of the Pennsylvania legislature proposed a bill to increase the salaries of *certain judges,* a member from the opposition party offered an amendment to make the salary increase apply to *uncertain judges* as well. He explained it this way: "My colleague's proposal will include very few judges, while my amendment will take in ninety-five per cent of those now sitting in our courts."

—*If Elected, I Promise,*
by JOHN F. PARKER
(Doubleday & Company, Inc.)

Chairman–Chairmanship

509. The hardest thing to stop is a temporary chairman.
—KIN HUBBARD

510. A chairman of a meeting is like the minor official at a bull-fight whose main function is to open and close the gates to let the bull in and out.

Chance

511. Chance is powerful. Let your hook always be cast.

512. Granted an omniscient Deity, there can be no such thing as accident or chance; even chance conforms to law. Nothing is chaotic, but rather only cosmic; nothing disorderly; only, in sum, orderly. Nothing occurs contrary to the foreknowledge of the Almighty; everything is predestined to conform to the totality of such foreknowledge.
—WM. RICHARD GORDON

Change

513. It is not the weathercock that changes; it is the wind.
—C. DESMOULINS

514. The world hates change, yet it is the only thing that has brought progress.
—CHARLES F. KETTERING

515. Change is inevitable. The great question of our time is whether the change will be by consent or coercion.
—BISHOP G. BROMLEY OXNAM

516. Consider how hard it is to change yourself and you'll understand what little chance you have trying to change others.
—ARNOLD GLASOW

517. All progress and growth is a matter of change, but change must be growth within our social and government concepts if it should not destroy them.
—HERBERT HOOVER

518. It seems to be our destiny never to love anything without seeking to alter it, and in altering it to make it other than what we first loved.

519. There is a certain relief in change, even though it be from bad to worse; as I have found in traveling in a stagecoach, that it is often a comfort to shift one's position and be bruised in a new place.

—Washington Irving

520. The wisest man may be wiser today than he was yesterday, and tomorrow than he is today. Total freedom from change would imply total freedom from error; but this is the prerogative of omniscience alone.

—Charles C. Colton

521. Everybody is a magician in his own right. Each of us keeps changing things into thoughts every day of his life. This is not only an ability we all have; it's a compulsion we can't avoid. Some folks change every minor event into a major crisis. Others change the same events into routine parades. This constant, unconscious conjuring is, of course, the major barrier to accurate communication by anybody with anybody else. We start changing the things and ideas we hear long before we have "seen" them—even with our mind's eye.

—Norman G. Shidle

522. There is nothing more permanent than change, and nothing that meets with more resistance. Yet nothing stands still. Everything either moves forward or falls backward. Man has progressed through the centuries because man has had the intelligence to meet change with change. Individuals, too, must heed that lesson of the race. And, of course, men can master change by training today for the opportunities which new conditions will open tomorrow. It was good advice a generation or so ago, and it is even better advice today.

Character

523. Men are what they were.

—George Bernard Shaw

524. Character is a victory, not a gift.

525. What a man has may be dependent upon others, but *what he is* depends upon himself alone.

526. You can't give character to another person, but you can encourage him to develop his own by possessing one yourself.

—Artemus Calloway

527. There must be a lot of good in some people, when you consider how little has ever come out of them.

528. Character is the one thing we make in this world and take with us into the next.

529. Character is pretty much like window glass—when it is cracked, it is cracked both inside and out.

530. The four cornerstones of character on which the structure of this nation was built are: Initiative, Imagination, Individuality and Independence.

—CAPTAIN EDWARD
RICKENBACKER

531.   When wealth is lost, nothing is lost;
When health is lost, something is lost;
When character is lost, all is lost!

532. Whatever your theology, you will find it hard to disagree with the old negro preacher who told his congregation: "There's an election going on all the time. The Lord votes for you and the devil votes against you, and you cast the deciding vote."

533. There is no such thing as a "self-made" man. We are made up of thousands of others. Every one who has ever done a kind deed for us, or spoken one word of encouragement to us, has entered into the make-up of our character and of our thoughts, as well as our success.

—GEORGE MATTHEW
ADAMS

534. A man's reputation, like his coat, may be soiled without touching the man himself, since the reputation is not the character, any more than the sleeve is the arm it envelops. The character may be soiled only by what the man himself does, while the reputation may have mud thrown upon it by anyone unmanly enough to injure the standing of another.

535. Like the beacon lights in harbors, which, kindling a great blaze by means of a few fagots, afford sufficient aid to vessels that wander over the sea, so, also, a man of bright character in a storm-tossed city, himself content with little, effects great blessings for his fellow-citizens.

—EPICTETUS

536. Instead of saying that man is the creature of circumstance, it would be nearer the mark to say that man is the architect of circumstance. It is character which builds an existence out of circumstance. From the same materials one man builds palaces, another hovels; one warehouses, another villas; bricks and mortar are mortar and bricks until the architect can make them something else.

—THOMAS CARLYLE

537. Character is revealed by very trivial actions. A boy applied to a banker for a position. He was told that there was no place vacant at the time. After thanking the banker he turned regretfully away, but, noticing a pin on the floor, stooped down, picked it up and laid it on the table. As he started out the officer of the bank called him back and said, "We want you. We will make a place for you." The boy became an outstanding banker, a successful businessman. His simple act showed a boy of careful habits. A boy of a courteous disposition.

—ALFRED BARRATT, "The
Importance of Courtesy,"
Wesleyan Methodist

538. A scorpion, being a very poor swimmer, asked a turtle to carry him on his back across a river. "Are you mad?" exclaimed the turtle. "You'll sting me while I'm swimming and I'll drown."

"My dear turtle," laughed the scorpion, "if I were to sting you, you would drown and I would go down with you. Now, where is the logic in that?"

"You're right!" cried the turtle. "Hop on!" The scorpion climbed aboard and halfway across the river gave the turtle a mighty sting. As they both sank to the bottom, the turtle resignedly said:

"Do you mind if I ask you something? You said there'd be no logic in your stinging me. Why did you do it?"

"It has nothing to do with logic," the drowning scorpion sadly replied. "It's just my character."

Charity. See also Giving

539. Charity sees the need; not the cause.

—*German Proverb*

540. The living need charity more than the dead.

—GEORGE ARNOLD

541. The highest exercise of charity is charity towards the uncharitable.

—J. S. BUCKMINSTER

542. If you haven't got any charity in your heart, you have the worst kind of heart trouble.

—BOB HOPE

543. True charity is to give all: not all that belongs to him who gives, but all that is due to him who receives.

—Constancio C. Vigil

544. The noblest charity is to prevent a man from accepting charity; and the best alms are to show and to enable a man to dispense with alms.

—*The Talmud*

Cheating

545. He who purposely cheats his friend would cheat his God.

—*Old Proverb*

546. Money is never so well spent as when you get cheated out of it—for at one stroke you have purchased prudence.

—Arthur Schopenhauer

547. The Indian who stopped scalping his enemies sometimes wonders why the white man still skins his friends.

Cheerfulness

548. Continual cheerfulness is a sign of wisdom.

—*Old Irish Saying*

549. Cheerfulness removes rust from the mind, lubricates our inward machinery, and enables us to do our work with fewer creaks and groans. If people were universally cheerful, probably there wouldn't be half the quarreling or a tenth part of the wickedness there is. Cheerfulness, too, promotes health and immortality. Cheerful people live longest here on earth, afterward in our hearts.

550.   'Tis well to walk with a cheerful heart
        Wherever our fortunes call,
    With a friendly glance and an open hand
        And a gentle word for all.
    Since life is a thorny and difficult path
        Where toil is the portion of man,
    We all should endeavor, while passing along,
        To make it as smooth as we can.

—*Author Unknown*

Child—Children

551. A baby is an angel whose wings decrease as his legs increase.

—*Early French Saying*

552. If a man leaves little children behind him, it is as if he did not die.

—*Moroccan Proverb*

553. Children not only make the home—they subject it to constant alterations.

—Herb Nelson

554. There is never much trouble in any family where the children hope some day to resemble their parents.

—William Lyon Phelps

555. If you make children happy now, you will make them happy twenty years hence by the memory of it.

—Kate Douglas Wiggin

556. The ingratitude of our children recalls to us the kindness of our fathers.

557. The older I grow, the more I appreciate children. Now, as I near my birthday, I salute them again. Children are the most wholesome part of the race, the sweetest, for they are freshest from the Hand of God. Whimsical, ingenious, mischievous, they fill the earth with joy and good humor. We adults live a life of apprehension as to what they will think of us; a life of defense against their terrifying energy; a life of hard work to live up to their great expectations. We put them to bed with a sense of relief—and greet them in the morning with delight and anticipation. We envy them the freshness of adventure and the discovery of life. In all these ways, children add to the wonder of being alive. In all these ways, they help to keep us young.

—Herbert Hoover

558. WHAT IS A CHILD?

(From a teacher's view)

A child is a combination of a thousand questions, all asked
    at the same time.
A miniature rocket blasting off exactly when you want quiet.
Ten little fingers, getting into trouble when at rest
Or else acting like ten thumbs when trying to do something
    extra special.
A head always full of ideas—not always appropriate at the time
But bursting from every seam.
A mouth that can't stay closed for even the slightest moment . . .

Giving information that won't be needed for at least another
    20 minutes.
A pair of ever-searching eyes that question your authority,
    your age, but with an
Innocent, calflike depth that breaks your heart when you
    want to scold.
A set of ears that never seem to be aimed in the right
    direction at the right time;
They never are on your wave length when you call his name
    or mention work.
But as soon as you say play, lunch or recess, he is the
    first to communicate
To the others what he has just received.
A nose that always seems to be sniffing or needing to be wiped
A body that never sits still, but is in perpetual motion
    and never seems to run
Down even when you haven't another bit of energy left, but
    is always completely
Tired when you are in an enthusiastic mood.
He has a voice which startles you, questions you, idolizes
    you and can
Melt the strongest, coldest heart to be found.
His feet are never on the floor, always the first thing
    he falls over
And can never get him to school on time.
His desk resembles the ingredients of an atomic bomb—a few
    erasers, two chewed-on
Pencils, a scratch pad with doodles, chalk, paper clips,
    rubber bands, a comb,
His lunch and, of course, a few old text-books.
He has the energy of a wild horse—sometimes he looks like he'd
    just raced one;
A temper as changeable as the weather,
The patience of a caged lion,
The smile of a new-born babe,
The laugh of a hyena,
But the pure heart of an angel.
He gives the teacher trouble, laughs, tears, a bad temper, a
    sore throat and a
Wish to resign.
But yet, he makes her life the most enjoyable with his ever-
    surprising moods

And whims about, "Well, I guess I do sort of like my teacher . . .
    even though
She makes me work!"

—FAYE HILLMAN

Child Care

559. Training the baby by the book is a good idea, only you need a different book for each baby.

560. If we had paid no more attention to our plants than we have to our children, we would now be living in a jungle of weeds.

—LUTHER BURBANK

561. The only trouble with all the new theories about bringing up children is that it leaves the job just as hard as ever.

—HEYWOOD BROUN

562. The first duty toward children is to make them happy. If you have not made them happy, you have wronged them; no other good they may get can make up for that.

—CHARLES BUXTON

563. A mother once asked a clergyman when she should begin the education of her child, who she told him was then four years old. "Madam," was the reply, "you have lost three years already. From the very first smile that gleams over an infant's cheek, your opportunity begins."

—ABIGAIL WHATELY

564. If a child is not disciplined and taught self-control early in the home, the grown-up world will take care of him later on, perhaps cruelly and when it is too late. A child curbed, taught obedience, spanked when he is young, rarely requires punishment when he hits his teens.

—JOHN WARREN HILL

Child Guidance

565. Children left to grow up like weeds are not likely to produce the fruits of genius.

566. The ones who will suffer most for the mistakes we make in raising our children will be our grandchildren.

—IMOGENE FEY

567. A judge who had a great number of cases involving families and homes once said: "We adults spend far too much time preparing the path for our youth and far too little time preparing our youth for the path."

568. There are really valid reasons why it is unwise to shield children from all violence, terror, sorrow, and death in their reading. The way to cure a child of fear of the dark is not to deny the existence of dark, but to walk with him in the dark and show him by example the restful quiet of it, and show him, too, how to avoid breaking his neck by stumbling over something he can't see.

—ROBERT G. MOOD, *Elementary English*

Child Training

569. When parents don't mind that their children don't mind, the children don't.

570. It isn't so hard to teach children right from wrong. The hard part is to remember what you taught them.

—CHARLES RUFFING

571. One reason why the upbringing of a child is so difficult nowadays is that no sooner have you taught it to talk than you have to start teaching it to keep quiet.

572. The best way of training the young, is to train yourself at the same time; not to admonish them, but to be seen always doing that of which you would admonish them.

—PLATO

573. In order to manage children well, we must borrow their eyes and their hearts, see and feel as they do, and judge them from their own point of view.

I pray God to make parents reasonable.

—EUGÉNIE DE GUERIN in *Thoughts* (Dodge)

574. Parents' discipline should be based on four F's: firmness, fondness, frankness, and fairness. Parents who cannot say no to a child often rear offspring who have contempt for authority. Parents who get too angry over minor infractions often fail to instill a sense of discipline in their children.

—ALEXANDER MARTIN

Choice

575. Man must have the right of choice, even to choose wrong, if he shall ever learn to choose right. The child walks as we unwind the swaddling clothes; the building stands in its full beauty as we remove the scaffolding. Let us beware lest we make gods of the scaffolding; lest by making more intricate the wrappings of law, more strong the rods of coercion, man himself remain feeble and imperfect.

—Josiah C. Wedgwood

576. A story is told in Benjamin Franklin's autobiography of a clergyman ordered to read the proclamation issued by Charles I, bidding the people to return to sports on Sunday. To the congregation's amazement and horror, he did read the royal edict in church, which many clergy had refused to do. But he followed it with the words, "Remember the Sabbath day to keep it holy," and added, "Brethren, I have laid before you the commandment of your king and the commandment of your God. I leave it to you to judge which of the two ought rather to be observed."

—W. J. Isbell, "Christians
Are Citizens, Too,"
Southern Baptist
Brotherhood Journal

Christianity

577. Christianity is a life, not a creed; a spirit, not a form.

—C. L. Goodell

578. Christianity is more than a storm cellar; it is a way of life.

—Rev. Gilbert S. Peters

579. Christianity could be condensed into four words: Admit, Submit, Commit and Transmit.

—William Wilberforce

580. It does not take a great mind to be a Christian, but it takes all the mind a man has.

—Bishop Richard C.
Raines

581. Christianity is like electricity. It cannot enter a person unless it can pass through.

—Bishop Richard C.
Raines

582. Christianity requires the participants to come out of the grandstand and on to the playing field.

583. Those who say they believe in Christianity and those who *practice* it are not always the same people.

584. Christianity teaches a man to spend the best part of his life preparing for the worst.

585. Christianity is either relevant all the time or useless anytime. It is not just a phase of life; it is life itself.
—RICHARD C. HALVERSON

586. Christianity has not been tried and found wanting; it has been found difficult and not tried.
—G. K. CHESTERTON

587. The Christian is like the ripening corn; the riper he grows, the more lowly he bends his head.
—GUTHRIE

588. A Christian should live so that instead of being a part of the world's problem he will be a part of the answer.
—REV. JACKSON BURNS

589. To the Christian, death is not an end, but an event in life; a new start with an extended knowledge, and a purer love.
—BISHOP OF LINCOLN

590. The whole history of Christianity proves that she has indeed little to fear from persecution as a foe, but much to fear from persecution as an ally.
—THOMAS B. MACAULAY

591. Nathaniel Hawthorne once described Christian faith as a "grand cathedral, with divinely pictured windows. Standing without, you can see no glory, nor imagine any, but standing within every ray of light reveals a harmony of unspeakable splendors."

592. Christ once compared Christians to salt, for just as a little salt permeates a dish and transforms all its flavor, so a few Christians can spread their influence throughout a community and change its character. Scientists tell us that less than one 200th of a dish's weight in salt is enough to give it an appetizing taste. A little Christianity will also go a long way.

Christmas

593. If you like to ponder past Christmases, go back to the first one.

594. Keeping Christmas is good, but sharing it is a great deal better.

595. He who has not Christmas in his heart will never find it under a tree.

—Roy L. Smith

596. Christmas season reminds us that a demonstration of religion is often better than a definition of it.

597. How many observe Christ's Birthday; how few His Precepts! O! 'tis easier to keep holidays than Commandments.

—Benjamin Franklin

598. A father's biggest difficulty at Christmastime is convincing the children that he is Santa Claus, and his wife that he isn't.

599. When we throw out the Christmas tree we should be especially careful not to throw out the Christmas spirit with it.

600. A happy child once asked, "Why can't Christmas come every day?" Men of good will might ask the same question. There is no reason why the warmth and good feeling of Christmas have to disappear as fast as a drumstick on a child's plate. Ben Franklin observed, "A good conscience is a continual Christmas." If we in America can develop the skill to make Tommy's sled and Suzy's skates last for years, can't we develop a spiritual force that will keep the Spirit of Christmas alive for 364 more days?

601. Back in 1659, three centuries ago, the colony of Massachusetts passed a law that read, "Whosoever shall be found observing any such day as Christmas, or the like, either by forbearing of labor, feasting, or in any other way, shall be fined five shillings." This law remained in force for over twenty years, and early American history records that numerous persons who refused to work on Christmas, either went to jail or paid fines. It wasn't until late in the first half of the nineteenth century that Chrismas was established as a legal holiday throughout the country.

602. On the day after Christmas last year, I boarded a bus in front of my office. It was fearfully crowded and I stood wedged into a niche behind the bus driver. When it was packed to capacity, a powerful, aggressive female started to leave. With unspeakable rudeness and irresistible force, she pushed through the crowd in the aisle and reached the door as incoming passengers tried to get aboard.

"Get off that platform," she shrieked, "or I'll shove all of you into the street."

Quietly, I commented to the bus driver, "Christmas came yesterday."

His reply was a superb understatement: "Some people never knew it was here."

—Dr. William B.
Lipphard

603. It wasn't until 440 A.D. that the fathers of the Church got around to selecting a date upon which to celebrate the birth of Christ— the day of the winter solstice, and even then the exact day and year have never been satisfactorily settled.

Christmas customs have descended from seasonal, pagan and religious ceremonies with legend and tradition woven heavily into the pattern. Association of the customs with pagan feasts of the winter solstice couple them to the beginning of time and link them very closely to the birth of Christ.

Church fathers exercised considerable wisdom in selecting the day of the solstice since it was the time of their most important festival. Flexibility in man-made calendars have caused the time of the solstice and the date of Christmas to vary by a few days.

Church

604. A church is God between four walls.

—Victor Hugo

605. The church that does not reach out, fades out.

—Rev. Allan K.
Williams

606. God put the church in the world. Satan seeks to put the world in the church.

607.
And whether it be a rich church
Or a poor church anywhere,
Truly it is a great church
If God is worshipped there.

—*Author Unknown*

Church Attendance

608. Some people go to church to see who didn't.

609. When a woman coughs in church, she either has a cold or a new hat.

610. Many come to bring their clothes to church rather than themselves.

611. Don't knock your church—it may have improved since the last time you were there.

612. Some people will bring to church a hymn book or a prayer book—but not a pocketbook.

—JACK HERBERT

613. Some people ask very little from any church—just a choice seat on Easter Sunday.

614. If absence really made the heart grow fonder, a lot of people would miss church more than any place in the world.

615. If the Church neglects the children, it is certain that the children will someday neglect the Church.

616. Many people who demand a front table in a night club try to even things up by taking a back seat in church.

617. If men took any real interest in what other men wear, I bet there would be as many men in church as there are women.

618. No, you don't have to attend church to be a good man. You don't have to cook your food to eat it, either, but it sure helps.

—OREN ARNOLD, *Presbyterian Life*

619. Church pews never skid into a ditch, smash against a telephone pole, or get tagged for speeding.

620. It's remarkable how few of the persons killed at grade crossings on Sundays are on their way to church.

621. Those who couldn't go to church in the winter because it was too cold won't be able to go in the summer either because it will be too hot.

622. The next time I canvass a new neighborhood and run into a chap who tells me he doesn't want to attend church because there are too many hypocrites in the church, I'm going to tell him very politely: "O, don't let that keep you away. We've always got room for one more."

623. When Dr. Pierce Harris of First Methodist Church, Atlanta, Georgia, spoke recently at a prison work camp, the prisoner introducing him recalled earlier days of association with the minister.

"Several years ago," he said, "two boys lived in the same community in north Georgia and attended the same school, played with the same bunch of fellows, and went to the same Sunday School.

"One of them dropped out of Sunday School because he felt he had outgrown it, and that it was 'sissy stuff.' The other boy kept on going because he felt that it really meant something in his life.

"The boy who dropped out is the one who is making this introduction today. The boy who kept going to Sunday School is the famous preacher who will preach to us this morning."

Church Membership

624. A church membership does not make a Christian any more than owning a piano makes a musician.

—Douglas Meador,
Matador (Texas)
Tribune

625. A small boy was asked by a friend why they never met at the Presbyterian church. He explained: "We belong to a different abomination."

Circumstances

626. Circumstances are the rulers of the weak; they are but the instruments of the wise.

—Samuel Lover

627. The space between virtue and vice is so narrow that there is just only room enough for circumstance to wedge itself in.

Citizenship

628. Whatever makes men good Christians, makes them good citizens.

—Daniel Webster

629. Every good citizen makes his country's honor his own, and cherishes it not only as precious but as sacred. He is willing to risk his life in its defense and is conscious that he *gains* protection while he gives it.

—Andrew Jackson

630. You can surmount the obstacles in your path if you are determined, courageous and hard-working. Never be fainthearted. Be resolute, but never bitter. Bitterness will serve only to warp your personality. Permit no one to dissuade you from pursuing the goals you set for yourselves. Do not fear to pioneer, to venture down new paths of endeavor. Demand and make good use of your rights, but never fail to discharge faithfully the obligations and responsibilities of good citizenship. Be good Americans.

—RALPH J. BUNCHE

Civilization

631. If we are to preserve civilization, we must first remain civilized.

—LOUIS ST. LAURENT

632. The future of civilization is, to a great extent, being written in the classrooms of the world.

—MILTON L. SMITH

633. Civilization is a movement and not a condition, a voyage and not a harbor.

—ARNOLD TOYNBEE

634. Civilization is made up of everything that we might get along without but would like to have.

—DAVID C. COYLE

635. Civilization is a state of society in which the only people who speak about the future with any confidence are the fortunetellers.

636. The true civilization is where every man gives to every other every right that he claims for himself.

—ROBERT G. INGERSOLL

637. No task is as difficult as striving to become a civilized person. But the lasting happiness which comes with that attempt makes the effort seem small indeed as compared with the value to be gained.

—LELAND P. STEWART

638. What is civilization? Its true signs are thought for the poor and suffering, chivalrous regard and respect for women, the frank recognition of human brotherhood, irrespective of race or color or nation or religion, the narrowing of the domain of mere force as a governing factor

in the world, the love of ordered freedom, abhorrence of what is mean
and cruel and vile, ceaseless devotion to the claims of justice.

—LORD RUSSELL
KILLOWEN

Clergy

639. Priests are no more necessary to religion than politicians to
patriotism.

—JOHN HAYNES HOLMES,
*Sensible Man's View of
Religion*

640. There is no adjusting a quarrel with the clergy save by grant-
ing their demands. Their cause, they always pretend, is the cause of God,
and they can therefore make no concession without sin.

—PAUL DE RAPIN DE
THOYRAS, *Histoire
d'Angleterre*

Cleverness

641. The desire to seem clever often keeps us from being so.

—FRANÇOIS DE LA
ROCHEFOUCAULD

642. There is no man really clever who has not discovered he is
also stupid.

Club Membership

643. The president of the Over-Eighty Club was challenged for
admitting two members who were only 78. He explained, "Well, every
organization needs some young blood."

—EUGENE P. BERTIN

644. A new pastor was invited by the local Kiwanians to join their
club. The membership secretary reminded him, however, that it was the
rule of the club to have only one representative from each profession and
that they already had one for the category of pastor. The only profession not represented at the moment was that of hog-caller. Would the
pastor mind? "Well," was the reverend gentleman's reply, "where I come
from, I was known as the shepherd, but, of course, you know your group
best."

College

645. A college education isn't essential. Just being a graduate sometimes will do.

—GLENN R. BERNHARDT

646. Nothing irks the college boy more than shaking out the envelope from home and finding nothing in it but news and love.

647. Not all educated men are college graduates, nor are all college graduates educated men. An educated man is one who is useful to humanity, his profession or trade, and to himself.

Comfort

648. The superior man thinks always of virtue; the common man thinks of comfort.

—CONFUCIUS

649. Everyone should own a really comfortable bed and a truly good pair of shoes, for he is in one or the other most of his life.

Commencement Exercises

650. The man who graduates today and stops learning tomorrow is uneducated the day after.

—NEWTON D. BAKER

651. You have only about 11,000 working days at your disposal if you graduate at age 22 and plan to retire at age 65. So you'd better get busy!

652. Part of the American myth is that people who are handed the skin of a dead sheep at graduation time think that it will keep their minds alive forever.

—JOHN MASON BROWN,
Seeing Things

653. The best advice I can give to any young man or young woman upon graduation from school can be summed up in exactly eight words, and they are—be honest with yourself and tell the truth.

—JAMES A. FARLEY

654. To the graduating class I bequeath the good advice that I gave to the students of former years. It really is as good as new, for very few have ever used it.

—RAYMOND L. NOONAN

655. I would feel that I had performed well the part that has providentially fallen to me if I could impress upon everyone who goes out this year with a diploma the thought that it is not a certificate of right to special favor and profit in the world but rather a commission of service.

—WARREN G. HARDING

Committee–Committees

656. Progress: what an inactive committee always reports.

657. Committee work is like a soft chair—easy to get into but hard to get out of.

658. If you live in a town run by a committee—be on the committee.

—WILLIAM GRAHAM
SUMNER

659. "Committee" is a noun of multitude, signifying many, but not signifying much.

660. Another nice thing about being quiet and dumb is that you'll not be picked to head a committee.

Common Man

661. Recently, in my opinion, there has been too much talk about the Common Man. It has been dinned into us that this is the Century of the Common Man. The idea seems to be that the Common Man has come into his own at last. But I have never been able to find out who this is. In fact, most Americans will get mad and fight if you try calling them common. . . . I have never met a father and mother who did not want their children to grow up to be uncommon men and women. May it always be so. For the future of America rests not in mediocrity, but in the constant renewal of leadership in every phase of our national life.

—HERBERT HOOVER

662. In calling the 20th century the "era of the common man," we tend to forget that it took the genius of very uncommon men to make this modern world possible. For example, an ordinary citizen can today buy at a corner drugstore, for a relatively small sum, a wonder drug for which Louis XIV would have given half of France. By any standard, Edison, Marconi, Pasteur and Salk were more gifted than we ordinary mortals, and certainly we all enjoy the fruits of their genius. What man could weave his own suit or construct his own electric light? These conveniences, these unearned rewards are so much a part of our daily lives that it seems to me each citizen's daily prayer should be, "Forgive me, O Lord, for taking so much for granted."

—JAMES A. FARLEY

Common Sense

663. Common sense is instinct; enough of it is genius.

—GEORGE BERNARD SHAW

664. A handful of common sense is worth a bushel of learning.

—*Old Proverb*

665. It is a thousand times better to have common sense without education than to have education without common sense.

—ROBERT G. INGERSOLL

666. Nature gives everybody five senses: touch, taste, sight, smell and hearing. But the other two—horse and common—you gotta acquire.

667. Common sense is only a modification of talent. Genius is an exaltation of it.

—EDWARD G. BULWER-LYTTON

668. If a man can have only one kind of sense, let him have common sense. If he has that and uncommon sense too, he is not far from genius.

—HENRY WARD BEECHER

Communism

669. The difference between communism and democracy is—plenty!

670. A Communist is a fellow who has given up all hope of becoming a capitalist.

671. Communism is where performance is promised. Democracy is where the promise is performed.

—JULIUS TANNEN

672. In America it's "Believe it or not," but in Communist countries it's "Believe it or else."

673. We must hate—hatred is the basis of Communism. Children must be taught to hate their parents if they are not Communists.

—NIKOLAI LENIN, speech to the Commissars of Education, Moscow, 1923

674. In a way, the Russians are quite helpful. If we didn't have them, how would we know whether we were ahead or behind?

675. The Communist, seeing the rich man in his fine home, says: "No man should have so much." The Capitalist, seeing the same thing, says: "All men should have as much."

—PHELPS ADAMS, *Forbes*

676. There is one redeeming feature about the Communist movement: As long as there are Communists there will always be ex-Communists.

677. At a Communist meeting one of the comrades in the audience stood up and addressed the chairman: "Comrade chairman, there is just one thing I'd like to know; what happens to my unemployment compensation when we overthrow the government?"

678. It has been finally determined what is meant by the hammer and sickle on the Russian flag. The sickle is to mow 'em down and the hammer is to keep 'em that way.

Companionship

679. People are also judged by the company they keep away from.

—JOSEPH C. SALAK

680. Carlyle and Tennyson once visited each other by the simple process of sitting before the fire for three hours without saying a word—each puffing his pipe!

681. Never associate with idiots on their own level because, being an intelligent man, you'll try to deal with them on their level—and on their level they'll beat you every time.

—JEAN COCTEAU

Comparison

682. To compare is not to prove.

—*French Proverb*

683. Comparison is the expedient of those who cannot reach the heart of the things compared.

—GEORGE SANTAYANA

Compassion

684. Compassion will cure more sins than condemnation.

—HENRY WARD BEECHER

685. An enemy's misfortune softens the rancor of the good, but strengthens that of the bad, as sun melts the snow and hardens mud.

686. The root of the matter, if we want a stable world, is a very simple and old-fashioned thing, a thing so simple that I am almost ashamed to mention it for fear of the derisive smile with which the wise cynics will greet my words. The thing I mean is love, Christian love, or compassion.

If you feel this, you have a motive for existence, a reason for courage, an imperative necessity for intellectual honesty.

—BERTRAND RUSSELL

Compensation

687.
   Each loss has its compensation
    There is healing for every pain,
   But the bird with a broken pinion
    Never soars so high again.

       —HEZEKIAH BUTTERWORTH
        (1839–1905)

688. For every grain of wit there is a grain of folly. For everything you have missed, you have gained something else; and for everything you gain, you lose something. . . . If the gatherer gathers too much, nature takes out of the man what she puts into his chest; swells the estate, but kills the owner. Nature hates monopolies and exceptions.

Competition

689. Most of us never recognize opportunity until it goes to work in our competitor's business.

—P. L. ANDARR

690. It isn't necessary to blow out the other person's light to let your own shine.

691. No man is in competition with another man, he is in conflict with his own errors.

692. He that wrestles with us strengthens our nerves and sharpens our skill. Our antagonist is our helper.

—EDMUND BURKE

693. By competition the total amount of supply is increased, and by increase of the supply a competition in the sale ensues, and this enables the consumer to buy at lower rates. Of all human powers operating on the affairs of mankind, none is greater than that of competition.

—Henry Clay

694. Sometimes I think my competitors do more for me than my friends do; my friends are too polite to point out my weaknesses, but my competitors go to great expense to advertise them.

My competitors are efficient, diligent, and attentive; they make me search for ways to improve my product and my service.

If I had no competitors, I might be lazy, incompetent, inattentive; I need the discipline they enforce on me.

I salute my competitors; they have been good to me. God bless them all!

695. A farmer walked into the hardware store of a midwestern town and asked to see an axe. After carefully examining a half-dozen, he chose one and asked its price.

"It is $1.50," said the storekeeper.

Producing a page torn from a mail-order catalogue, the farmer said, "Here is the same axe for only $1.33."

The hardware man looked at the picture, pondered, then said, "If they can sell it for that, so can I."

"O.K. I'll take it," said the farmer.

The storekeeper picked up the axe, weighed it on a scale behind the counter and began to make out a sale bill, $1.33, plus 15 cents, total $1.48.

"Hey!" shouted the farmer. "What's that 15 cents for?"

"For postage. If you sent off for it you'd have to pay postage, wouldn't you?"

The farmer had to admit he would. He counted out the $1.48. The storekeeper wrapped up the axe—and calmly laid it on a shelf.

"Say, what's the big idea?" asked the farmer.

With a twinkle in his eye, the storekeeper replied, "Come back in three days and you can have it."

—"Life in These United States" anecdote, April 1944, page 65, contributed by Ben Shatzman. Copyright 1944 by *The Reader's Digest Association, Inc.* Reprinted with permission.

Complaint–Complaints

696. Those who do not complain are never pitied.

—Jane Austen

697. Don't complain. Every time the lamb bleats he loses a mouthful of hay.

698. The usual fortune of complaint is to excite contempt more than pity.

—Dr. Samuel Johnson

699.
The wheel that squeaks the loudest
Is the one that gets the grease.

—Josh Billings

700. Those who complain about the way the ball bounces are often the ones who dropped it.

701. A Spaniard dared to question the tenderness of a steak served him in the dining car of the Madrid-Paris express. The waiter, with scorn and a show of wounded pride, informed him that if he were not satisfied with the service there was a suggestion and complaint box at the end of the car.

Whereupon the Spaniard seized the steak from his plate, stalked down the car and stuffed it inside the complaint box.

Compliment—Complimentary

702. I can live for two months on a good compliment.

—Mark Twain

703. Compliments cost nothing, yet many pay dearly for them.

704. Tell a lady with a handsome face that she is pretty, she only thinks it is her due. Assure a lady, whose visage is something more than plain, that she looks killing today, she feels the flattery the whole day after.

Compliments which we think are deserved we accept only as debts; those which conscience informs us we do not merit we receive with the same gratitude that we do favors given away.

—Oliver Goldsmith

Compromise

705. Life cannot subsist in society but by reciprocal concessions.

—Dr. Samuel Johnson

706. In our spirit of compromise, the Reverend Vance Havner likens us to the uncertain soldier in our *un*-Civil War who, figuring to play it safe, dressed himself in a blue coat and gray pants and tiptoed out onto the field of battle. He got shot from both directions!

707. Two heads are not always better than one, despite the old saying that they are. When two members of a church committee both thought they could write the better slogan for the outdoor bulletin boards, the chairman of the committee remembered the old saying and suggested a compromise. He asked one member to put his slogan on the side bulletin board while the other member put a second slogan on the front board. *Result:* One board urged readers to "Make your worst enemy your best friend." The other announced, "Drink is man's worst enemy."

Compulsion

708. Bodily exercises, when compulsory, do no harm to the body; but knowledge which is acquired under compulsion obtains no hold on the mind.

—PLATO

709. No human power can force the intrenchments of the human mind: compulsion never persuades; it only makes hypocrites.

—FRANÇOIS DE FÉNÉLON

710. A wise man will so act that whatever he does may rather seem voluntary and of his own free will than done by compulsion, however much he may be compelled by necessity.

—NICCOLO MACHIAVELLI

Conceit

711. The person who knows everything has a lot to learn.

712. He who gets too big for his breeches will be exposed in the end.

713. We admire the man who knows, but we hate the man who *knows* he knows.

714. It is a strange commentary that the head never begins to swell until the mind stops growing.

Concentration

715. Concentration is my motto—first honesty, then industry, then concentration.

—ANDREW CARNEGIE

716. The one prudence in life is concentration; the one evil is dissipation; and it makes no difference whether our dissipations are coarse or fine; property and its cares, friends, and a social habit, or politics, or music, or feasting. Everything is good which takes away one plaything and delusion more, and drives us home to add one stroke of faithful work.

Concentration is the secret of strength in politics, in war, in trade, in short, in all management of human affairs.

—RALPH WALDO
EMERSON, *Power*

Conduct. See *also* Behavior

717. Loose conduct can do a fine job of getting you in tight places.

718.
This day is mine to mar or make,
    God keep me strong and true;
Let me no erring by-path take,
    No doubtful action do.

Grant me when the setting sun
    This fleeting day shall end,
I may rejoice o'er something done,
    Be richer by a friend.

Let all I meet along the way
    Speak well of me tonight.
I would not have the humblest say
    I'd hurt him by a slight.

Let there be something true and fine
    When night slips down to tell
That I have lived this day of mine
    Not selfishly, but well.

—*Anonymous*

Conference

719. Conference: a big business term for swapping stories in somebody's private office.

720. A conference is a meeting at which people talk about what they should already be doing.

721. No grand idea was ever born in a conference, but a lot of foolish ideas have died there.

—F. SCOTT FITZGERALD

Confession

722. What use to confess our faults at the moment the vessel is sinking?

—CLAUDIUS CLAUDIANUS

723. Confession is good for the soul, but more profitable for the psychiatrist.

724. We confess our little faults only to persuade others that we have no great ones.

—FRANÇOIS DE LA
ROCHEFOUCAULD

725. Confession may be good for the soul, but it doesn't get one much reputation for sense.

Confidence

726. Trust men, and they will be true to you; treat them greatly, and they will show themselves great.

—RALPH WALDO EMERSON

727. Trust him little who praises all, him less who censures all, and him least who is indifferent about all.

—JOHANN KASPAR
LAVATER

Conformity

728. Either do as your neighbors do, or move away.

—*Moroccan Proverb*

729. If a man does not keep pace with his companions, perhaps it is because he hears a different drummer. Let him step to the music which he hears, however measured or far away.

—HENRY DAVID THOREAU

730. Everybody is criticizing conformity these days, but there is one thing that can be said in favor of it—you can practice it without making a fool of yourself.

731. We are discreet sheep; we wait to see how the drove is going, and then go with the drove. We have two opinions: one private, which we are afraid to express; and another one—the one we use—which we force ourselves to wear to please Mrs. Grundy, until habit makes us comfortable in it, and the custom of defending it presently makes us love it, adore it, and forget how pitifully we came by it. Look at it in politics.

—MARK TWAIN

732. The great football star and coach, "Bo" Macmillan, told some years ago of being nearly drowned as a boy when swept over a dam. Caught in a whirlpool below, he vainly tried to fight his way back to the surface. Each time he was pulled under again. Finally there flashed into his mind the thought, "Maybe if I let myself go with the current it will bring me out someplace." Exactly this happened. Ceasing his struggles to go back, he found himself in a few minutes coming to the surface in a quiet pool downstream. He then made his way easily to shore.

733. Charles the Fourth, after his abdication, amused himself in his retirement at St. Juste, by attempting to make a number of watches go exactly together. Being constantly foiled in this attempt, he exclaimed, "What a fool have I been to neglect my own concerns, and to waste my whole life in a vain attempt to make all men think alike on matters of religion when I can't even make a few watches keep time together."

—CHARLES C. COLTON

Confusion

734. When a man's knowledge is not in order, the more of it he has the greater will be his confusion.

—HERBERT SPENCER

735. No wonder we are confused these days. We are admonished to sit tight, hold tight, and sleep tight—then warned that we *must* relax.

—CAROLINE CLARK

Conquest

736. A conqueror, like a cannon-ball, must go on. If he rebounds his career is over.

—DUKE OF WELLINGTON

737. When we conquer enemies by kindness and justice we are more apt to win their submission than by victory in the field. In the one case, they yield only to necessity; in the other, by their own free choice.

—POLYBIUS, *Histories*

Conscience

738. A twinge of conscience is a glimpse of God.

739. By the verdict of his own breast no guilty man is ever acquitted.

—JUVENAL

740. Conscience warns us as a friend before it punishes us as a judge.

—KING STANISLAS I of Poland

741. Conscience doesn't keep you from doing anything wrong; just keeps you from enjoying it!

Conservatism

742. Oaks are the true conservatives; they hold old leaves till summer gives a green exchange.

—ROY HELTON

743. There is danger in reckless change but greater danger in blind conservatism.

—HENRY GEORGE

Consistency

744. Consistency is a paste jewel that only cheap men cherish.

—WILLIAM ALLEN WHITE

745. Then there was the good little girl who had been saying "no" so long that she almost loused up her wedding ceremony.

746. The extraordinary thing about my father is that his public face and his private face have been the same. He has been the same man to the world that he has been to his family. And that is harder than it sounds. It is the very definition of integrity.

—CHARLES VAN DOREN

Consolation

747. The remembrance of the good done those we have loved is the only consolation left us when we have lost them.

—DEMOUSTIER

748. We like to know the weaknesses of eminent persons; it consoles us for our inferiority.

—MME. DE LAMBERT

Constructive—Constructiveness

749.   TEN POINTS

1. You cannot bring about prosperity by discouraging thrift.
2. You cannot strengthen the weak by weakening the strong.

3. You cannot help small men by tearing down big men.

4. You cannot help the poor by destroying the rich.

5. You cannot lift the wage-earner by pulling down the wage-payer.

6. You cannot keep out of trouble by spending more than your income.

7. You cannot further the brotherhood of man by inciting class hatred.

8. You cannot establish sound security on borrowed money.

9. You cannot build character and courage by taking away a man's initiative and independence.

10. You cannot help men permanently by doing for them what they could and should do for themselves.

—WILLIAM J. H.
BOETCKER

750.   I watched them tearing a building down,
  a gang of men in a busy town.
With a ho-heave-ho and a lusty yell
  they swung a beam and the sidewall fell.
I asked the foreman, "Are those men skilled,
  and the men you'd hire if you had to build?"
He gave a laugh, said "No, indeed;
  just common labor is all I need.
I can easily wreck in a day or two
  what builders have taken a year to do."
I thought to myself as I went my way,
  "Which of these roles have I tried to play?
Am I a builder who works with care,
  measuring life by the rule and square?
Am I shaping my deeds to a well-made plan,
  patiently doing the best I can?
Or am I a wrecker, who walks the town
  content with the labor of tearing down?"
—*Author Unknown*

Contamination

751.   In fighting with a chimeysweep, you are blackened whether you win or lose.

752.   Unless your cask is perfectly clean, whatever you pour into it turns sour.

—HORACE

Contempt

753. Contempt is the subtlest form of revenge.

—Baltasar Gracián, *The Art of Worldly Wisdom*

754. "I have the greatest contempt for Aristotle," said a non-classical scholar. "But not" retorted a bystander, "the kind of contempt bred by familiarity."

Contentment

755. Contentment is natural wealth, luxury is artificial poverty.

—Socrates

756. Contentment is a matter of hoping for the best and making the best of what you get.

757. Contentment does not consist in heaping up more fuel, but in taking away some fire.

—Thomas Fuller

Controversy

758. A long dispute means that both parties are wrong.

—Voltaire

759. Every quarrel begins in nothing and ends in a struggle for supremacy.

—Elbert Hubbard

760. Most controversies would soon be ended, if those engaged in them would first accurately define their terms, and then adhere to their definitions.

—Tryon Edwards

Conversation

761. Conversation without thought is just gossip.

762. At a dinner party one should eat wisely, but not too well— and talk well, but not too wisely.

—W. Somerset Maugham

763. A bore talks mostly in the first person, a gossip in the third, and a brilliant conversationalist in the second.

764. That literary genius, George Bernard Shaw, is credited with the statement that he found it "more interesting to talk to a scullery maid, ignorant but fearless, who spoke what she pleased, in a way that was distinctly her own, even if illiterate, than to talk to an educated duchess who talked banal things in the usual conventional manner."

765. As a young man, actor William Gillette studied stenography. He was living then in a boardinghouse, so he decided to practice his shorthand evenings by taking down every word spoken in the drawing room. "Years later," Gillette told a friend, "I went over my notebooks, and found that in four months of incessant conversation, no one had said anything that made any difference to anybody."

Conviction—Convictions

766. It is important that people know what you stand for; it is equally important that they know what you *won't* stand for.

767. One man with a belief is a social force superior to ninety-nine men who have only an interest.

—John Stuart Mill

Cooperation

768. Cooperation is spelled with two letters—WE.

—George M. Verity

769. Three helping one another bear the burden of six.

—George Herbert

770. We are made for cooperation, like feet, like hands, like eyelids, like the rows of the upper and lower teeth. To act against one another then is contrary to Nature, and it is acting against one another to be vexed and turn away.

—Marcus Aurelius

771. Two neighbors, one blind and the other lame, were called to another place. The sightless one carried the cripple, the latter directing the way, and thus they made the trip together in safety. By each doing what he could, their objective was attained.

772. Without the help of others, any one of us would die, naked and starved. Consider the bread upon our tables, the clothes upon our backs, the luxuries that make life pleasant; how many men worked in sunlit fields, in dark mines, in the fierce heat of modern metal, and among the looms and wheels of countless factories, in order to create them for our use and enjoyment.

—ALFRED E. SMITH

Cosmetics

773. Cosmetics are a woman's way of keeping a man from reading between the lines.

774. A dear old Quaker lady who was asked what gave her such a lovely complexion and what cosmetic she used replied sweetly: "I use for the lips, truth; for the voice, prayer; for the eyes, pity; for the hands, charity; for the figure, uprightness; and for the heart, love."

775. Although cosmetics may appear to be non-essential, even the dictator nations were unable to stop the trade by decree. In the early days of the Soviet Union, cosmetics were banned, and immediately a large bootleg traffic sprang up from Poland, so the business was finally turned into a government monopoly. In Germany cosmetics were also banned with no more success than the prohibition of liquor in America, and at last reports Germany was still one of the largest cosmetic markets in the world.

Courage

776. One man with courage makes a majority.

—ANDREW JACKSON

777. Bravery has no place where it can avail nothing.

—DR. SAMUEL JOHNSON

778. Ofttimes the test of courage becomes rather to live than to die.

—VITTORIO ALFIERI,
Oreste

779. To keep standing up after being counted is the true test of courage.

780. Courage is not the *absence* of fear; it is the *mastery* of it.

781. The best reason for holding your chin up when in trouble is that it keeps the mouth closed.

—IVERN BOYETT

782. A rather fragile looking gent was hailed into court for striking his wife, a large, buxom woman.

"Why did you strike your wife?" the surprised judge asked after appraising the couple.

"Well, your honor," said the defendant softly, "she had her back to me, the broomstick was handy and the back door was wide open. So I took the chance."

Courtesy

783. An excess of courtesy is discourtesy.

—*Japanese Proverb*

784. Courtesy is to business what oil is to machinery.

785. Courtesy costs nothing, yet it buys things that are priceless.

786. It is better to have too much courtesy than too little, provided you are not equally courteous to all, for that would be injustice.

—BALTASAR GRACIÁN

Courtship

787. When a girl begins to count on a man, his number is up.

788. Some girls are unmarried for the same reason some drivers run out of gas. They pass too many filling stations looking for their favorite brand.

789.
Act I
The man is on his knees.

Act II
The woman is on his knees.

Act III
Both are on their knees.

Cowardice

790. Remember that every hard-boiled egg is yellow inside.

791. To know what is right and not to do it is the worst cowardice.

—CONFUCIUS

792. It is cowardly to fly from a living enemy or to abuse a dead one.

—*Danish Proverb*

793. It is better to be a coward for a minute than dead the rest of your life.

—*Irish Proverb*

794. An Englishman and a Frenchman, having quarrelled, were to fight a duel. Being both great cowards, they agreed (for their mutual safety) that the duel should take place in a perfectly dark room. The Englishman had to fire first. He groped his way to the fireplace, fired up the chimney, and brought down the Frenchman, who had taken refuge there.

Credit

795. Buying on trust is the way to pay double.

—*Old Proverb*

796. Credit is like a looking glass, which when once sullied by a breath, may be wiped clear again; but if once cracked can never be repaired.

—Scott

Credo

797. My code of life conduct is simply this: work hard, play to the allowable limit; disregard equally the good and bad opinions of others; never do a friend a dirty trick; never grow indignant over anything; live the moment to the utmost of its possibilities; and be satisfied with life always, but never with oneself.

—George Jean Nathan

798. I would be true, for there are those who trust me;
I would be pure, for there are those who care;
I would be strong, for there is much to suffer;
I would be brave, for there is much to dare.

I would be friend of all—the poor, the friendless;
I would be giving and forget the gift;
I would be humble, for I know my weakness;
I would look up—and laugh—and love—and lift.

—Howard Arnold
Walter

799.   TEN THINGS TO REMEMBER

There are ten things for which no one has ever been sorry:

1. For doing good to all.
2. For speaking evil of none.
3. For hearing before judging.
4. For thinking before speaking.
5. For holding an angry tongue.
6. For being kind to the distressed.
7. For asking pardon for all wrongs.
8. For being patient toward everybody.
9. For stopping the ears to a talebearer.
10. For disbelieving most of the ill reports.

Crime. See also Crime–Punishment

800.   One is never criminal in obeying the law of Nature.
—Honoré de Balzac

801.   What is crime amongst the multitude, is only vice among the few.

—Benjamin Disraeli

802.   Most people fancy themselves innocent of those crimes of which they cannot be convicted.

—Seneca

803.   "People can't fool a burglar by leaving lights on in the hall or living room of their homes when they go out for the evening," a professional burglar once said.

"There are several ways we can check this—ringing the doorbell and asking for a tip, ringing up on the telephone, and so forth. The best place to leave a light to prevent burglary is an upstairs bathroom and adjoining bedroom, with the blinds so arranged that the light shows just a little at the sides. It's easy to spot a bathroom in almost any house, and when there's a light there—well, we'd rather not take a chance."

Crime–Punishment. See also Crime

804.   He who profits by a crime, commits it.
—*Ancient Proverb*

805.   The sin they do by two and two they must pay for one by one.
—Rudyard Kipling

806. He who overlooks a crime, encourages the commission of another.

—*Ancient Proverb*

807. When the judge passes sentence—that's when a felon needs a friend.

808. To punish and not prevent is to labor at the pump and leave open the leak.

—THOMAS FULLER

809. It is better that ten guilty persons escape than that one innocent suffer.

—WILLIAM BLACKSTONE,
Commentaries on the Laws of England

810. A miscarriage of mercy is as much to be guarded against as a miscarriage of justice.

—ROBERT LYND

811. We enact many laws that manufacture criminals, and then a few that punish them.

—BENJAMIN R. TUCKER

812. To punish a man, you must injure him; to reform him, you must improve him. To injure him is not to improve him.

—GEORGE BERNARD SHAW

813. When we execute a murderer it may be that we fall into the same mistake as the child that strikes a chair it has collided with.

—G. C. LICHTENBERG

814. In passing sentence upon two rogues, Philip of Macedon ordered one of them to leave the country with all speed and the other to try to catch him.

Criticism

815. You have to be little to belittle.

816. Instead of putting others in their place, put yourself in their place.

817. If you are not afraid to face the music, you may get to lead the band some day.

—EDWIN H. STUART

818. Most people resent being called down, but it's much better than to be shown up.

819. The trouble with most of us is that we would rather be ruined by praise than saved with criticism.

820. It is much easier to criticize a sermon than it is to write one once a week for fifty-two weeks of the year.

—Jaspar B. Sinclair

821. Any baseball team could use a man who plays every position superbly, never strikes out and never makes an error; but there's no way to make him lay down his hot dog and come out of the grandstand.

822. I always said that I'd like Barrymore's acting till the cows came home. Well, ladies and gentlemen, last night the cows came home.

—George Jean Nathan's angry review on John Barrymore's clowning performance in *My Dear Children*

823. Don't be afraid of criticism. Anyone who can fill out a laundry slip thinks of himself as a writer. Anyone who can't fill out a laundry slip thinks of himself as a critic.

—George Seaton

824. Here's how the *Chicago Times* in 1865 evaluated Lincoln's Gettysburg Address in commenting on it the day after its delivery: "The cheek of every American must tingle with shame as he reads the silly, flat, and dish-watery utterances of a man who has to be pointed out to intelligent foreigners as President of the United States."

825. When you go into an orchard and see lots of sticks and stones under a tree you know that tree has borne some fruit. This little observation should be consolation to those who tend to get discouraged under criticism. No one bothers much about throwing verbal brickbats at people who are doing nothing. The more active and fruitful your life the more you will receive criticism.

Cruelty

826. All cruelty springs from weakness.

—Seneca

827. Find a cruel man and you see a coward.

—*Ancient Proverb*

Culture

828. Culture is not just an ornament; it is the expression of a nation's character, and at the same time it is a powerful instrument to mould character. The end of culture is right living.

—W. Somerset Maugham

829. The most distinctive mark of a cultured mind is the ability to take another's point of view; to put one's self in another's place, and see life and its problems from a point of view different from one's own. To be willing to test a new idea; to be able to live on the edge of difference in all matters intellectually; to examine without heat the burning question of the day; to have imaginative sympathy, openness and flexibility of mind, steadiness and poise of feeling, cool calmness of judgment, is to have culture.

—A. H. R. Fairchild

Curiosity

830. Where necessity ends, curiosity begins; and no sooner are we supplied with everything that nature can demand than we sit down to contrive artificial appetites.

—Dr. Samuel Johnson

831. There are two kinds of curiosity. One arises from interest, which makes us desirous to learn what may be useful to us; the other from pride, which makes us desire to know what others are ignorant of.

—François de la
Rochefoucauld

Cynicism

832. It takes a clever man to turn cynic and a wise man to be clever enough not to.

—Fannie Hurst, *Wisdom*

833. Cynics are only happy in making the world as barren to others as they have made it for themselves.

—George Meredith

834. Beware of the confirmed cynic—a menace to any organization. His misanthropic outlook spreads like a virus to all unfortunate enough to work near him. It has well been said cynicism is the small change of shallow minds. Is there a cure? Perhaps the only way is to put the victim in such a position he must work till he drops. Then he will be so occupied with the job he may forget his poison darts, and in doing so forget himself for a while.

Dancing

835. Dancing is one of the few remaining activities in which men lead women.

836. Gracefulness is a gift not shared by everybody. For instance there was the man who tried to learn how to dance. He followed the directions of his instructor, using a chair to serve as his partner, while practicing in privacy. He was so awkward and ungainly that he broke every chair in the house. The man? None other than Napoleon!

Danger

837. In this world, there is always danger for those who are afraid of it.

—GEORGE BERNARD SHAW

838. We cannot banish dangers, but we can banish fears. We must not demean life by standing in awe of death.

—DAVID SARNOFF

839. A timid person is frightened before a danger, a coward during the time, and a courageous person afterward.

—JEAN PAUL RICHTER

Death

840. Life is a dream; death, an awakening.

—LA BEAUMELLE

841. Death: Patrick Henry's second choice.

842. Good men must die, but death cannot kill their names.

—*Old Proverb*

843. Dead he is not, but departed,—for the artist never dies.

—HENRY WADSWORTH
LONGFELLOW,
Nuremberg

844. The ancients dreaded death; the Christian can only fear dying.

—AUGUSTUS HARE

845. To a father, when his child dies, the future dies; to a child, when his parents die, the past dies.

—BERTHOLD AUERBACH,
On the Heights

846. I look upon life as a gift from God. I did nothing to earn it. Now that the time is coming to give it back, I have no right to complain.
—JOYCE CARY (shortly before he died)

847. They that love beyond the world cannot be separated by it.

Death cannot kill what never dies. Nor can spirits ever be divided, that love and live in the same divine principle, the root and record, of their friendship. . . .

Death is but crossing the world, as friends do the seas; they live in one another still. . . .

This is the comfort of friends, that though they may be said to die, yet their friendship and society are, in the best sense, ever present because immortal.

—WILLIAM PENN

Debt

848. He is rich who owes nothing.

—Hungarian Proverb

849. Debt is the slavery of the free.

—PUBLILIUS SYRUS

850. Research shows that tall men are just as short at the end of the month as anybody else.

Debtor—Creditor

851. If one half of the world knew how the other half lived, they wouldn't pay their bills either.

852. There are some men who spend half their lives borrowing money and the other half in not paying it back.

Deception

853. It is a double pleasure to deceive the deceiver.

—JEAN DE LA FONTAINE

854. He is not deceived who knows himself to be deceived.

—Legal Maxim

855. If a man deceive me once shame on him, if he deceive me twice shame on me.

—Ancient Proverb

Decision—Decisions

856. We ought to weigh well what we can only once decide.
—PUBLILIUS SYRUS

857. When possible make the decisions now, even if action is in the future. A reviewed decision usually is better than one reached at the last moment.
—WILLIAM B. GIVEN, JR.

858. Never make a decision yourself, if you don't have to. When one of your men asks you a question, ask him what is the answer. There is only one answer to many questions, and, therefore, this method answers many questions before they are asked. It not only develops your men, but also enables you to measure their ability.
—HENRY L. DOHERTY

Defeat

859. When you cannot get a thing, then is the time to have contempt for it.
—BALTASAR GRACIÁN

860. What is defeat? Nothing but education; nothing but the first step to something better.
—WENDELL PHILLIPS

861. I would rather lose in a cause that I know some day will triumph than to triumph in a cause that I know some day will fail.
—WENDELL L. WILLKIE

Defeatism

862. The worst possible result of failure is defeatism. History is laden with examples of men who, having failed, tried again . . . with achievements which brought established benefits to mankind.

863. Besides the practical knowledge which defeat offers, there are important personality profits to be taken. Defeat strips away false values and makes you realize what you really want. It stops you from chasing butterflies and puts you to work digging gold.
—WILLIAM MOULTON
MARSTON

Delay

864. Delay is hateful, but it gives wisdom.
—PUBLILIUS SYRUS

865. Deliberation is not delaying.

—Ancient Proverb

866. Where duty is plain, delay is dangerous; where it is not, delay may be wise and safe.

—Old Proverb

Democracy

867. The number one principle of democracy is that even a wrong guy has rights.

868. Man's capacity for justice makes democracy possible, but man's inclination to injustice makes democracy necessary.

—Reinhold Niebuhr

869. One of the evils of democracy is that you have to endure the man you elected, whether you like him or not.

—Will Rogers

870. In free countries, every man is entitled to express his opinions —and every other man is entitled not to listen.

—G. Norman Collie

Despair

871. The darkest hour is only sixty minutes.

872. Never despair. But if you do, work on in despair.

—Edmund Burke

873. Despair is the absolute extreme of self-love. It is reached when a man deliberately turns his back on all help from anyone else in order to taste the rotten luxury of knowing himself to be lost.

—Thomas Merton, *Seeds of Contemplation.* Copyright by Abbey of Gethsemane, 1949

Despicability

874. A man must make himself despicable before he is despised by others.

—*Chinese Proverb*

875. In the footprints on the sands of time some people leave only the marks of a heel.

Destiny

876. Destiny leads the willing but drags the unwilling.

—Ancient Proverb

877. We sow our thoughts and reap our actions. We sow our actions and reap our habits. We sow our habits and reap our characters. We sow our characters and reap our destiny.

—C. A. HALL

878. Remember that you are but an actor, acting whatever part the Master has ordained. It may be short or it may be long. If he wishes you to represent a poor man, do so heartily; if a cripple or a magistrate, or a private man, in each case act your part with honor.

—EPICTETUS

Determination

879. Back of ninety-nine out of one hundred assertions that a thing cannot be done is nothing but the unwillingness to do it.

—WILLIAM FEATHER

880. It is a lot better to say "I must" than to wait until you have to listen to somebody else saying to you, "You must!"

881. A young doctor chose to make Japan his field of work. His friends tried to dissuade him from going there.

"Look," they said, "you are absolutely helpless against the suffering of that giant nation. You disappear in that vast mass of humanity. What can you do about their epidemics? What can you accomplish against war, famine, flood?"

As he started up the gangplank, the young man gave them his confident answer: "When it is dark about me, I do not curse at the darkness; I just light my candle."

—THOMAS DREIER

Dictatorship

882. Dictators always look good until the last ten minutes.

—JAN MASARYK

883. If I were a dictator the first book I would burn would be the Bible. I'd burn it because I'd realize that the whole concept of democracy came from that book. "Democracy" is a Greek word which means rule by the people, but even at the height of its ancient glory

Athens was not a democracy. The Greeks gave us a word for it, but the Bible gave us the philosophy for the way of life.

—QUENTIN REYNOLDS

884. An ancient ruler of a troublesome people sent an ambassador to a neighboring ruler to seek his secret of success as a dictator. Without wasting a word, the dictator took the ambassador to a nearby wheatfield. Wherever he saw one head of grain standing taller than the rest, he cut it off. The ambassador was quick to get the point.

Diet–Dieting. See *also* Overweight

885. Seconds count—especially when dieting.

886. When a woman is on a diet, that sneaked snack is the pause that refleshes.

887. Some people are no good at counting calories—and have the figures to prove it.

888. The world's most effective diet consists of exactly four words: "No more, thank you."

—KATE SMITH

Difference–Differences

889. Two things, well considered, would prevent many quarrels: first, to have it well ascertained whether we are not disputing about terms rather than things and, second, to examine whether that on which we differ is worth contending about.

—CHARLES C. COLTON

890. In every country where man is free to think and to speak, difference of opinion will arise from difference of perception, and the imperfection of reason; but these differences, when permitted, as in this happy country, to purify themselves by free discussion, are but as passing clouds overspreading our land transiently, and leaving our horizon more bright and serene.

—THOMAS JEFFERSON

891. Many people with different backgrounds, cultures, languages, and creeds combine to make a nation. But that nation is greater than the sum total of the individual skills and talents of its people. Something more grows out of their unity than can be calculated by adding the assets of individual contributions. That intangible additional quantity is often due to the differences which make the texture of the nation rich. Therefore, we must never wipe out or deride the differences amongst us—for where there is no difference, there is only indifference.

—Louis Nizer

Difficulty—Difficulties

892. Difficulties are meant to rouse, not discourage.

—William E. Channing

893. Be thankful if you have a job a little harder than you like. A razor cannot be sharpened on a piece of velvet.

Dignity

894. The fellow who stands on his dignity finds he has poor footing.

895. The two things that a healthy person hates most between heaven and hell are a woman who is not dignified and a man who is.

—G. K. Chesterton

896. It is of very little use in trying to be dignified, if dignity is no part of your character.

—Christian Nevell Bovée

Dilemma

897. If you can't lick them and they won't let you join them, what then?

898. Whereas the wheel that does the squeaking is the one that gets the grease, it is also true that the fly that does the buzzing is the fly that gets swat.

899. A man is known by the company he keeps. But . . . if a good man keeps company with a bad man, is the good man bad because he keeps company with the bad man, or is the bad man good because he keeps company with the good man?

Diplomacy

900. Diplomacy is the art of saying "Nice doggie!" until you can find a rock.

—Robert Phelps

901. Diplomacy is the art of convincing people you really don't want something you know you can't get.

902. If you have the advantage over someone, and you lead him to think that he has the advantage over you, without giving him the chance to take advantage of you—you are a diplomat.

Direction

903. It's easy to tell when you're on the right road—it's all up-grade.

904. A man was sailing in the channel between Southern California and Catalina Island in a fog when a new 40-foot power boat loomed up.

"Which way to Catalina Island?" shouted the man at the wheel of the power boat.

The yachtsman got out his parallel rule and laid a course on the chart.

"West by north by half a north."

"Don't get technical," the other man shouted. "Just point."

Disagreement

905. Honest differences of views and honest debate are not dis-unity. They are the vital process of policy-making among free men.
—HERBERT HOOVER

Disappointment

906. Too many people miss the silver lining because they're expecting gold.
—MAURICE SEITTER

907. Disappointment to a noble soul is what cold water is to burning metal; it strengthens, tempers, intensifies, but never destroys it.
—ELIZA TABOR

Discipline

908. Either you will teach your children discipline or the world will teach them discipline in ways that will be destructive to their individual happiness.
—J. EDGAR HOOVER

909. No horse gets anywhere until he is harnessed. No steam power drives anything until it is confined. No Niagara is ever turned into light and power until it is focused, dedicated and disciplined.
—HARRY EMERSON
FOSDICK

910. Spanking as a means of discipline is unknown among so-called primitive peoples. It is the civilized man's method, anthropologists tell us. Perhaps we civilized people resort to spanking because we are too much in a hurry about too many little things. And hurry is not a child's way of living.

> —GEORGE SHEVIAKOV in "How Early Does Discipline Begin?" *National Parent-Teacher*

911. Even Stonewall Jackson, transcendent military genius though he was—whose Valley Campaign with its wonderful succession of brilliant victories, is now studied by the military colleges of Europe as the supreme specimen of modern strategy—even Jackson, with all his genius, did not rely upon his sagacity alone, nor upon the unexcelled bravery of his men alone; he knew the value of discipline as few men have known it, and when asked to what degree of proficiency soldiers ought to be drilled, he answered: "Until they cannot make a mistake."

Discontent

912. Restlessness and discontent are the first necessities of progress.

> —THOMAS A. EDISON

913. Discontent is the want of self-reliance: it is infirmity of will.

> —RALPH WALDO EMERSON

914. The root of discontent is self-love; the more self is indulged the more it demands.

> —*Old Proverb*

Discouragement

915. The lowest ebb is the turn of the tide.

> —HENRY WADSWORTH LONGFELLOW

916. A man's caliber may be measured by the amount of opposition it takes to discourage him.

917.   CARRY THROUGH

There is no use in vain regret,
  In hot remorse or bitter tears;
There is no sense in looking back
  To stir the memories and the tears;
What you have done, then, you have done,
  And all your tears won't wash it out.
You cannot make a forward step
  Burdened by fear or chained by doubt.

There is no courage in the weak,
　No strength in that regretting mood;
Wise men go forward though they faint,
　And only weaklings sit and brood.
What you have been, too, you have been,
　What you're to be is up to you—
So get up, dust yourself, and work;
　Forget it all, and carry through!

—*Anonymous*

Discovery

918.　A great mathematician, Bertrand Russell, when asked how he accounted for his many new discoveries in what to the layman seems an already completely explored and fixed science, answered "I challenge the axioms."

919.　Don't keep forever on the public road, going only where others have gone. Leave the beaten path occasionally and dive into the woods. You will be certain to find something you have never seen before. It will be a little thing but do not ignore it. Follow it up, explore around it, one discovery will lead to another and before you know it, you will have something really worth thinking about.

—Alexander Graham Bell

Discretion

920.　Better lose the anchor than the whole ship.

—*Dutch Proverb*

921.　It's better to tighten your belt than to lose your pants.

Dissatisfaction

922.　If you would but exchange places with the other fellow, how much more you would appreciate your own position.

—Victor E. Gardner

923.　A fair amount of griping is a wonderful thing. It is healthy and a good way to let off steam. Dissatisfaction with the *status quo* leads to improvements and then we have progress.

—Stephen Baker

Distortion

924.　More and more we're learning that we can't tell a book by its movie.

925. A Nazi officer in occupied Paris was shown on the screen addressing a large group of rebellious Frenchmen. He asked those in the group desiring additional food coupons to raise their right hands. Naturally, the response was automatic. But when the newsreel was distributed by the Nazis, it was entitled "French citizens welcomed us to Paris with upraised hands in the Nazi salute." Thus can we be misled by the wiles of propaganda.

Distrust

926. If we distrust people, we justify their deceiving us.
—François de la
Rochefoucauld

927. Women distrust men too much in general, and not enough in particular.
—P. Commerson

Disunity

928. If a house be divided against itself, that house cannot stand.
—*New Testament*

Diversification

929. We ought never to fasten our ships to one small anchor, nor our life to a single hope.
—Epictetus

930. A tradesman wants to know why one often sees six or seven clocks in a main street each of which shows a different time. Well, if they all showed the same time, one would be enough.

Divorce

931. Love at first sight usually ends with divorce at first slight.

932. If a marriage gives out, usually there hasn't been enough give in.

933. There would be fewer divorces if the husband tried as hard to keep his wife as he did to get her.
—Rob Prewitt

934. Judging by the number of divorces, too many couples were mispronounced man and wife.

935. The divorce rate might go down if, instead of marrying for better or worse, young people would try to marry for good.

936. The divorce problem exists because there are too many husbands and wives and not enough married couples.

937. "If there was only some way of getting a divorce," snapped the woman to her lawyer, "without making *him* happy!"

938. Divorce is quite useless. One gets married for lack of judgment. Then one gets divorced for lack of patience. And finally one remarries for lack of memory!

—Armand Salacrou,
Réalités

Doctor–Patient

939. At today's medical prices, an ounce of prevention is worth about $18.50.

940. The doctor had a small boy in his office into whose knee he inserted a needle to draw off a little fluid.

The boy's mother and the doctor's nurse held the youngster while the doctor performed his painful task. The boy let out a yell, of course, even though he was more offended than hurt.

The task completed, the doctor sought to take the boy's mind off his troubles. "You're a nice looking chap," he told the youngster. "What do you expect to do when you grow up?"

His eyes wet with tears, the boy looked at the doctor with grim determination and muttered, "I'm going to kill you."

941. When a doctor writes a prescription he usually puts first a big capital R with a long tail. Across the tail is a short stroke. This has a tradition thousands of years old.

The R stands for the Latin Recipe, or Recipe in the imperative. And the stroke across the tail is actually an invocation to the great god Jove. It represents a J. Doctors no longer place any reliance on the help of Jove, but the custom persists.

A patient often regards a doctor's handwriting as bad merely because he cannot read the prescription. He is not meant to, anyway. The doctor uses abbreviations which are quite well understood by the druggist to whom the prescription is addressed. Doctors are not wilfully obscure in their handwriting, but subconsciously they may develop obscurity because they are aware that it is frequently not good for a patient to know too much about the drug he is getting.

Dog–Dogs

942. Money will buy a fine dog, but only love will make him wag his tail.

943. My line of thoughts about dogs is analogous. A dog reflects the family life. Whoever saw a frisky dog in a gloomy family, or a sad dog in a happy one? Snarling people have snarling dogs, dangerous people have dangerous ones. And their passing moods may reflect the passing moods of others.

—Sherlock Holmes

944. I hope that I retain my reason about dogs, but whether I do or not, I know this, that I would not be without these animals at any price. Their companionship is delightful, and their affection extraordinarily moving.

To be welcomed home by three little dogs that stand in the hall and wag their tails and utter barks of pleasure at one's return is among the happiest experiences a man can enjoy. It is a happiness I do not intend, if I can help it, ever to forego.

There are people, and I am sorry for them, to whom a dog is only a nuisance. Well, they have their nature, and it is absurd to complain of them for it, but they are unenviable. They are missing a great happiness.

—St. John Ervine

Doubt–Doubts

945. Better be despised for too anxious apprehensions, than ruined by too confident security.

—Edmund Burke

946. Doubt is like the dark. A room may be dark because the sun is not shining—or it may be dark because the windows are dirty. One cannot turn on the sun, but one can wash the windows.

947. I think one of the troubles of the world has been the habit of dogmatically believing something or other . . . we ought always to entertain our opinions with some measure of doubt.

—Bertrand Russell

Dream–Dreams–Dreaming

948. The best way to make your dreams come true is to wake up.

949. Add sputniks and missiles to all the other good reasons for not building castles in the air.

950. We sometimes congratulate ourselves at the moment of waking from a troubled dream: it may be so the moment after death.
—NATHANIEL HAWTHORNE

951. I have read a pathetic farewell letter which my mother, as a young girl, wrote to her parents. She dreamed that she saw a tombstone with a date upon it, and the date was approaching. She lived to be eighty-three.
—DEAN W. R. INGE

Drinking

952. A fool and his money are saloon parted.

953. We drink to one another's health and spoil our own.
—JEROME K. JEROME

954. Some battle their way to the top—others bottle their way to the bottom.

955. A cocktail party starts out with people mixing drinks and ends up with drinks mixing people.

956. It is unfortunate today that some regard alcoholism as a disease like cancer. It may end as a disease, but it begins with an act of will, namely to take a drink.
—BISHOP FULTON J. SHEEN

957. Drink because you are happy, but never because you are miserable. Never drink when you are wretched without it, or you will be like the grey-faced gin-drinker in the slum; but drink when you would be happy without it, and you will be like the laughing peasants of Italy. Never drink because you need it, for this is rational drinking, and the way to death and hell. But drink because you do not need it, for this is irrational drinking, and the ancient health of the world.
—GILBERT K. CHESTERTON

Drunkenness

958. Don't drink to the good health of so many people that you lose your own.

959. Every moderate drinker can stop if he would; every inebriate if he could.
—*Old Proverb*

960. A man past middle life came to Dante Gabriel Rossetti, bringing with him some sketches and drawings. The fumes of liquor were on his breath; his eyes were bloodshot, his hands unsteady. Rossetti saw at a glance that the drawings were hopeless, and told him so. For a moment the visitor hesitated. Then he drew from an inside pocket another portfolio of drawings, saying they were the work of a young student. Rossetti was delighted and asked that the youth be sent to him. "Ah, sir," said the man, "I am, or rather I was, that youth. Your words, sir, have only confirmed my own suspicions. I have thrown away my best talents."

Duty–Duties

961. A sense of duty is useful in work, but offensive in personal relations.

—BERTRAND RUSSELL

962. The man who is "all wool and a yard wide" doesn't shrink from doing his duty.

963. Doing a thing from mere sense of duty is like eating when you are not hungry.

964. One trouble with the world is that so many people who stand up vigorously for their rights fall down miserably on their duties.

965. A farmer was walking over his farm with a friend, exhibiting his crops, herds of cattle, and flocks of sheep. His friend was greatly impressed and highly pleased, especially with the splendid sheep. He had seen the same breed frequently before, but never had seen such fine specimens. With great earnestness he asked the farmer how he had succeeded in rearing such fine sheep. The simple answer was, "I take care of my lambs."

966. Someone tells the story about the time when a rider who headed a hunting party in England commanded a boy at a gate to open it.

"I'm sorry, sir," answered the boy, "but my father sent me to say that you must not hunt on his grounds."

"Do you know who I am?" demanded the man gruffly.

"No, sir," answered the boy.

"I am the Duke of Wellington."

The boy took off his cap, but he did not open the gate. "The Duke of Wellington will not ask me to disobey my father's orders," he said quietly.

Slowly the man took off his hat, and smiled. "I honor the boy who is faithful to his duty," said the great man, and with that he and his party rode away.

—Nashua Cavalier

Earnestness

967. Earnestness alone makes life eternity.

—Thomas Carlyle

968. Patience is only one faculty; earnestness the devotion of all the faculties.

—Christian Nevell
Bovée

969. The shortest and surest way to prove a work possible is strenuously to set about it; and no wonder if that proves it possible that for the most part makes it so.

—Robert South

Eating

970. We used to say "What's cooking?" when we came home from work. Now it's "What's thawing?"

971. It was shortly after Thanksgiving Day that someone asked the little boy to define the word "appetite." His reply was prompt and enthusiastic.

"When you're eating you're 'appy; and when you get through your tight—that's appetite."

Economy. *See also* Thrift

972. Economy is a way of spending money without getting any pleasure out of it.

—Armand Salacrou,
Réalités

973. In this free-spending age, the man who preaches economy might as well start by saving his breath.

974. Economy is going without something you do want, in case you should some day want something which you probably won't want.

—Anthony Hope

Education

975. He who opens a school, closes a prison.

—Victor Hugo

976. Education should be exercise; it has become massage.
—Martin H. Fischer, M.D.

977. All the average youngster wants out of school is himself.

978. Even to rebuild the Temple, the schools must not be closed.
—*The Talmud*

979. By nature all men are alike, but by education become different.

—*Old Proverb*

980. Jails and prisons are the complement of schools; so many less as you have of the latter, so many more you must have of the former.
—Horace Mann

981. Education is not intended to make lawyers or clergymen, soldiers or schoolmasters, farmers or artisans, but men.
—Sir John Lubbock

982. An education doesn't always teach one what to do, but if a person is smart it will give him some hints as to how to undo what he should not have done.

983. Pour water hastily into a vessel with a narrow neck, little enters; but pour gradually, and in small quantities, and the vessel is filled. Such was the simile employed by Quintilian, to show the folly of teaching children too much at a time.

Efficiency

984. Doubtless the world was made in seven days. There were no efficiency experts then.

985. A sense of the value of time—that is, of the best way to divide one's time into one's various activities—is an essential preliminary to efficient work; it is the only method of avoiding hurry.
—Arnold Bennett

Effort

986. Genius begins great works; labor alone finishes them.
—Joseph Joubert

987. If you would have things come your way, go after them.

988. The trouble with people these days is that they want to get to the promised land without going through the wilderness.

989. A law of nature rules that energy cannot be destroyed. You change its form from coal to steam, from steam to power in the turbine, but you do not destroy energy. In the same way, another law governs human activity and rules that honest effort cannot be lost, but that some-day the proper benefits will be forthcoming.

—Paul Speicher

Egotism

990. The more you speak of yourself, the more you are likely to lie.

—Johann von Zimmerman

Employer—Employe

991. The employer generally gets the employes he deserves.

—Sir Walter Bilbey

992. If you want to get the best out of a man, you must look for the best that is in him.

—Bernard Haldane

993. *Sign on a secretary's desk:* The boss may not always be right, but the boss is always the boss.

994. It's always easier to arrive at a firm conviction about a problem after you know what the boss thinks.

995. We would rather have one man or woman working with us than three merely working for us.

—J. Dabney Day

996. A modern employer is one who is looking for men and women between the ages of 21 and 30 with 40 years' experience.

997. The question, "Who ought to be boss?" is like asking "Who ought to be the tenor in the quartet?" Obviously, the man who can sing tenor.

—Henry Ford

998. The boss put a new sign in the office: "Don't hesitate; do it now!" The first employe to see it hit him for a raise, the second went home immediately, and the third punched him in the nose.

999. Be alert, work hard, do a good job every day, and who knows? Some day you may own the company, work in a big private office, and have the privilege of worrying about staying in the black, the pleasure of meeting the payroll, and the happy task of beating competition.

1000. Annie, the maid, was straightening up the living room, when suddenly her mistress, who had looked in from the hall, exclaimed: "You didn't wind that clock, Annie. You know it's an 8-day clock, but you gave the key only one or two turns."

"Haven't you forgotten I'm leavin' tomorrow, Ma'am?" Annie airily rejoined. "I can't be doin' any of the new girl's work!"

1001. *To all employes:* Due to increased competition and a desire to stay in business, we find it necessary to institute a new policy. We are asking that somewhere between starting and quitting time, and without infringing too much on the time usually devoted to Lunch Periods, Coffee Breaks, Rest Periods, Story Telling, Ticket Selling, Vacation Planning and the re-hashing of yesterday's TV programs, each employe endeavor to find some time that can be set aside and known as the "Work Break."

—George Fuermann

1002. If you work for a man, in heaven's name work
    for him;
Speak well of him and stand by the institution
    he represents.
Remember, an ounce of loyalty is worth a pound
    of cleverness.
If you must growl, condemn, and eternally find
    fault, why—resign your position.
And when you are outside, damn to your heart's
    content—
But as long as you are a part of the institution
    do not condemn it.
If you do, the first high wind that comes along
    will blow you away and probably you will
    never know why.

—Elbert Hubbard

Employment

1003. Work! The job you save may be your own.

1004. There is no future in any job; the future lies in the man who holds the job.

—Dr. G. W. Crane, *Psychology Applied* (Hopkins, Inc.), 1960, p. 692

1005. For every man who has worked himself out of a job, a hundred have talked themselves out of one.

1006. Always remember the soundest way to progress in any organization is to help the man ahead of you to get promoted.

—L. S. HAMAKER

1007. The nearest to perfection most people ever come is when filling out an employment application.

1008. You can buy a man's time, you can buy a man's physical presence at a given place; you can even buy a measured number of skilled muscular motions per hour; but you cannot buy enthusiasm, loyalty or the devotion of hearts, minds and souls. You have to earn these things.

—CLARENCE FRANCIS

Emulation

1009. Your son will follow your footsteps more easily than he will follow your advice.

1010. There is much difference between imitating a good man, and counterfeiting him.

—BENJAMIN FRANKLIN

1011. He who imitates what is evil always goes beyond the example that is set; on the contrary he who imitates what is good always falls short.

—FRANCESCO GUICCIARDINI

Encouragement

1012. Correction does much, but encouragement does more.

—JOHANN WOLFGANG VON
GOETHE

1013. The truth is that for everything that can be accomplished by showing a person when he's wrong, ten times as much can be accomplished by showing him where he is right. The reason we don't do it so often is that it's more fun to throw a rock through a window than to put in a pane of glass.

—ROBERT T. ALLEN, "But
—I Do Mind Criticism!"
Farm Journal

Enemy—Enemies

1014. You can meet friends everywhere but you cannot meet enemies anywhere—you have to make them.

1015. It is much safer to reconcile an enemy than to vanquish him; victory may deprive him of his poison, but reconciliation of his ill-will.

1016. The enemies a man makes by taking a decided stand generally have more respect for him than the friends he makes by being on the fence.

Enlightenment

1017. There are two ways of spreading light: to be the candle, or the mirror that reflects it.

—EDITH WHARTON

1018. We may receive so much light as not to see, and so much philosophy as to be worse than foolish.

—WALTER SAVAGE LANDOR

Enthusiasm

1019. Enthusiasts without capacity are the really dangerous people.

—JOHN MORLEY

1020. A man who allows himself to be carried away with enthusiasm often has to walk back.

1021. The English novelist, J. B. Priestly, was once asked why it was that several gifted writers who were young with him had not matured in their art as he had. His answer was this: "Gentlemen, the difference between us was not in ability, but in the fact that they merely toyed with the fascinating idea of writing. I cared like blazes! It is this caring like the blazes that counts."

Envy

1022. To envy anybody is to confess ourselves his inferior.

—JULIE JEANNE ELÉONORE
DE LESPINASSE

1023. Few men have the strength to honor a friend's success without envy.

—AESCHYLUS

1024. For one man who sincerely pities our misfortunes, there are a thousand who sincerely hate our success.

—CHARLES C. COLTON

1025. When the grass looks greener on the other side of the fence, it may be that they take better care of it over there.

Equality

1026. The only real equality is in the cemetery.

—*German Proverb*

1027. Equality of opportunity is an equal opportunity to prove unequal talents.

—SIR HERBERT SAMUEL

1028. Equal opportunities become unequal in the hands of unequal men.

1029. Equality is not a law of nature. Nature has made no two things equal: its sovereign law is subordination and dependence.

—LUC DE CLAPIERS
VAUVENARGUES

1030. If all men were on an equality, the consequence would be that all must perish; for who would till the ground? who would sow it? who would plant? who would press wine?

—*From the Latin*

Equivocation

1031. Equivocation is first cousin to a lie.

—*Ancient Proverb*

1032. Equivocation is half way to lying, as lying is the whole way to Hell.

—WILLIAM PENN

Error. See *also* Mistake

1033. There is no harm in being sometimes wrong—especially if one is promptly found out.

—JOHN MAYNARD KEYNES

1034. To err is human, but when the eraser wears out ahead of the pencil, you're overdoing it.

—JOSH JENKINS

Eternity

1035. Life is the preface to the book of eternity.

—LOISELEUR

1036. The thought of eternity consoles for the shortness of life.

—LUC DE CLAPIERS
VAUVENARGUES

Etiquette

1037. Good manners are made up of petty sacrifices.

—RALPH WALDO EMERSON

1038. A man's own good breeding is the best security against other people's ill manners.

—LORD CHESTERFIELD

Evil

1039. Evil often triumphs, but never conquers.

—JOSEPH ROUX, *Meditations of a Parish Priest*

1040. A little evil is often necessary for obtaining a great good.

—VOLTAIRE

Exaggeration

1041. We always weaken whatever we exaggerate.

—JEAN FRANÇOIS DE
LAHARPE

1042. There are people so addicted to exaggeration that they can't tell the truth without lying.

Example

1043. Example is not the main thing in influencing others. It is the only thing!

—DR. ALBERT SCHWEITZER

1044. No man is completely worthless. He can always serve as a horrible example.

1044a. When Benjamin Franklin wished to interest the people of Philadelphia in street lighting, he didn't try to persuade them by talking about it—instead, he hung a beautiful lantern on a long bracket before his own door. Then he kept the glass brightly polished, and carefully and religiously lit the wick every evening at the approach of dusk. Thus recounts Cole D. Robinson in *World Horizons.*

People wandering about on the dark street saw Franklin's light a long way off and came under the influence of its friendly glow with grateful hearts. To each one it seemed to say: "Come along, my friend! Here is a safe place to walk. See that cobblestone sticking up? Don't stumble over it! Good-bye! I shall be here to help you again tomorrow night, if you should come this way."

It wasn't long before Franklin's neighbors began placing lights in brackets before their homes, and soon the entire city awoke to the value of street lighting and took up the matter with interest and enthusiasm.

Excess–Excessiveness

1045. Too much is seldom enough. Pumping after your bucket is full prevents its keeping so.

—Augustus Hare

1046. The excesses of our youth are draughts upon our old age, payable with interest, about thirty years after date.

—Charles C. Colton

1047. Excessive ambitions necessarily entail great sacrifices. Much hoarding must be followed by heavy loss. He who knows when he has enough will not be put to shame.

—Lao Tzû

Excuse–Excuses

1048. Excellence is the perfect excuse. Do it well, and it matters little what.

—Ralph Waldo Emerson

1049. An excuse is worse and more terrible than a lie; for an excuse is a lie guarded.

—Alexander Pope

1050. The man who really wants to do something finds a way, the other kind finds an excuse.

Executive

1051. The big shots are only the little shots who keep shooting.

—Christopher Morley

1052. The limit of work an executive can delegate to subordinates is what he can—if need be—undo himself.

1053. No man will ever be a big executive who feels that he must, either openly or under cover, follow up every order he gives and see that it is done—nor will he ever develop a capable assistant.

—John Lee Mahin

Expectation

1054. As long as prosperity is built on people spending all they *hope* to earn, people will have to have faith or they may need charity.

1055. Any man will usually get from other men just what he is expecting of them. If he is looking for friendship he will likely receive it. If his attitude is that of indifference, it will beget indifference. And if a man is looking for a fight he will in all likelihood be accommodated in that. Men can be stimulated to show off their good qualities to the leader who seems to think they have good qualities.

—John Richelsen

Expediency

1056. Expedients are for the hour; principles for the ages.

—Henry Ward Beecher

1057. No man is justified in doing evil on the grounds of expedience.

—Theodore Roosevelt

Experience

1058. Smart people speak from experience—smarter people, from experience, don't speak.

1059. Experience may be a good teacher, but some people never graduate from kindergarten.

Extravagance

1060. Today's extravagance becomes tomorrow's necessity.

1061. He who buys what he needs not, sells what he needs.

—*Japanese Proverb*

1062. One reason why so many people are extravagant these days is that there are a thousand ways to spend money and only one way to save it.

Fact–Facts

1063. Digging up facts may be a hard job, but it's much better than jumping at conclusions.

1064. We should keep so close to facts that we never have to remember the second time what we said the first time.
—F. Marion Smith, D.D.

1065. The possession of facts is knowledge; the use of them is wisdom; the choice of them, education. Knowledge is not power but riches, and like them, has its value in spending.

Failure

1066. Success is a public affair; failure is a private funeral.
—Rosalind Russell

1067. Failure is only the opportunity to begin again, more intelligently.
—Henry Ford

1068. A man may fall many times but he won't be a failure until he says that someone pushed him.
—Elmer G. Letterman

1069. In a western town there's a new automatic ice plant with a number of slots that take coins of different denominations for ice of assorted sizes and kinds. Instructions are printed over each slot, but in the center is the boldest sign of all: *"When all else fails, try reading directions."*

1070. The pattern for failure has four corners: The unwillingness to accept help; the belief that force is a substitute for gentleness; the endeavor to escape from reality; and finally, self-pity, where only the dignity of confession can bring healing and self-respect.

Faith

1071. Living without faith is like driving in the fog.

1072. Small faith will take you to heaven but great faith will bring heaven to you.

1073. A minister noticed a little boy holding securely the end of a long string. The attached kite was indistinguishable in the evening twilight. When he inquired of the lad why he was acting so, the boy said he was flying a kite. "I can't see it; but I know it's there, for I feel the pull."

—Rev. Bernard L.
Dunham

Falsehood. See *also* Veracity

1074. Half a fact is a whole falsehood.

—*Old Proverb*

1075. The cruelest lies are often told in silence.

1076. Falsehood is never so successful as when she baits her hook with truth.

—Charles C. Colton

1077. The liar's punishment is not that no one will believe him, but that he will believe no one else.

1078. The most mischievous liars are those who keep sliding on the verge of truth.

—J. C. and A. W. Hare,
Guesses at Truth

Fame

1079. Fame like a river is narrowest at its source and broadest afar off.

—*Ancient Proverb*

1080. Happy is the man who hath never known what it is to taste of fame—to have it is a purgatory, to want it is a hell.

—E. G. Bulwer-Lytton

1081. The halls of fame are very wide and are always very full. Some go in by the door called "Push," and some by the door called "Pull."

1082. It is said that Lord Northcliffe in a dinner-table discussion was told by a lady that "Thackeray awoke one morning and found himself famous."

Northcliffe answered promptly: "When that morning dawned, dear lady, Thackeray had been writing eight hours a day for fifteen years. The man who wakes up one day to find himself famous hasn't been asleep."

1083. "Literary fame is not always highly regarded by the people," once wrote William Dean Howells. "I remember when I was in San

Remo, some years ago, seeing in a French newspaper this notice by a rat-trap maker of Lyons:

"'To whom it may concern: M. Pierre Loti, of Lyons, begs to state that he is not the same person and that he has nothing in common with one Pierre Loti, a writer.'"

Family

1084. In the modern home a father knows better than to know best.

1085. The average household consists of a husband who makes the money, and a wife and kids who make it necessary.

Family Life

1086. The happy family is but an earlier heaven.
—SIR JOHN BOWRING

1087. If you would have a happy family life, remember two things: in matters of principle, stand like a rock; in matters of taste, swim with the current.

Farm—Farmer—Farming

1088. The farmer doesn't go to work. He wakes up surrounded by it.

1089. When tillage begins, other arts follow. The farmers therefore are the founders of human civilization.
—DANIEL WEBSTER,
September 1849

1090. There's only one way to get rich farming, and that's to sell your corn as whiskey, your potatoes as vodka, your barley as beer, your fruit as brandy, your sorghum as rum.

Fashion

1091. *Friend whispering warning to girl in barest of evening gowns:* "Someone is talking about your back behind you."

1092. The modern woman's clothes are like barbed wire fence—they protect the property without obstructing the view.

1093. Women dress less to be clothed than to be adorned. When alone before their mirrors, they think more of men than of themselves.
—ROCHEBRUNE

Fatalism

1094. Prepare for the worst; expect the best; and take what comes.

1095. Take things as they come—the past is gone, tomorrow is an uncertainty, and today is no sure thing.

Fatherhood

1096. No father has to be much of an actor to play a supporting role.

1097. *One dad to another:* "I'm no model father. All I'm trying to do is behave so that when people tell my son that he reminds them of me, he'll stick out his chest instead of his tongue."

1098. The words that a father speaks to his children in the privacy of home are not heard by the world, but, as in whispering-galleries, they are clearly heard at the end and by posterity.
—JEAN PAUL RICHTER

1099. FATHERS OF GREAT MEN

The father of *Shakespeare* was a wool merchant.
The Emperor *Diocletian* was the son of a slave.
Abraham Lincoln's father was a poor farmer and laborer.
Cardinal Antonelli's father was an Italian bandit.
The father of *Adrian,* the ascetic pontiff, was a beggar.
Virgil's father was a porter and for years a slave.
Demosthenes' father was a blacksmith and swordmaker.
Ben Franklin was the son of a soapboiler.
Daniel Webster was the son of a poor farmer.
Christopher Columbus was the son of a weaver.
Sophocles, the Greek poet, was the son of a blacksmith.

Father–Son

1100. Fathers should not get too discouraged if their sons reject their advice. It will not be wasted; years later the sons will offer it to their own offspring.

1101. A doctor was busy in his study when his small son came in and stood silently by. The doctor, preoccupied with his work, put his hand into his pocket, took out a coin and offered it to the boy. "I don't want any money, daddy," the lad said.

After a few moments the doctor opened a drawer of his desk, took out a candy bar and offered this to his son. Again he was refused.

A little impatient, the busy doctor asked, "Well, what *do* you want?"

"I don't want anything," replied the boy. "I only wanted to be with you."

—From *Treasury of the Christian World,* by A. GORDON NASBY. Copyright by Harper & Brothers. Used by permission.

1102.
A careful man I ought to be;
A little fellow follows me;
I do not dare to go astray
For fear he'll go the self-same way.

I cannot once escape his eyes,
Whate'er he sees me do he tries.
Like me he says he's going to be,
The little chap who follows me.

He thinks that I am good and fine,
Believes in every word of mine.
The base in me he must not see,
That little chap who follows me.

I must remember as I go
Thru Summer's sun and Winter's snow
I am building for the years to be;
That little chap who follows me.

—*Author Unknown*

Fault–Faults

1103. A fault denied is twice committed.

—*Spanish Proverb*

1104. He who overlooks one fault invites another.

—PUBLILIUS SYRUS

1105. No man is born without faults; he is the best who has the fewest.

—HORACE

1106. The first faults are theirs that commit them;
The second faults are theirs that permit them.

—THOMAS FULLER

Fault-Finding

1107. Don't find fault with what you don't understand.

—*French Proverb*

1108. If you are pleased at finding faults, you are displeased at finding perfections.

—JOHANN KASPAR
LAVATER

1109. We are likely to find fault with our neighbors for trifling shortcomings and to overlook serious faults in ourselves.

We want to get a good price when we sell, and to buy cheaply; we want others to be dealt with severely when they are in trouble, but for ourselves we desire mercy and patience.

We expect our word to be accepted unquestioningly, but we are uppish and unpleasant when it comes to accepting some one else's word.

—ST. FRANCIS DE SALES

Favor—Favors

1110. To accept a favor is to sell one's freedom.

—PUBLILIUS SYRUS

1111. A favor is half granted when gracefully refused.

—PUBLILIUS SYRUS

1112. The greater the favor, the greater the obligation.

—CICERO

Fear

1113. It is better to have a right destroyed than to abandon it because of fear.

—PHILLIP MANN

1114. Fear isn't cowardice. Cowardice is failure to fight fear. The weakling feels fear and quits. The man of courage feels fear and fights.

—ARNOLD H. GLASOW,
Thoughts for Today

1115. They conquer who believe they can. He has not learned the lesson of life who does not each day surmount a fear.

—RALPH WALDO EMERSON

Fellowship

1116. With some people you spend an evening, with others you invest it.

1117. What men call . . . good fellowship is commonly but the virtue of pigs in a litter, which lie close together to keep each other warm.
—Henry David Thoreau

Firmness

1118. The greatest firmness is the greatest mercy.
—Henry Wadsworth Longfellow

1119. The superior man is firm in the right way, and not merely firm.

—Confucius

Fishing

1120. There was once a fisherman who told the truth. He called another fisherman a liar.

1121. Small men have one great advantage as anglers. They make the fish look bigger when they are photographed.

1122. Once upon a time, the Roman goddess, Pales, held her annual feast attended by people from miles around. Everyone it seemed was there, just as Pales required.

But in the midst of festivities she suddenly noticed that two fishermen were missing. In great indignation the goddess set out to learn the reason. Along a stream she finally found the two contentedly fishing and earnestly hoping that their absence from the feast would not be noticed. Great was their consternation at the approach of the goddess. She, in her fury, promptly turned them into an alder and a willow. To this day both these trees continue to grow along streams, leaning out as though to watch for fish, and sometimes lazily dipping their branches, like fish lines, into the water.

Flag, U. S.

1123. The flagstaff over the west entrance of the United States Capitol probably flies more American flags than any flagpole in the United Staates. It is customary that all flags given to schools, veterans' organizations and other deserving groups or individuals by the United

States Government be carefully unfurled, raised to the top of the Capitol staff and flown for several minutes before packing for shipment. There are several flags flying day and night over the U. S. Capitol—one of the few places where the flying of the flag at night is authorized. Some of them have special significance. For example, American flags are flown over both the Senate and House wings of the Capitol to signify that the particular legislative bodies are in session. They are lowered when the groups adjourn.

1124. THE FLAG SPEAKS

I stand for a world-shaking idea that is creating a new earth, putting kings to flight, bursting the shackles of slaves, making men gods, glorifying human personality and lifting all humanity to a higher plane of more abundant living. I stand for a new experiment in the laboratory of life which has exploded old theories of government and set men free. I have kindled, and kept burning in the hearts of men, the fires of liberty, unity, justice and brotherhood. Men have lived and toiled and died to keep alive the things I symbolize. A great host of heroes, with the help of God, have kept me gallantly flying in the face of every threat and challenge to the democratic way of life which I represent. The blood spilled at Valley Forge, Gettysburg, San Juan Hill, Chateau Thierry, Bataan, and in all the other great battles for freedom on land and sea, is in my red stripes. The shining white light of concentrated sunshine penetrating the blackest night is in my white stripes, which in the nation's darkest hours are radiant with eternal hope. The vast sweeping infinity of the heavens is in my stars, inspiring mankind to continue climbing courageously up the spiral staircase of history to a world of gleaming promise. I am the emblem of man's finest dream. I am the standard of the "last best hope of earth." I am the *American Flag.*

—WILFERD A. PETERSON, in *The Art of Getting Along*

Flattery

1125. When a man is really important, the worst adviser he can have is a flatterer.

—GERALD W. JOHNSON

1126. Flatterers say to your face that which they would never think of saying behind your back.

—*If Elected, I Promise* by JOHN F. PARKER (Doubleday & Company, Inc.)

1127. He who praises me on all occasions is a fool who despises me or a knave who wishes to cheat me.

—*Chinese Proverb*

1128. Never praise a woman too highly. If you stop, she'll think you don't love her any more; if you keep it up, she'll think she's too good for you.

Flower–Flowers

1129. Flowers are the sweetest things that God ever made, and forgot to put a soul into.

—Henry Ward Beecher

1130. Flowers are often sensitive to noise. If you set a vase of carnations close to a noisy orchestra, you will find that in time they will turn away from the music, as if the sound was too much for them.

Flowers are much like human beings; they catch cold from draughts, are stupefied by chloroform, and become intoxicated with alcohol.

Folly

1131. Every man is a fool in some man's opinion.

—*Spanish Proverb*

1132. A fool with money to burn soon meets his match.

1133. When a poor fool acquires riches he becomes a rich fool.

—Abraham Miller

1134. There's no fool like an old fool. You just can't beat experience.

1135. We know that a fool and his money are soon parted, but what would be interesting to learn is how they got together in the first place.

Fool–Fools. See Folly

Forbearance

1136. Forbearance is a part of justice.

—Marcus Aurelius

1137. Next to knowing when to seize an opportunity, the most important thing in life is to know when to forego an advantage.

—Benjamin Disraeli

Foresightedness

1138. It is a mistake to look too far ahead. Only one link in the chain of destiny can be handled at a time.

1139. Men become bad and guilty because they speak and act without foreseeing the results of their words and their deeds.

—Franz Kafka

Forgetting

1140. Life cannot go on without much forgetting.

—Honoré de Balzac

1141. My skirt with tears is always wet—
I have forgotten to forget.

—*Japanese Proverb*

Forgiveness

1142. So long as one loves, one forgives.

—François de la
Rochefoucauld

1143. To forgive all is as inhuman as to forgive none.

—Seneca

1144. Forgiving the unrepentant is like drawing pictures on water.

—*Japanese Proverb*

1145. He who has not forgiven an enemy has never yet tasted one of the most sublime enjoyments of life.

—Johann Kaspar
Lavater

1146. William Makepeace Thackeray and Charles Dickens, toward the middle of the nineteenth century, became rivals and estranged. Just before Christmas, 1863, they met in London, and frigidly failed to recognize each other. Thackeray turned back, seized the hand of Dickens and said he could no longer bear the coldness that existed between them. Dickens was touched; they parted with smiles. The old jealousy was destroyed. Almost immediately afterward Thackeray suddenly died. Sir Thomas Martin later wrote, "The next time I saw Dickens he was looking down into the grave of his great rival. He must have rejoiced, I thought, that they had shaken hands so warmly a day or so before." Is it not always well to seek forgiveness now? Are we sure that another opportunity will be afforded?

Fortitude

1147. There is a certain blend of courage, integrity, character and principle which has no satisfactory dictionary name but has been called different things at different times in different countries. Our American name for it is "guts."

1148. One of man's greatest qualities is described by the simple word "guts"—the ability to take it. If you have the discipline to stand fast when your body wants to run, if you can control your temper and remain cheerful in the face of monotony or disappointment, you have "guts" in the soldiering sense. This ability to take it must be trained—the training is hard, mental as well as physical. But once ingrained, you can face and flail the enemy as a soldier, and enjoy the challenges of life as a civilian.

—COL. JOHN S. ROOSMA

Fortune, Good. See Luck

Fourth of July

1149. The United States is the only country with a known birthday. All the rest began, they know not when, and grew into power, they know not how. If there had been no Independence Day, England and America combined would not be so great as each actually is. There is no Republican, no Democrat, on the Fourth of July—all are Americans.

—JAMES G. BLAINE

1150. On July 4, 1776, 56 serious-minded and dedicated men signed their names to a simple, impassioned document which they had named the Declaration of Independence. They were fully aware of the fact that this document would either bring freedom to all Americans, or else it would leave all 56 of them hanging from a gallows, to prove that their dream of national sovereignty had been folly. Only time would tell—and it did.

Frankness

1151. Be not ashamed to say what you are not ashamed to think.

—MICHEL DE MONTAIGNE

1152. Often our worst enemies are the friends we once talked to as only a friend should.

Freedom

1153. The free man is not he who defies the rules . . . but he who, recognizing the compulsions inherent in his being, seeks rather to read, mark, learn, and inwardly digest each day's experience.

—BERNARD I. BELL

1154. Liberty of conscience cannot mean liberty to *do* what I like. . . . It is from my likings that I must be emancipated if I would be a free man.

—FREDERICK D. MAURICE

1155. To stand up for the freedom of others is one of the marks of those who are free, just as to fail to do so is one of the marks of those who are ready to be enslaved.

—ALAN PATON

1156.
Stone walls do not a prison make,
　　Nor iron bars a cage;
Minds innocent and quiet take
　　That for an hermitage;
If I have freedom in my love
　　And in my soul am free,
Angels alone that soar above,
　　Enjoy such liberty.

—RICHARD LOVELACE

1157. The difference between a river and a swamp is that a river is confined within banks, while a swamp is not . . . Because a river is confined, and channeled, it has life. It is a mighty, moving, living thing. Because a swamp has no restrictions, it becomes thin and stagnant. . . . In our modern life we boast of freedom. We want life without restrictions and without confinement. Only we forget that such living becomes stagnant.

—LEONARD COCHRAN

Freedom of Speech. See Speech, Freedom of

Freedom of the Press. See Press, Freedom of

Friendship

1158. When we lose a friend we die a little.

1159. Friendship is like two clocks keeping time.

1160. When a friend asks, there is no tomorrow.
—*Ancient Proverb*

1161. Friends are made by many acts—and lost by only one.

1162. The more hot arguments you win, the fewer warm friends you'll have.
—Burton Hillis in *Better Homes & Gardens*

1163. He will never have true friends who is afraid of making enemies.
—William Hazlitt

1164. He who for his own sake would expose a friend deserves not to have one.
—Jean Jacques Rousseau

1165. Friendship between two women is always a plot against each other.
—Alphonse Karr

1166. Having money and friends is easy. Having friends and no money is an accomplishment.

1167. Friends are not made. They are only recognized. That may be one of the difficulties of lonely people. They often fail to recognize the friendliness of those about them.

1168. Be not jealous of thy friend's friendship for another; surely the more friends he hath, the better friend he is to have.
—Christopher Bannister

1169. Three men are my friends—he that loves me, he that hates me and he that is indifferent to me.
Who loves me, teaches me tenderness; who hates me, teaches me caution; who is indifferent to me, teaches me self-reliance.

1170. Do not save your loving speeches
For your friends till they are dead;
Do not write them on their tombstone,
Speak them rather now instead.
—Anna Cummins

1171. When Socrates was building himself a house at Athens, being asked by one that observed the littleness of the design why a man so eminent would not have an abode more suitable to his dignity, he replied that he should think himself sufficiently accommodated if he could see that narrow habitation filled with real friends.

—Dr. Samuel Johnson

1172. Make no man your friend before inquiring how he has used his former friends; for you must expect him to treat you as he treated them. Be slow to give your friendship, but when you have given it, strive to make it lasting; for it is as reprehensible to make many changes in one's associates as to have no friends at all. Neither test your friends to your own injury nor be willing to forego a test of your companions.

—Isocrates

Fund-Raising

1173. Money still talks—the problem is sometimes to get enough volume through.

1174. Whenever he was asked which of his possessions he treasured most, the late Chief Justice Charles Evans Hughes, a twinkle in his eye, would lead the visitor into his study and point to a beautifully framed letter written in Spencerian script:

"In order to raise money for the church, our members are making aprons from the shirttails of famous men. We would be so pleased if you could send us one of your shirttails. Please have Mrs. Hughes mark them with your initials and also pin on them a short biography of the famous occasions in which they have been intimately associated with your life."

Furniture

1175. Times do change: Once upon a time, Grandpa fixed the chair with a piece of wire. Now, the wire is the chair.

1176. "I ache all over," a man complained. "What's the trouble?" his companion inquired sympathetically.

"A couple of weeks ago we bought a lot of ultra-modern furniture," he explained, "and I've just found out that all this time I've been sleeping in the bookcase."

Future, The

1177. Give the best you've got today. That's a recipe for a better tomorrow.

1178. If you've mortgaged the future to buy folly, don't complain when the foreclosure comes.

1179. Nobody can really guarantee the future. The best we can do is size up the chances, calculate the risks involved, estimate our ability to deal with them, and then make our plans with confidence.
—HENRY FORD II

Gambling

1180. Losing comes of winning money.
—*Chinese Proverb*

1181. There is no better gambling than not to gamble.
—*German Proverb*

1182. He who hopes to win what belongs to another deserves to lose his own.
—RICHARDSON

1183. People who can afford to gamble don't need money, and those who need money can't afford to gamble.

1184. There is a secret advantage that every gambling house has over the people who gamble in it. Known only to big operators and called the "hidden percentage," it lies in the fact that a person who gambles is not willing to win as much as he is willing to lose. A person will usually send a lot of money after his losses trying to get even, but will stop and run with a small amount of winnings. The average gain is far below the average loss.

Garden—Gardens—Gardening

1185. To live off of a garden, you must live in it.

1186. Experience teaches that love of flowers and vegetables is not enough to make a man a good gardener. He must also hate weeds.

1187. The real purpose of a back garden is to provide a place where a man can go and chop wood after a row with his wife.

Generalization

1188. He who accuses too many accuses himself.

1189. Nothing is so useless as a general maxim.

Generosity

1190. Generosity during life is a very different thing from generosity in the hour of death; one proceeds from genuine liberality and benevolence, the other from pride or fear.

—HORACE MANN

1191. What appears to be generosity is often nothing but a disguised ambition, which despises petty interests in order to reach greater ones.

—FRANÇOIS DE LA
ROCHEFOUCAULD

1192. There is wisdom in generosity, as in everything else. A friend to everybody is often a friend to nobody; or else, in his simplicity, he robs his family to help strangers, and so becomes brother to a beggar.

—CHARLES H. SPURGEON

Genius

1193. Genius may sometimes need the spur, but more often he needs a curb.

—DIONYSIUS CASSIUS
LONGINUS, *On the
Sublime*

1194. Sometimes men come by the name of genius in the same way that certain insects come by the name of centipede—not because they have a hundred feet, but because most people can't count above fourteen.

—GEORG CHRISTOPH
LICHTENBERG

Gentleman

1195. I can create a nobleman, but Deity alone can form a gentleman.

—KING JAMES I

1196. Being a gentleman is like being happy—if you must try to be, you aren't.

1197. One of the marks of a gentleman is his refusal to make an issue out of every difference of opinion.

—ARNOLD H. GLASOW

Gentleness

1198. Power will accomplish more by gentle than by violent means, and calmness will best enforce the imperial mandate.

—CLAUDIUS CLAUDIANUS

1199. Gentleness brings victory to him who attacks, and safety to him who defends. Those whom Heaven would save, it fences round with gentleness.

—LAO TZŮ

Geriatrics

1200. The person fears death most who fears life most, and the one who lives with the realization that he has but one life to enjoy is the person who, in his waning years, is as happily satisfied as ever.

—JOHN M. DORSEY

1201. Discussing the problems of older people, Dr. Robert T. Monroe, of the Age Center of New England, made this fascinating psychological point: "A person can be compared with a totem pole, of which you see only the top figure. But in his subconscious mind, a man has many other images of himself which are just as real. For example, the retired banker may still picture himself by turns as the shrewd businessman, the loving grandparent, the graceful rhumba dancer, the successful college athlete. He'll enjoy talking to you as a contemporary about football, dancing and business and you'll compliment him by doing so."

—LAURENCE O. PRATT,
"Seven Sins Against
Older People." Reprinted
from *This Week* maga-
zine. Copyright 1957 by
the United Newspapers
Magazine Corporation.

Gift—Gifts

1202. Better give than have to give.

—SENECA

1203. Gifts should be handed, not thrown.

—*Danish Proverb*

1204. Carve your name on hearts, and not on marble.

—CHARLES H. SPURGEON

1205. As the purse is emptied, the heart is filled.

—VICTOR HUGO

1206. He that hath pity on the poor lendeth to the Lord.

—*The Bible*

1207. People seldom think alike until it comes to buying wedding presents.

—*Wall Street Journal*

1208. Not only is it more blessed to give than to receive—it is also deductible.

1209. We make a living by what we get, but we make a life by what we give.

1210. Some people who give the Lord credit are reluctant to give him cash.

—JACK HERBERT

1211. The use of money is all the advantage there is in having money.

—BENJAMIN FRANKLIN

1212. More people would give to charity anonymously if it were well publicized.

1213. The way to judge of a man's charity is not what he gives, but what he keeps.

1214. A kind thought has more value than a material gift, because it cannot be bought.

—N. SRI RAM

1215. Give a man alms and you give him temporary relief, but give him work and you save him.

1216. If we bestow a gift or a favor and expect a return for it, it is not a gift but a trade.

1217. Money-giving is a very good criterion, in a way, of a person's mental health. Generous people are rarely mentally ill people.

—DR. KARL MENNINGER

1218. We often excuse our own want of philanthropy by giving the name of fanaticism to the more ardent zeal of others.

—HENRY WADSWORTH
LONGFELLOW

1219. You give me nothing during your life, but you promise to provide for me at your death. If you are not a fool, you know what I wish for.

—MARTIAL

1220. The question is not how little can I give or how much is the most I have to give. The question is how much dare I keep and live like a Christian.

1221. He that will not permit his wealth to do any good to others while he is living, prevents it from doing any good to himself when he is dead; and by an egotism that is suicidal and has a double edge, cuts himself off from the truest pleasure here and the highest happiness hereafter.

—CHARLES C. COLTON

1222. A man whose labor has acquired riches and whose charity disperses them is like the revolving sun, which draws the water from the ocean at the hour of noon, to dispense it over the earth in the evening dews.

1223. A Community Chest volunteer was calling on a tough prospect. "Our financial report shows," she said, "that you had an income of over $30,000 last year and made no contribution to the Community Chest."

The prospect stared coldly back at the volunteer. "Does your financial report also show that my mother has an incurable sickness that will cost thousands of dollars in operations and hospital care if she is to recover?"

"No, it doesn't," the volunteer admitted.

"Does it show that my brother was so badly wounded in the war that he refuses to return to America until certain plastic surgery can be completed and paid for?"

"No," said the volunteer deeply moved. "How terrible to have one's family so afflicted."

"Does it show that my daughter's husband faces ruin unless he can raise money to pay for flood damage to his little shop?"

"No, it doesn't." The embarrassed volunteer got up to leave. "I want you to know that we understand," she faltered.

"I knew you would," the prospect answered. "After all, if I am not giving any money to them, how can I justify contributing to the Community Chest?"

Glory

1224. When glory comes, loss of memory follows.

—*French Proverb*

1225. Glory paid to our ashes comes too late.

—MARTIAL

1226. The greatest baseness of man is his seeking for glory: but even this is the greatest indication of his excellence; for, whatever possession he may have on earth, whatever health and essential comfort he may have, he is not satisfied without the esteem of men.

—BLAISE PASCAL

God

1227. God often visits us, but most of the time we are not at home.

—JOSEPH ROUX, *Meditations of a Parish Priest*

1228. If you aren't as close to God as you once were, don't make a mistake about which one has moved.

1229. It is highly convenient to believe in the infinite mercy of God when you feel the need of mercy, but remember also his infinite justice.

—B. R. HAYDON, *Table Talk*

1230. A little boy asked his mother how many gods there were. A younger brother answered, "Why, one to be sure." "But how do you know that?" inquired the other. "Because," answered the younger, "God fills every place, so that there is no room for any other."

1231. Rabbi Eliezer said, "Turn to God *one day* before your death." His disciples said, "How can a man know the day of his death?" He answered them, "Then you should turn to God *today;* perhaps you may die *tomorrow;* thus every day will be employed in returning."

God–Man

1232. God tries you with a little, to see what you'd do with a lot.

1233. The love of wealth makes bitter men; the love of God, better men.

—W. L. HUDSON

1234. Once when Lord Moynihan, great British surgeon, had finished operating before a gallery full of distinguished visiting doctors he was asked how he could work with such a crowd present. He replied: "You see, there are just three people in the operating room when I operate—the patient and myself." "But that is only two!" his questioner commented; "Who is the third?" Moynihan responded, "The third is God."

Golden Rule

1235. Unless the Golden Rule is accepted by *both* sides in a controversy, it doesn't do either any good.

1236. The trouble with the Golden Rule is that before most men are ready to live by it they have lead in their legs and silver in their hair.

1237. THE GOLDEN RULE IN SEVEN WORLD
FAITHS

Christianity: All things whatsoever ye would that men should do to you, do yet even so unto them.

Hinduism: Men gifted with intelligence . . . should always treat others as they themselves wish to be treated.

Buddhism: In five ways should a clansman minister to his friends and families: by generosity, courtesy and benevolence, by treating them as he treats himself, and by being as good as his word.

Taoism: Regard your neighbor's gain as your own gain, and regard your neighbor's loss as your own loss.

Confucianism: What you do not want done to yourself, do not do to others.

Judaism: Thou shalt love thy neighbor as thyself.

Islamism: No one of you is a believer until he loves for his brother what he loves for himself.

—RUTH CRANSTON in
World Faiths

Golf

1238. There's always room for a good man except on a public golf course.

1239. If golf is played for exercise, how is it that the player who manages to get the least of it wins?

1240. Golf is what letter-carrying, ditch-digging, and carpet-beating would be if those three tasks had to be performed on the same hot afternoon in short pants and colored socks by gouty-looking gentlemen who required a different implement for every mood.

1241. Once, when General Ulysses S. Grant was visiting Scotland, his host gave him a demonstration of a game, new to Grant, called golf. Carefully, the host placed the ball on the tee and took a mighty swing, sending chunks of turf flying but not touching the ball.

Grant watched the exhibition quietly, but after the sixth unsuccessful attempt to hit the ball, he turned to his perspiring, embarrassed host and commented: "There seems to be a fair amount of exercise in the game, but I fail to see the purpose of the ball."

1242. This prayer was given before dinner at a golf installation party:

O God, Who made the earth round and hurled it into space with infinite power and accuracy, bless us who are gathered here tonight, whose aim is to imitate Thy divine action on the golf course.

Grant us a portion of Thy power, smoothness and accuracy. Give us poise, perseverance and patience in our golfing efforts. Implant in our hearts a love for this great game—but a greater love for our fellow-man on and off the golf course. May brotherly love reign supreme in all our golfing and kindred activities.

Bless our staff, our officers, our champions, our duffers. Increase their proficiency and decrease their scores. Lengthen their woods and straighten their irons. Control their approaches and guide their putts. But above all, O Lord, bestow on them a saving sense of humor and balance so that they may always golf in the spirit of charity, humility and reverence for Thy name.

Finally, O Lord, bless this spirited social gathering and this food that we are about to take in the realization that all good things—even a good golf score—come from You. Amen.

—FATHER GEORGE
MONAGHAN, Pastor of
Our Lady of Perpetual
Help Church, *Weekly
Calistogan*, Calistoga,
California

Goodness

1243. Good men die but death cannot kill them.

—THOMAS FULLER

1244. The sorrow of knowing that there is evil in the best is far out-balanced by the joy of discovering that there is good in the worst.

—AUSTEN RIGGS

1245. There is no man so good, who, were he to submit all his thoughts and actions to the laws, would not deserve hanging ten times in his life.

—MICHEL DE MONTAIGNE

1246. Some people think that they are good if they are doing good; others often think that they are doing good if they simply are good. Both are frequently mistaken.

—ALICE WELLINGTON
ROLLINS

Goodwill

1247. Today's profits are yesterday's goodwill ripened.

1248. Goodwill is the mightiest practical force in the universe.

—C. F. DOLE

1249. Goodwill is the one and only asset that competition cannot undersell nor destroy.

—MARSHALL FIELD

Gossip

1250. One reason the dog has so many friends: he wags his tail instead of his tongue.

1251. Great minds discuss ideas; normal minds discuss events; small minds discuss people.

1252. If what we see is doubtful, how can we believe what is spoken behind the back.

—*Chinese Proverb*

1253. When it comes to spreading gossip the female of the species is much faster than the mail.

1254. Never tell evil of a man, if you do not know it for certainty, and if you know it for a certainty, then ask yourself, "Why should I tell it?"

—JOHANN KASPAR
LAVATER

Government

1255. One should always remember that what the government gives, it must first take away.

1256. It is the duty of government to make it difficult for people to do wrong, easy to do right.

—William E. Gladstone

1257. Our government is one of checks and balances—Congress writes the checks and we supply the balances.

1258. DECLARATION OF JEWISH
INDEPENDENCE

We, the members of the National Council, representing the Jewish people in Palestine and the Zionist movement of the world, met together in solemn assembly by virtue of the natural and historic right of the Jewish people and the resolution of the General Assembly of the United Nations, hereby proclaim the establishment of the Jewish State in Palestine, to be called Israel.

We hereby declare that as from the termination of the mandate at midnight this night of the 14th to 15th of May, 1948, and until the setting up of duly elected bodies of the State in accordance with a constitution to be drawn up by a Constituent Assembly not later than the 1st day of October, 1948, the present National Council shall act as the Provisional State Council, and its executive organ, the National Administration, shall constitute the provisional government of the State of Israel.

The State of Israel will promote the development of the country for the benefit of all its inhabitants; will be based on precepts of liberty, justice and peace taught by the Hebrew prophets; will uphold the full social and political equality of all its citizens without distinction of race, creed or sex; will guarantee full freedom of conscience, worship, education and culture; will safeguard the sanctity and inviolability of shrines and holy places of all religions, and will dedicate itself to the principles of the Charter of the United Nations.

The State of Israel will be ready to co-operate with the organs and representatives of the United Nations in the implementation of the resolution of November 29, 1947, and will take steps to bring about an economic union over the whole of Palestine.

We appeal to the United Nations to assist the Jewish people in the building of its State and to admit Israel into the family of nations.

In the midst of wanton aggression we call upon the Arab inhabitants of the State of Israel to return to the ways of peace and play their part in the development of the State, with full and equal citizenship and due representation in all its bodies and institutions, provisional or permanent.

We offer peace and amity to all neighboring states and their peoples, and invite them to cooperate with the independent Jewish nation for the common good of all. The State of Israel is ready to contribute its full share to the peaceful progress and reconstruction of the Middle East. Our call goes out to the Jewish people all over the world to rally to our side in the task of immigration and development, and to stand by us in the great struggle for the fulfillment of the dream of generations—the redemption of Israel.

Graduation. See Commencement Exercises

Gratitude

1259. When you drink from the stream remember the spring.
—*Chinese Proverb*

1260. Let every man speak well of the bridge he goes over.

1261. It is better to say "thank you," and not mean it, than to mean it and not say it.

1262. If you can't be thankful for what you receive, be thankful for what you escape.

1263. If you do good to a man, look not for gratitude, for you have discovered his weakness. You know his nothingness and he'll never forgive that.
—ELBERT HUBBARD

Greatness

1264. The price of greatness is responsibility.

1265. The great are great only because we are on our knees. Let us rise!
—PRUD'HOMME

1266. *Description of a great man:*
"When I met him, I was looking down.
When I left him, I was looking up."

1267. At the funeral of Louis XIV the great cathedral was packed with mourners paying final tribute to the king whom they all considered great. The room was dark, save for one lone candle which illumined the great gold casket that held the mortal remains of the monarch.
At the appointed time, Massilion, court preacher, stood to address

the assembled clergy of France. As he rose, he reached from the pulpit and snuffed out the one candle which had been put there to symbolize the greatness of the king. Then from the darkness came just four words, "God only is great!"

—HOMER J. R. ELFORD,
pastor, Trinity Meth-
odist Church, Youngs-
town, Ohio, in *New
Christian Advocate*

Greed. See also Avarice

1268. If you chase two hares, both will escape you.

1269. People who have little and want less are happier than those who have much and want more.

1270. In Tolstoy's *Man and Dame Fortune* the hero is told he can have the right to all of the land around which he can plow a furrow in a single day. The man started off with great vigor, and was going to encompass only that which he could easily care for. But as the day progressed he desired more and more rights. He plowed and plowed, until at the end of the day he could in no possible way return to his original point of departure, but struggling to do so, he fell, the victim of a heart attack. The only right he secured was the right to 18 square feet of land in which to be buried.

—RUSSELL T. LOESCH

Grief. See also Sorrow

1271. Grief diminishes when it has nothing to grow upon.

—PUBLILIUS SYRUS

1272. Grief is the agony of an instant; the indulgence of grief the blunder of a life.

—BENJAMIN DISRAELI

Guilt

1273. He confesses his guilt who evades a trial.

1274. He who is guilty believes all men speak ill of him.

—*Italian Proverb*

1275. Guilt cannot keep its own secret, suicide is confession.

—DANIEL WEBSTER

Gullibility

1276. It is an equal failing to trust everybody, and to trust nobody.

1277. Some people believe everything you tell them—if you whisper it.

1278. When Carter L. Burgess resigned as Assistant Secretary of Defense to become president of Trans World Airlines, he was awarded an exceptional civilian service medal by the Army. After listening to the long and glowing tribute paid him by Army Secretary Brucker, Burgess said: "I am sorry my mother is not here. She not only would have enjoyed this ceremony, but she would have believed every word of it."

—WALTER TROHAN, Chiccago Tribune-New York News Syndicate in *The Reader's Digest*

Habit—Habits

1279. Good habits result from resisting temptation.
—*Ancient Proverb*

1280. The chains of habit are too weak to be felt till they are too strong to be broken.
—DR. SAMUEL JOHNSON

1281. I tried to stop smoking cigarettes by telling myself I just didn't want to smoke—but I didn't believe myself!
—BARBARA KELLY

1282. A wise old man was once taking a stroll through a forest with a shiftless youth by his side. The man suddenly stopped and pointed to four plants. The first was a tiny sprout. The second had rooted itself quite firmly. The third was a small shrub. The fourth had grown into a well-developed tree.

The old man said, "Pull up this first plant." The youth pulled it up easily with his fingers."

"Now pull the second," said the man. The youth obeyed, and with slight effort the plant came up, roots and all.

"And now the third," continued the elderly gentlemen. The boy pulled with one hand then with the other, but it would not come. Then he took both hands, and the plant yielded to all his strength.

"And now," said the old man, "try the fourth." The youth grasped the trunk with all his might, but hardly a leaf shook. "I cannot move it," he exclaimed.

"Just so, my son," said the wise old man, "with our bad habits. When they are young and small, we can cast them out but when they are full grown, they cannot be uprooted."

Handicap–Handicaps

1283. Sometimes we do handicapped persons a disservice when we offer them too much sympathy. They need *courage,* not sympathy. Some soldiers in ancient Greece once were twitting another soldier because of his withered foot. The twitting stopped when he said, "I am here to fight, not to run."

1284. Among the students at a well-known college was a young man on crutches. A homely fellow, he had a talent for friendliness and optimism. He won many scholastic honors and the respect of his classmates. One day a classmate asked the cause of his deformity.

When the fellow said briefly, "Infantile paralysis," the friend questioned further.

"With a misfortune like that, how can you face the world so confidently?"

"Oh," he replied, smiling, "the disease never touched my heart."

1285. When a young man, Robert Ripley was entering upon a career in big-league baseball. He fractured his arm in the first game he pitched. Doctors warned him not to do any work that would strain his arm.

Bob taught himself to draw. A job as a newspaper sports cartoonist was the first training for his highly successful feature. His radio work-pictures and pencil drawings of oddities brought him world-wide fame.

Robert Ripley was inclined to regard his fractured arm at the first game of ball he pitched as a "lucky break."

1286. History is full of men who triumphed over handicaps. Pope was a hopeless invalid, unable to stand without the aid of a cruel brace. Cervantes stuttered but he became a public speaker of remarkable power. Look at the two sickly, puny children with scarcely a chance for maturity who turned out to be Chopin and Theodore Roosevelt. Stephen A. Douglas, hunchback and statesman; Edison, deaf and perfecting the phonograph; Milton, blind and writing England's greatest poem; Franklin D. Roosevelt, crippled by infantile paralysis and becoming President of the United States—all of them were victors over handicaps.

Happiness

1287. The only true happiness comes from squandering ourselves for a purpose.

—John Mason Brown, in
Words to Live By

1288. Why is it that when your cup of happiness is full, *somebody* always jogs your elbow.

—Helen Rowland

1289. The thing that counts most in the pursuit of happiness is choosing the right traveling companion.

—Adrian Anderson

1290. When we look at what we want and then compare that with what we have, we shall be unhappy. When we think of what we deserve, then of what we have, we shall thank God.

1291. Youth and old age should be periods of intensive happiness. The one is easy because we do not know what is before us, and the other because so much misery is behind us.

—Viscount Castlerosse

Hardship

1292. The difficulties of life are intended to make us better, not bitter.

—George Gritter,
Moody Monthly

1293. It is easy to endure hardships if you have courage and money, and the hardships belong to somebody else.

Haste

1294. Hasty climbers have sudden falls.

—*English Proverb*

1295. There's no use hurrying—you pass by more than you overtake.

1296. He who pours water hastily into a bottle spills more than goes in.

—*Spanish Proverb*

1297. Composer Igor Stravinsky's publisher urged him to hurry the completion of a new composition.

"Hurry!" he cried angrily. "I never hurry. I have no time to hurry."

Hate—Hatred

1298. Hatred is a coward's revenge for being intimidated.

—GEORGE BERNARD SHAW

1299. Whatever you love, you are its master; whatever you hate, you are its slave.

—DAGOBERT D. RUNES

1300. Booker T. Washington, the great Negro educator, was walking down a street with a white friend when he was roughly elbowed into the gutter by a passing pedestrian. His friend was furious, exclaiming, "How can you tolerate such an insult?" To which Washington replied, "I defy any man to make me hate."

—JAY SABO, *Goodwill Cannot Hate*

Health

1301. Cultivate health instead of treating disease.

—JOHN RUSKIN

1302. The human body is wonderfully strong. Even when it is defective it will go on for thirty or forty years. The late John D. Rockefeller had gastritis and nervous dyspepsia at forty, but he lived to be nearly ninety-eight. Cecil Rhodes had lung trouble at twenty-one. A doctor told him he had only six months to live. But he lived to be forty-nine. Herbert Spencer was an invalid all his life, but he wielded a world-wide influence and lived to be eighty-three.

1303.
We squander Health
In search of Wealth,
We scheme and toil and save;
Then squander Wealth
In search of Health,
And all we get's a grave.
We live and boast of what we own
We die and only get a stone.

—*Anonymous*

Heaven

1304. To get to heaven, turn right and keep straight.

1305. Some people hope to be elected to heaven when they aren't even running for office.

Helpfulness

1306. Julia Ward Howe one day was talking to Charles Sumner, the distinguished senator from Massachusetts. She asked him to interest himself in the case of a person who needed some help. The senator answered, "Julia, I've become so busy I can no longer concern myself with individuals." Julia replied, "Charles, that is quite remarkable. Even God hasn't reached that stage yet."

—RALPH W. SOCKMAN

1307. Such help as we can give each other in this world is a debt to each other; and the man who perceives a superiority or a capacity in a subordinate, and neither confesses nor assists it, is not merely the withholder of kindness, but the committer of injury.

—JOHN RUSKIN, *The Two Paths*

1308. William D. Boyce, a Chicago publisher, became lost one night in a London fog. A boy touched him and asked, "Can I help you, sir?" He escorted the publisher to his hotel, and upon arrival refused pay for his services. "I am a Boy Scout," he explained. "We do not accept pay for rendering a service to anyone in need."

Boyce was impressed. He called on Sir Robert Baden-Powell, founder of British scouting, to learn more about the movement. Returning to America, he became one of the leaders in establishing Boy Scouting in this country.

—*The Speaker's Book of Illustrative Stories,* edited by MAXWELL DROKE (Droke House)

Heredity

1309. A man can't very well make for himself a place in the sun if he keeps continually taking refuge under the family tree.

1310. A Sunday school teacher suddenly stopped reading a passage in the Bible and asked the youngsters: "Why do you believe in God?"

She got a variety of answers, some full of simple faith, others obviously insincere. The one that stunned her came from the son of a padre. He answered apologetically: "I guess it just runs in our family."

Hero-Worship

1311. Teen-age talk is mostly idol gossip.

1312. Pure hero-worship is healthy. It stimulates the young to deeds of heroism, stirs the old to unselfish efforts, and gives the masses models of mankind that tend to lift humanity above the common-place meanness of ordinary life.

—DONN PIATT, *Memories of Men Who Saved the Union*

Hesitancy—Hesitation

1313. He who hesitates is bossed.

1314. He who hesitates isn't always lost—sometimes he is just smart.

1315. In 1863, when Secretary Seward placed the Emancipation Proclamation before President Lincoln for his signature, Lincoln dipped his pen in ink and moved his hand in place to affix his signature. Then he drew his hand away and dropped the pen. He repeated the procedure a few moments later. As he stopped the pen for the second time, he said to Seward: "I have been shaking hands since 9 o'clock this morning and my right arm is almost paralyzed. If my name ever goes into history, it will be for this act, and my whole soul is in it. If my hand trembles when I sign the proclamation, all who examine the document hereafter will say: 'He hesitated.'"

High Cost of Living. See Living, High Cost of

History

1316. He that would know what shall be must consider what hath been.

—*Ancient Proverb*

1317. Not to know what has been transacted in former times is to continue always a child.

—SENECA

1318. History was a lot easier when we were in school. Not only was there less of it, but it seemed to stay put more.

History, American. *See American History*

Hobby—Hobbies

1319. The way to a person's pocketbook is through his hobby.

1320. Everybody who has a hobby that is losing money wants to call it a business, but everyone who has one that is making money wants to call it a recreation.

1321. Men are born collectors. First it's bugs, toads, and marbles; then girls, kisses, and ties; then money, worries, and a family; then golf trophies, jokes, and hair tonics; and finally pains, symptoms, and memories.

Home

1322. Children may wreck a house but they make a home.

1323. All that keeps some families from having a home of their own is a teen-age daughter.

1324. Home is a mighty test of character. What you are at home you are everywhere, whether you demonstrate it or not.
—THOMAS DEWITT
TALMADGE

1325. The word "home" means more than the word "house." A house is a place to live; a home is a place to love. Governments can build houses, but only people can make homes. And the strength of our nation lies in the character of our people who want their houses to be homes.

Honesty. *See also* Integrity

1326. It pays to be honest, but it's slow pay.
—*Old Proverb*

1327. Honor and honesty are derived from the same Latin word.

Honor

1328. No person was ever honored for what he received. Honor has been the reward for what he gave.
—CALVIN COOLIDGE

1329. When a virtuous man is raised, it brings gladness to his friends, grief to his enemies, and glory to his posterity.

—BEN JONSON

Hope

1330. A misty morning does not signify a cloudy day.

—*Ancient Proverb*

1331. Of all the forces that make for a better world, none is so indispensable, none so powerful, as hope. Without hope men are only half alive. With hope they dream and think and work.

—CHARLES SAWYER

Hospitality

1332. Who practices hospitality entertains God himself.

—*The Talmud*

1333. A man who stays a week with another makes himself a slave for a week.

—DR. SAMUEL JOHNSON

1334. Hospitality is a wonderful thing. Concern for the pleasure and comfort of a guest is an extremely admirable trait. However, I think the Eskimos carry it a little too far. As for example, when a man traveling alone stops for a period at the house of a friend, the host offers to share his wife with his guest. The offer usually is accepted. A refusal might be considered insulting. As women are somewhat scarce in the Arctic, wife-sharing is not unusual. At times, three or four Eskimos share a wife. They all live together. The men do the housework.

—E. V. DURLING, *King Features Syndicate*

Human Being

1335. Every man is to be respected as an absolute end in himself; and it is a crime against the dignity that belongs to him as a human being, to use him as a mere means for some external purpose.

—IMMANUEL KANT

1336. If you're an adult of average weight, here is what you accomplish in 24 hours:

Your heart beats 103,689 times.
Your blood travels 168,000,000 miles.
You breathe 23,040 times.
You inhale 438 cubic feet of air.

You eat 3¼ pounds of food.
You drink 2.9 quarts of liquids.
You lose ⅞ pound of waste.
You speak 4,800 words, including some unnecessary ones.
You move 750 muscles.
Your nails grow .000046 inch.
Your hair grows .01714 inch.
You exercise 7,000,000 brain cells.
. . . feel tired?

Human Nature

1337. It's easier to understand human nature by bearing in mind that almost everybody thinks he's an exception to most rules.

1338. One of the saddest things about human nature is, that a man may guide others in the path of life, without walking in it himself; that he may be a pilot, and yet a castaway.

1339. A simple experiment will distinguish two types of human nature. Gather a throng of people and pour them into a ferryboat. By the time the boat swings into the river you will find that a certain proportion have taken the trouble to climb upstairs in order to be out on deck and see what is to be seen as they cross over. The rest have settled indoors, to think what they will do upon reaching the other side, or perhaps lose themselves in apathy or tobacco smoke. But leaving out those apathetic, or addicted to a single enjoyment, we may divide all the alert passengers on the boat into two classes—those who are interested in crossing the river, and those who are merely interested in getting across.

—MAX EASTMAN in *Enjoyment of Poetry*, published by Charles Scribner's Sons, 1913

Human Relations

1340. To handle yourself, use your head; to handle others, use your heart.

1341. The foundation of good human relations is friendliness and goodwill. The right conception of business, in my judgment, is a transaction—or a series of transactions—carried out in the spirit of friendliness. There are, I know, some people in all walks of life who are so cold-blooded in their attitude that dealings with them chill the blood. There is much more to business than the exchange of material values. We can do business, just as we can carry on all other aspects of our lives, in a wholesome and friendly attitude. When we do so, our days become brighter and happier, more meaningful and more worthwhile.

—CHARLES G. REIGNER.
Reproduced from *The Rowe Budget* by special arrangement with, and permission of, the publishers—The H. M. Rowe Company, Baltimore and Chicago

Human Rights

1342. The existence and validity of human rights are not written in the stars. . . . A large part of history is therefore replete with the struggle for those human rights, an eternal struggle in which a final victory can never be won. But to tire in that struggle would mean the ruin of society.

—ALBERT EINSTEIN

1343. The principle of equality of rights is quite simple. Every man can understand it, and it is by understanding his rights that he learns his duties; for where the rights of men are equal, every man must finally see the necessity of protecting the rights of others as the most effectual security of his own.

—THOMAS PAINE

Humility

1344. Falling hurts least those who fly low.

—*Chinese Proverb*

1345. True humility isn't the boast that you don't know anything, but the simple admission that you do know only some things.

1346. A humble man is like a good tree—the more full of fruit the branches are the more they bend down.

Humor. See *also* Wit and Humor

1347. He must not laugh at his own wheeze:
A snuff box has no right to sneeze.

—KEITH PRESTON

1348. Humor is the most philosophic of all the emotions. It is a recognition in our instinctive nature of what our minds in their purest contemplation can inform us, that pleasure and pain are, except for the incidental purpose of preserving us, indifferent—that failure is just as interesting as success.

—MAX EASTMAN, *The*
Sense of Humor

Humor, Sense of

1349. A sense of humor is what makes you laugh at something which would make you mad, if it happened to you.

1350. A sense of humor is the pole that adds balance to our steps as we walk the tight rope of life.

Husband. *See also* Husband—Wife

1351. A husband is one who thinks twice before saying nothing.

1352. All men make mistakes—husbands just find out about them sooner.

1353. Men who are called model husbands, needn't get all puffed up over it; according to the dictionary, "model" is "a small imitation of the real thing."

Husband—Wife

1354. When a wife sins the husband is never innocent.

—*Italian Proverb*

1355. A woman raises her standard of living by lowering her husband's resistance.

1356. The husband who boasts that he never made a mistake has a wife who did.

1357. The more a wife loves her husband, the more she seeks to correct his faults.

1358. Women don't really look for too much in a husband: just someone to spend with the rest of their lives.

1359. The happiest wife is not the one who marries the best man. She is the one who makes the best man out of the one she married.

—SIR NOEL BOWATER

1360. When a wife tells her husband she has given him the best years of her life, he may be rightfully concerned about the future.

Hypocrisy

1361. Every man alone is sincere; at the entrance of a second person hypocrisy begins.

—Ralph Waldo Emerson

Idea—Ideas

1362. Little words never hurt a big idea.

—Howard Newton

1363. An idea isn't responsible for the people who believe in it.

—Don Marquis

1364. The force of ideas is never felt till they are voted down.

Ideals—Idealism

1365. Efficiency without ideals is brutal. Ideals without efficiency are futile.

1366. When they come downstairs from their Ivory Towers, idealists are very apt to walk straight into the gutter.

—Logan Pearsall Smith

1367. As I have come to understand men, it is clear to me that there is much more goodwill in them than appears. As the waters of visible streams are small compared with those that flow below the ground, so also the visible idealism of men in comparison with that which they cherish within them unrevealed or barely so.

—Albert Schweitzer

Idleness

1368. Idleness is the nest in which mischief lays its eggs.

—Goold Brown

1369. One of the things that worry businessmen is the number of unemployed on the payroll.

1370. Too much idleness, I have observed, fills up a man's time much more completely, and leaves him less his own master, than any sort of employment whatsoever.

—Edmund Burke

1371. The higher men climb the longer their working day. And any young man with a streak of idleness in him may better make up his mind at the beginning that mediocrity will be his lot. Without immense, sustained effort he will not climb high. And even though fortune or chance were to lift him high, he would not stay there. For to keep at the top is harder almost than to get there. There are no office hours for leaders.

—James Cardinal
Gibbons

Ignorance

1372. None are less eager to learn than they who know nothing.

1373. An illiterate wise man is not half so dangerous as an educated fool.

—*Old Proverb*

1374. Whenever you argue with another wiser than yourself in order that others may admire your wisdom, they will discover your ignorance.

—Saadi

Imagination

1375. He who has imagination without learning, has wings and no feet.

—Barthelemy Catherine
Joubert

1376. Imagination was given to man to compensate him for what he is not; a sense of humor, to console him for what he is.

1377. Our imagination is one of our most important functions. We can use it to worry with or we can use it to work with. If we let it become a source of worry, we invite destruction; but if we put it to work we will create something useful—something we can always be proud of.

Imitation

1378. No man ever became great by imitation.

1379. Don't worry because a rival imitates you. As long as he follows in your tracks, he can't pass you.

Immaturity

1380. A person remains immature, whatever his age, as long as he thinks of himself as an exception to the human race.
—HARRY A. OVERSTREET

1381. The mark of the immature man is that he wants to die nobly for a cause, while the mark of the mature man is that he wants to live humbly for one.
—WILLIAM STEKEL

Immigration

1382. Immigration is the sincerest form of flattery.

1382a. About twenty years hence the immigrants now coming in will be worried about the flood of aliens coming to our shores.

Immortality

1383. If there was no future life, our souls would not thirst for it.
—JOHANN RICHTER

1384. The day which we fear as our last, is but the birthday of our eternity.
—SENECA

1385. To believe in immortality is one thing; but it is first needful to believe in life.
—ROBERT LOUIS
STEVENSON

Impatience

1386. If we should take away from the length of our days those which the impatience of our desires has wished away, the longest life would be much shortened.

1387. It is not generally considered that impatience is a virtue, yet it has real value in some circumstances. In a world so beset with delays and excuses, an impatient man will often find a way to cut through the tangle of red tape and indifference that confronts him. Impatience, if exercised by men who are thoroughly capable, can be of considerable value in modern business.

Imperfection–Imperfections

1388. He censures God who quarrels with the imperfections of men.

—EDMUND BURKE

1389. If we wish to be just judges of all things, let us first persuade ourselves of this: that there is not one of us without fault.

—SENECA

Impossible, The

1390. By asking for the impossible we obtain the possible.

—*Italian Proverb*

1391. It is difficult to say what is impossible, for the dream of yesterday is the hope of today and the reality of tomorrow.

—ROBERT H. GODDARD

Impulsiveness

1392. Jumping to conclusions doesn't make for happy landings.

1393. Obey the spur of the moment. . . . Let the spurs of countless moments goad us incessantly into life.

—HENRY DAVID THOREAU

Inaction

1394. Doing nothing is doing evil.

—*Ancient Proverb*

1395. Iron rusts from disuse; stagnant water loses its purity and in cold weather becomes frozen; even so does inaction sap the vigors of the mind.

—LEONARDO DA VINCI

1396. He who is silent is forgotten; he who abstains is taken at his word; he who does not advance falls back; he who stops is overwhelmed, distanced, crushed; he who ceases to grow greater becomes smaller; he who leaves off, gives up; the stationary condition is the beginning of the end.

—HENRI FRÉDÉRIC AMIEL

Incentive

1397. There's no incentive to success these days—one can live too comfortably as a failure.

1398. In a Missouri brickworks, each brickmaker is permitted to sign his own product. Bricks are turned out with names such as Smith and O'Dowd baked right into them.

The company has found that now that the men get personal credit for them, all its bricks are models of workmanship.

1399. Years ago Gerald Stanley Lee told about an American employer in Mexico who was driven almost crazy by the dilatory actions of his workmen on a construction job. They were paid a daily wage to wheel loads of dirt to a dump. They worked as if engaged in a slow race.

When he figured out what it was worth to haul and dump one wheelbarrow load, he placed a man with a bag of coins at the dump and paid each workman for each wheelbarrow load dumped. After that he had trouble keeping the men from working themselves to death.

All this employer did was to give recognition to the truth that the lower in the scale of intelligence men are, the closer to their work must be placed the reward for that work.

Income Tax

1400. The idea is to file an income tax return, not to chisel.

1401. About the time a man is cured of swearing, another income tax payment is due.

1402. We owe more than we can tell to the government of this wonderful nation, and the payment date is April 15th.

1403. The Internal Revenue Service, like God, must love poor people. It makes so many of them.

1404. A lot more people would pay their taxes with a smile—if the government didn't insist on cash.

1405. It may be true that George Washington never told a lie, but there were no income tax blanks in his day.

—JACK HERBERT

1406. Another thing that hasn't survived the income tax is the old theory that you couldn't be wounded by a blank.

1407. Behind every successful man there stands a woman—and the Internal Revenue Service: one to take the credit and the other the cash.

1408. Every man's income runs into four figures: the figure he reports to the income tax collector, the correct one, the one he tells his wife, and the figure she passes along to her bridge club.

Indecision

1409. Indecision is the graveyard of good intentions.
—Old Proverb

1410. While we consider when to begin, it becomes too late.
—Latin Proverb

1411. Better take the wrong street than stand forever on the corner.
—E. W. HELMS

Independence

1412. Self-government, self-discipline, and self-responsibility are the triple safeguards of the independence of man.
—BERNICE MOORE

1413. It is easy in the world to live after the world's opinions; it is easy in solitude to live after our own; but the great man is he who, in the midst of the crowd, keeps with perfect sweetness the independence of solitude.
—RALPH WALDO EMERSON

Independence Day. See Fourth of July

Indifference

1414. A story is often told of the Devil. He was auctioning his weapons to those who were interested. Hate, greed, and lust were among those weapons on his counter. Someone noticed that he was keeping one of them back and not showing it for sale. An interested spectator asked about this particular weapon.

"Oh," replied the Devil, "that is my favorite and most effective one."

On closer inspection, it turned out that this weapon carried the label, "Indifference."

—The Speaker's Book of Illustrative Stories, edited by MAXWELL DROKE (Droke House

Indispensability

1415. Make yourself indispensable and you will move up. Act as though you were indispensable and you will move out.

1416. Anyone who thinks he's indispensable should try sticking his finger in a bowl of water and noticing the hole it leaves when he takes it out.

Individuality

1417. Whatever crushes individuality is despotism, by whatever name it may be called.

—John Stuart Mill

1418. Every individual has a place to fill in the world, and is important in some respect, whether he chooses to be so or not.

—Nathaniel Hawthorne

1419. Mountains never shake hands. Their roots may touch, they may keep together some way up, but at length they part company and rise into individual, isolated peaks. So it is with great men; at first they grow up together, seeming to be animated by the same spirit—to have the same desires and anticipations, the same purposes and ends. But after a while the genius of each begins to show itself and to follow its own bent. They separate and develop more and more; and those who, when young, worked in concert, stand alone in their old age. But if mountains do not shake hands, neither do they kick each other.

Indolence. See also Laziness

1420. *Tacitus, describing life in Rome under Domitian:*
The charm of indolence creeps over the mind, and we end by living the inaction which at first we detested.

1421. It is an undoubted truth that the less one has to do the less time one finds to do it in. One yawns, one procrastinates, one can do it when one will, and, therefore, one seldom does it at all; whereas those who have a great deal of business must (to use a vulgar expression) buckle to it; and then they always find time enough to do it in.

—Lord Chesterfield

Inflation

1422. If the doctor tells you that you're "sound as a dollar"— you'd better take it easy!

1423. Inflation is like sin; every government denounces it and every government practices it.

—Sir Frederick
Leith-Ross

1424.   If you're going to teach your children the value of a dollar, you'll have to do it awfully fast.

1425.   By the time a family acquires a nest egg these days, inflation has turned it into chicken feed.

1426.   People in 1939 who thought the dollar was their best friend are finding out it isn't half the friend they thought it was.

1427.   Inflation means that instead of having the money you haven't got, you have twice as much, but it's worth only half of what you would have had if you had what you haven't got.

1428.   Any housewife knows that to increase the amount of soup available for the family dinner it is necessary only to add more water. But she also knows that as the water is added the quality of the soup is reduced. The value of money is affected very much in the same manner, with inflation playing the role of water in the currency soup.
—RALPH HENDERSHOT

Influence

1429.   I am a part of all I have met.
—ALFRED, LORD TENNYSON

1430.   One man can completely change the character of a country, and the industry of its people, by dropping a single seed in fertile soil.
—JOHN C. GIFFORD

1431.   The career of a great man remains an enduring monument of human energy. The man dies and disappears, but his thoughts and acts survive, and leave an indelible stamp upon his race.
—SAMUEL SMILES, *Character*

Ingratitude

1432.   A thankless man rarely does a thankful deed.
—*Old Proverb*

1433.   One ungrateful man does an injury to all who stand in need of aid.
—PUBLILIUS SYRUS

1434.   The one sure way to escape ingratitude is to do good without expecting gratitude as your reward. If you do not get your joy out of the act of self-expression you cannot find it elsewhere.

Inheritance

1435. He who waits for a dead man's shoes is in danger of going barefoot.

—*Danish Proverb*

1436. Many a man's good fortune is due to the will power of a deceased relative.

Initiative

1437. If you have nothing else to do, look about you and see if there isn't something close at hand that you can improve! It may make you wealthy, though it is more likely that it will make you happy.

—George Matthew Adams

1438. A man should learn to detect and watch that gleam of light which flashes across his mind from within, more than the lustre of the firmament of bards and sages. Yet he dismisses without notice his thought, because it is his. In every work of genius we recognize our own rejected thoughts: they come back to us with a certain alienated majesty.

—Ralph Waldo Emerson

Inquisitiveness

1439. The things most people want to know about are usually none of their business.

—George Bernard Shaw

1440. He who asks a question is a fool for five minutes; he who does not ask a question remains a fool forever.

—*Chinese Proverb*

Installment Purchase

1441. Getting things on the cuff is the quickest way to lose your shirt.

1442. Wealthy people miss one of life's greatest thrills—paying the last installment.

1443. When a wife buys things on credit, she is merely displaying confidence in her husband.

1444. There are two kinds of people in this country—those who have new cars and all the latest appliances, and those who pay cash.

Insult–Insults

1445. A well-known television star once devised a wonderful system for coping with vicious and insulting poison-pen letters. He mailed the offending missive right back to the sender with this note of his own: "The enclosed letter arrived on my desk a few days ago. I am sending it to you in the belief that as a responsible citizen you should know that some idiot is sending out letters over your signature. Cordially . . ."

Insurance

1446. The uninsured are in no more peril than the insured, but their families are.

1447. The man with money to burn is usually the kind who keeps up the payments on his fire insurance.

Insurance, Life. See Life Insurance

Integrity. See also Honesty

1448. One thing you can keep and still give is your word.

1449. A true test of integrity is to leave your parrot with a neighbor while you go on your holidays.

1450. A commentary on the times is that the noun "honesty" now is usually preceded by "old-fashioned."

1451. It is surprising to find that great heights may be attained merely by remaining on the level.

1452. No public man can be just a little crooked. There is no such thing as a no-man's-land between honesty and dishonesty. Our strength is not in politics, prices, or production, or price controls. Our strength lies in spiritual concepts. It lies in public sensitiveness to evil.
—HERBERT HOOVER

1453. A client went to his attorney and said: "I am going into a business deal with a man I do not trust. I want you to frame an air-tight contract which he can't break and which will protect me from any sort of mischief which he may have in his mind."

"Listen, my friend," said the attorney, "there is no group of words in the English language which will take the place of plain honesty between men, or which will fully protect either of you if you plan to deceive each other."

—ERNEST HAYCOCK

1454. When he was 24 years old, Abraham Lincoln served as the postmaster of New Salem, Illinois, for which he was paid an annual salary of $55.70.

Even then, 24 years before he entered the White House, the rail splitter was showing the character that earned him the title of "Honest Abe."

The New Salem post office was closed in 1836, but it was several years before an agent arrived from Washington to settle accounts with ex-postmaster Lincoln, who was a struggling lawyer not doing too well.

The agent informed him that there was $17 due the government. Lincoln crossed the room, opened an old trunk and took out a yellowed cotton rag bound with string.

Untying it, he spread out the cloth and there was the $17. He had been holding it untouched for all the years.

"I never use any man's money but my own," he said.

Intelligence

1455. The intelligent have a right over the ignorant, namely, the right of instructing them.

—RALPH WALDO EMERSON

1456. Intelligence is a lot like money—if you don't let on how little you've got people will treat you as though you have a lot.

Interdependence

1457. Singer Marian Anderson nearly always refers to herself as "one" or "we." Explaining this habit, she says, "When you realize that whatever you do in life is never something you do absolutely alone, you do not like to be saying, 'I did this . . . I . . . I . . . I.'"

1458. A hundred times a day I remind myself that my inner and outer life depend on the labors of other men, living and dead, and that I must exert myself in order to give in the same measure as I have received and am receiving.

—DR. ALBERT EINSTEIN

Intolerance

1459. If there is anything the nonconformist hates worse than a conformist it's another nonconformist who doesn't conform to the prevailing standards of nonconformity.

1460. The highest result of education is tolerance. Long ago men fought and died for their faith; but it took ages to teach them the other kind of courage—the courage to recognize the faiths of their brethren and their rights of conscience. Tolerance is the first principle of community; it is the spirit which conserves the best that all men think. No loss by flood and lightning, no destruction of cities and temples by the hostile forces of nature has deprived man of so many noble lives and impulses as those which his intolerance has destroyed.

—HELEN . KELLER, *The Open Door* (Doubleday & Company, Inc.)

Invention

1461. The right of an inventor to his invention is no monopoly . . . in any other sense than a man's house is a monopoly.

—DANIEL WEBSTER

1462. A tool is but the extension of a man's hand, and a machine is but a complex tool. And he that invents a machine augments the power of a man and the well-being of mankind.

—HENRY WARD BEECHER

1463. Once Thomas A. Edison was seeking a solvent for hard rubber. Other scientists were also engaged in the same effort. Whereas they were seeking the solution to their problem through theory and formula, Edison proceeded along a more direct route. He went to his impressive and remarkably complete storeroom of chemicals where he immersed a small fragment of hard rubber in a vial of each one of these many chemicals. The number was enormous but he stuck to it and eventually found his solvent.

Investment

1464. One never makes a bad investment—some of them just turn out that way.

1465. Most people who loaned money to Robert Fulton for the development of his proposed steamboat did so with the stipulation that their names be kept secret, for fear they might be ridiculed for backing such an absurd idea.

1466. Benjamin Franklin left a fund of $5,000 to the City of Boston in 1791. His will provided that interest from this fund be allowed to accumulate for 100 years. By 1891 the $5,000 had grown to almost $400,000. A school was established with part of the accumulated fund and the balance, $92,000, was invested for a second century. It is reported that by 1950 the $92,000 had increased to almost a million. Apparently Ben knew what he was talking about when he said: "Money begets money and its offspring begets more."

Jealousy

1467. The jealous man poisons his own banquet, and then eats it.

1468. No man is a complete failure until he begins disliking men who succeed.

1469. Unconsciously a jealous person always hopes to be proven right in his suspicions.

1470. For every executive's wife allegedly jealous of her husband's secretary, there are a dozen secretaries who envy their bosses' wives.

Joint Effort

1471. Behind an able man there are always other able men.
—*Chinese Proverb*

1472. A man had just arrived in Heaven, told St. Peter how grateful he was to be in such a glorious place, and asked St. Peter to give him one glimpse into Hades in order that he might appreciate his good fortune even more. This St. Peter did. In Hades he saw a long table extending as far as the eye could reach, laden down with the most delicious of all varieties of foods. But everyone around the table was starving to death. When asked for an explanation, St. Peter said, "Everyone is required to take food from the table only with four-foot long chopsticks. They are so long that no one can reach the food from the table to his mouth, and therefore each one is dying of starvation."

Quickly they returned to Heaven, and behold, the new arrival saw an identical table, laden down with identical foods, but everyone around the table was happy and well fed. Then he said to St. Peter: "With what do they take the food from the table?" and St. Peter answered, "Only with four-foot long chopsticks." At that the new arrival inquired: "Then why are all those in Hades starving to death while all those up here are so well fed and happy?" Whereupon St. Peter replied: "In Heaven we feed each other."

—HARRY C. MABRY

Journalism

1473. Remember, son, many a good story has been ruined by over-verification.

—JAMES GORDON BENNETT

1474. If you see an editor who pleases everybody, there will be a glass plate over his face and he will not be standing up.

1475. If words were invented to conceal thought, newspapers are a great improvement on a bad invention.

—HENRY DAVID THOREAU

1476. Journalism consists in buying white paper at two cents a pound and selling it at ten cents a pound.

—CHARLES A. DANA

Judge—Judges

1477. A good and faithful judge prefers what is right to what is expedient.

—HORACE, *Carmina*

1478. We must remember that we have to make judges out of men, and that by being made judges their prejudices are not diminished and their intelligence is not increased.

—ROBERT G. INGERSOLL

1479. As the laws are above magistrates, so are the magistrates above the people; and it may truly be said, that the magistrate is a speaking law, and the law a silent magistrate.

—CICERO

Judgment

1480. Good judgment comes from experience—and experience comes from poor judgment.

1481. Some men build up a reputation for having good judgment by using the good judgment of others.

1482. When you meet a man, you judge him by his clothes; when you leave, you judge him by his heart.

—*Russian Proverb*

Judiciary. See Judge—Judges

July, Fourth of. See Fourth of July

Justice

1483.   Rigid justice is rank injustice.

—Old Proverb

1484.   When a jury permit a guilty man to escape, they augment the danger of the innocent.

—Ancient Proverb

1485.   I hear much of people's calling out to punish the guilty, but very few are concerned to clear the innocent.

—Daniel Defoe, *An Appeal to Honor and Justice*

Juvenile Delinquency

1486.   A good man dies when a boy goes wrong.

1487.   Few of us oldsters are qualified to discourse on juvenile delinquency. We've been away from it too long.

—D. O. Flynn

1488.   Juvenile delinquency sets in when a youngster stops asking adults where he came from and starts telling them where to go.

1489.   There is no such thing as a problem boy. When we speak of a problem boy what we really mean is a boy with problems.

Kindness

1490.   Never return a kindness. Pass it on.

1491.   You cannot do a kindness too soon, for you never know how soon it will be too late.

—Ralph Waldo Emerson

1492.   A convict from Darlington, England, just released from jail, happened to pass Mayor John Morel on the street. Three long years had been spent by the convict in prison for embezzlement and he was sensitive about the social ostracism he expected to get from the people in his home town.

"Hello," greeted the mayor in a cheery tone, "I'm glad to see you!

How are you?" The man appeared ill at ease and the discussion stopped.

Years later, according to the story told by J. H. Jowett, Mr. Morel, the mayor, and the released man accidentally met in another town, and the latter said, "I want to thank you for what you did for me when I came out of prison."

"What did I do?" asked the mayor.

"You spoke a kind word to me and it changed my life," replied the grateful man.

—REV. PURNELL BAILEY

Kiss–Kisses–Kissing

1493. If you can kiss the mistress, do not kiss the maid.

1494. The sound of a kiss is not so loud as that of a cannon, but its echo lasts a deal longer.

—OLIVER WENDELL HOLMES, *The Professor at the Breakfast Table*

1495. The only difference between a kiss on the brow and a kiss on the lips is that, whereas the first has finished its travels in the act, the second has only just started out.

Know-how

1496. We need all the technical training we can lay hold of. But let us not mistake qualification for ability; it is the use of a tool rather than the possession of it which gets a job done.

—VINCENT TAYLOR

1497. Ralph Waldo Emerson, a philosopher who had a very deep respect for the practical side of life, once tried to lead a young heifer into his barn. His son Edward grasped the animal by the ears and attempted to pull her from the front, while his father pushed with all his might and main from behind. But the stubborn beast refused to budge.

Pulling and hauling, they were interrupted by a laughing Irish servant girl who had been brought up on a farm. Motioning the two men aside, she thrust her finger into the heifer's mouth, and the creature, expecting to obtain nourishment from the proffered digit, obediently followed her into the barn.

That night, Emerson wrote in his diary: "I like people who can get things done!"

1498. There once was a restaurant famous for a steak which came as close to perfection as sirloin was intended to come. There was a widespread rumor that the chef used some complicated abracadabra to turn out the beef wonder. For years enterprising fellow chefs tried to worm the secret out of him.

In time the great chef retired, and in a moment of sentimental generosity, agreed to tell a few close associates the "how" and "why."

"I use the best meat I can get," he said, "take plenty of time and care in trimming it and preparing it for the fire. I watch and baste it carefully until it's done just right. That's all . . . there isn't any secret to it!"

Knowledge

1499. Oddly enough, it's the person who knows everything who has the most to learn.

1500. Whatever I did not know, I was not ashamed to inquire about, so I acquired knowledge.

—*Persian Philosopher*

1501. Knowledge without common sense is folly; without method it is waste; without kindness it is fanaticism; without religion it is death. But with common sense, it is wisdom; with method it is power; with character it is beneficence; with religion, it is virtue, life and peace.

1502. If anyone tell thee that he has searched for knowledge and not attained it, believe him not; if he tell thee that he has attained knowledge without searching for it, believe him not; but if he tell thee that he has searched for knowledge and attained it, thou mayest believe him.

—*The Talmud*

Labor

1503. Without labor nothing prospers.

—Sophocles

1504. I pity that man who wants a coat so cheap that the man or woman who produces the cloth shall starve in the process.

—Benjamin Harrison

1505. Labor Day is the only national holiday dedicated to plain people, rather than heroes and historic events. It provides an opportunity for all of us to recognize and honor the working men and women who have built America to its present stature and keep it going with such steady efficiency. We need this annual reminder because during the rest of the year the contributions made to our well-being by the unsung workers of our country are taken for granted. Only when some dramatic interruption takes place, do we begin to realize how dependent we are in our daily lives upon the continuous miracle of production and service rendered by the great army of free American workers.

—George Meany

Labor–Capital. See Capital–Labor

Language

1506. If an American had uttered Winston Churchill's famous line, "Give us the tools and we will finish the job," it would have come out, "Donate the implements and we shall finalize the solution of the matter."

—Lord Conesford, M.P.

1507. "It's absolutely silly to think that one year of a foreign language is going to do you any good," a college foreign language instructor told a balky freshman. "I studied 'beginner's French' in school, but, when I went to Paris, unfortunately I couldn't find anyone who spoke 'beginner's French.'"

Laughter

1508. The young man who has not wept is a savage, and the old man who will not laugh is a fool.

—George Santayana,
Dialogues in Limbo

1509. The reason man is the only animal that laughs and weeps is that he is immediately struck with the difference between what things are and what they ought to be.

1510.

A laugh is just like sunshine,
It freshens all the day,
It tips the peak of life with light
And drives the clouds away;
The soul grows glad that hears it
And feels its courage strong;
A laugh is just like sunshine,
For cheering folks along.

A laugh is just like music,
It lingers in the heart,
And where its melody is heard,

The ills of life depart;
And happy thoughts come crowding
Its joyful notes to greet;
A laugh is just like music
For making living sweet.

—*Anonymous*

Law—Laws

1511. Petty laws breed great crime.

—OUIDA, *Pipistrello*

1512. Law is not law, if it violates the principles of eternal justice.

—LYDIA MARIA CHILD

1513. English law punishes vice; the Chinese laws do more, they reward virtue.

1514. The precepts of law are these: to live honorably, to injure no other man, to render every man his due.

—JUSTINIAN

Law Enforcement

1515. The execution of the laws is more important than the making of them.

—THOMAS JEFFERSON

1516. Think of the number of laws it takes in our civilized world just trying to enforce the Ten Commandments.

1517. The trouble seems to be that too many people think the law should be enforced, and not enough think it should be observed.

Lawyer—Lawyers

1518. Do as adversaries do in law. Strive mightily, but eat and drink as friends.

—WILLIAM SHAKESPEARE

1519. As in all the learned professions, most lawyers are not lawyers, but practitioners out of their depth in cases they have not to deal with every day. They soon lose all sense of law. That is why judges should be retired at thirty.

—GEORGE BERNARD SHAW

1520. A lawyer has no business with the justice or injustice of the cause which he undertakes unless his client asks his opinion, and then he is bound to give it honestly. The justice or injustice of the cause is to be decided by the judge.

—Dr. Samuel Johnson

1521. The young lawyer had been delivering a long and tiresome dissertation on the merits of his case when, noting the apparent lack of interest on the part of the judge, he asked: "Is it the pleasure of the court that I continue?"

The judge sighed and replied: "Pleasure, my dear sir, has long been out of the question, but you may proceed."

Laziness. See *also* Indolence

1522. Easy street is a blind alley.

—Wilson Mizner

1523. The man who waits for things to turn up finds his toes do it first.

1524. Too many people fashion their lives after French bread— one long loaf!

1525. A river becomes crooked by following the line of least resistance. So does man.

1526. There must be something to reincarnation, judging by the way some people come back to life at quitting time.

Leadership

1527. A strong leader knows that if he develops his associates he will be even stronger.

—James F. Lincoln

1528. Leadership: The art of getting someone else to do something that you want done because he wants to do it.

—President Dwight D. Eisenhower at Annual Conference of the Society for Personnel Administration, Washington, D. C., May 12, 1954

1529. There are two kinds of leaders—those interested in the flock and those interested in the fleece.

1530. Civilization is always in danger when those who have never learned to obey are given the right to command.

—BISHOP FULTON J. SHEEN

1531. A good leader inspires other men with confidence in him; a great leader inspires them with confidence in themselves.

1532. Any commander who fails to obtain his objective, and who is not dead or severely wounded, has not done his full duty.

—GENERAL GEORGE S. PATTON

1533. A psychologist who studied three types of leaders—criminals, army officers, and student leaders—found three traits that were common to all: (1) speed of decision, (2) finality of decision, (3) self-confidence.

Learning

1534. He who adds not to his learning diminishes it.

—*The Talmud*

Legislation

1535. It is useless to make good laws for bad people.

1536. The passing of an unjust law is the suicide of authority.

—*Pastoral Letter of the American Roman Catholic Hierarchy, February 1920*

1537. Be sure you obey good laws before you seek to alter bad ones.

—JOHN RUSKIN

1538. Let all laws be clear, uniform, and precise; to interpret laws is almost always to corrupt them.

—VOLTAIRE

1539. Everybody says this country has too many laws, and yet every man thinks he knows of a law that ought to be passed.

1540. A law not repealed continues in force, not because it cannot be repealed, but because it is not repealed, and the non-repealing passes for consent.

—THOMAS PAINE, *The Rights of Man*

1541. Nick Longworth used to get quite a laugh out of his remark about sitting near politicians at banquet tables. "It's no fun sitting near a congressman," he often said, "because it takes them so damn long to pass anything."

—*If Elected, I Promise*
by JOHN F. PARKER
(Doubleday and
Company, Inc.)

Leisure

1542. The difference between existence and life is the intelligent use of leisure.

1543. Leisure is what you make it. It may be your greatest blessing or your greatest curse. You determine its quality, and its quality determines you. In the old era, the job determined the worker. In the new, leisure determines the man.

—WALTER B. PITKIN

Liberty. *See also* Freedom

1544. Liberty must be limited in order to be possessed.

—EDMUND BURKE

1545. Liberty may be endangered by the abuse of liberty as well as by the abuse of power.

—JAMES MADISON, *The Federalist*

1546. We must keep in the forefront of our minds the fact that whenever we take away the liberties of those whom we hate, we are opening the way to loss of liberty for those we love.

—WENDELL L. WILLKIE

1547. If men use their liberty in such a way as to surrender their liberty, are they thereafter any less the slaves? If people by plebiscite elect a man despot over them, do they remain free because the despotism was of their own making? Are the coercive edicts issued by him to be regarded as legitimate because they are the ultimate outcome of their own votes?

—HERBERT SPENCER

Library

1548. A great library contains the diary of humanity.

1549. A man's library consists of all the books he has that no one wants to borrow.

1550. Hammers and tongs instead of library cards would have been needed in medieval times to "borrow" a library book. In the 15th century library books were laid on the desk and chained to a horizontal bar. Chains were still in use for this purpose in church libraries in England down to the early part of the 18th century.

Lie—Lies. See *also* Falsehood

1551. Better a lie that soothes than a truth that hurts.
—*Czech Proverb*

1552. The man who fears no truths has nothing to fear from lies.
—THOMAS JEFFERSON

Life

1553. There is no cure for birth or death save to enjoy the interval.
—GEORGE SANTAYANA

1554. To the wise, life is a problem, to the fool a solution.

1555. Life lets us ask for what we want, but gives us what we deserve.

1556. To be able to look back on one's past life with satisfaction is to live twice.
—MARTIAL

1557. It's easy to find your station in life—sooner or later someone will tell you where to get off.

1558. Life doesn't consist in holding good cards but in playing a poor hand well.

1559. We make death uneasy by thinking of life, and life uneasy by thinking of death.

1560. Some people spend half their lives complaining about the shortness of life's span, and the other half killing time.

1561. Biology defines *life* as "the metabolic activity of protoplasm." But there are times when it seems even worse than that.

1562. Only those are fit to live who do not fear to die; and none are fit to die who have shrunk from the joy of life. Life and death are parts of the great adventure.

—THEODORE ROOSEVELT

1563.
Among life's dying embers
These are my regrets
When I'm right, no one remembers
When I'm wrong no one forgets.

1564.   LIFE'S JOURNEY

Life is like a journey on a train,
With two fellow travelers at each window pane.
I may sit beside you all the journey through,
Or I may sit elsewhere, never knowing you.
But should fate mark me to sit by your side,
Let's be pleasant travelers—'tis so short a ride!

—*Author Unknown*

1565.   SUCH IS LIFE

Man comes into this world without his consent, and leaves it against his will. When he is little, the big girls kiss him, and when he is big, the little girls kiss him. If he makes a lot of money, he is dishonest; if he is poor, he is a bad manager. If he needs credit, he can't get it; if he is rich, everyone wants to do something for him. If he is religious, he is a hypocrite; if he doesn't go to church, he is a hardened sinner. If he gives to charity, it is for show; if he doesn't, he is a stingy cuss. If he is affectionate, he is a soft specimen; if he doesn't care for anyone, he is cold-hearted. If he dies young, there was a great future before him; if he lives to a ripe age, he is an old fogey. If he saves money, he is a tightwad; if he spends it, he is a spendthrift. If he has money, he is a grafter; if he hasn't got it, he is a bum. So what the H—l's the use.

Life Insurance

1566. Wives may object to the purchase of life insurance, but widows never do.

1567. Life insurance, very often, is the last thing on earth a man wants, but it's too late then.

1568. A man who dies without life insurance abandons his family and absconds with their support.

1569. Life insurance was created so that "live and let live" could be changed to "live and help live."

1570. Most investments are geared to provide a return on your money while life insurance is geared to provide a return of your money.

1571. "The only dependable fortuneteller I have known," said Theodore Roosevelt, "is the life insurance man. He tells you what is going to happen, and it does."

Limitation—Limitations

1572. An acorn cannot make much headway in a flower-pot.
—G. F. TRAIN

1573. When a man puts a limit on what he will do, he puts a limit on what he can do.

Literature

1574. Literature is the immortality of speech.
—FRIEDERICH SCHLEGEL

1575. No literature is complete until the language in which it is written is dead.
—HENRY WADSWORTH LONGFELLOW

Litigation

1576. Fools and obstinate men make lawyers rich.
—H. G. BOHN, *Handbook of Proverbs*

1577. He who has the worst cause makes the most noise.
—*Old Proverb*

1578. The only thing certain about litigation is its uncertainty.

Little Things

1579. It matters not how small the beginning may seem to be; what is once well done is done forever.
—HENRY DAVID THOREAU

1580. Those who apply themselves too closely to little things often become incapable of great things.
—FRANÇOIS DE LA ROCHEFOUCAULD

1581. In striving to attain big things, the little things come easy, but in striving to attain only little things, even they become hard.

—C. T. GILBREATH

1582. An old gardener while laying a stone wall in a country estate was asked by the owner why he used so many small stones along with the large ones. "It's like this," he said, "these stones are like men. Many small men like me are needed to keep the big ones in place. If I leave small stones out, the big ones will not stay in place and the wall will fall."

—S. KENRICK GUERNSEY

1583. One day in Colorado a great, stalwart tree fell down. It was a sapling when Columbus landed at San Salvador. It had been struck by lightning fourteen times. It had braved storms, defied earthquakes, and bent beneath the fierce onslaughts of mountain torrents. But in the end, tiny beetles killed it. They bored under the bark, dug into its heart, ate away its mighty fibers—and one day down toppled the great king of the forest.

1584.   THE LITTLE THINGS

If any little word of mine
    May make a life the brighter,
If any little song of mine
    May make a heart the lighter,
God help me speak the little word
    And take my bit of singing,
And drop it in some lonely vale
    To set the echoes ringing.

If any little love of mine
    May make a life the sweeter,
If any little care of mine
    May make a friend's the fleeter
If any little lift may ease
    The burden of another,
God give me love, and care, and strength
    To help my toiling brother.

—Anonymous

Livelihood

1585. Not everyone who wants to make a good living wants to earn it.

1586. It's not so hard to make money these days. It's making a living that's so difficult.

Living, High Cost of

1587. We haven't yet heard of anybody who wants to stop living on account of the cost.

1588. The cost of living is always a problem. With inflation you worry about the cost, and with deflation you worry about the living.

Loneliness

1589. The man who spends his life building walls instead of bridges has no right to complain if he is lonely.

Longevity

1590. One incentive for living indefinitely is to see what the meek will do with the earth.

1591. Possibly man could live twice as long if he didn't spend the first half of his life acquiring habits that shorten the other half.

—MARY L. WRIGHT

1592.   HOW LONG THEY LIVE

Pike: Perhaps the longest lived of all creatures—one was known to have lived for 267 years.

Tortoises: About 200 years.

Crocodiles: About 100 years.

Eagles and Falcons: About 100 years.

Parrots and Swans: About 80 years.

Crabs: About 50 years.

Lions: About 30 years.

Cattle: Live between 25 and 30 years.

Pigs: Live up to 20 years.

Ants: One was kept alive for 15 years.

Deer: Live between 10 and 15 years.

Wild Goats: Live between 12 and 14 years.

Queen Bees: About 5 years.

Rats and Mice: Live up to 5 years.

Oysters: About 4 years.

Long-Windedness. See *also* Public Speaking

1593. Speeches that are measured by the hour will die with the hour.

—THOMAS JEFFERSON

1594. When a fellow says, "Well, to make a long story short," it's too late.

—DON HEROLD

1595. "Do you object to your wife having the last word?" "Not at all. I'm delighted when she gets to it."

Loquacity

1596. Loquacity and lying are cousins.

—*German Proverb*

1597. During World War II, when food rationing was in effect, point values were: Brains, 3 points. Tongue, 6 points. That seems to be the usual ratio.

Love

1598. In love we often doubt what we most believe.

—FRANÇOIS DE LA ROCHEFOUCAULD

1599. The love that lasts longest is the love that is never returned.

1600. Love is just a chemical reaction. But it's fun trying to find the formula.

—J. D. SHANTEL, Professor of Chemistry

1601. A man in love makes the mistake of thinking one woman is different from all others.

1602. In matters of love, the beginning of the end often turns out to be but the end of the beginning.

1603. What's so remarkable about love at first sight? It's when people have been looking at each other for years that it becomes remarkable.

1604. Love is like a poker game. It starts with a pair, she gets a flush, he shows diamonds, and it ends with a full house.

Loyalty

1605. Fidelity purchased with money, money can destroy.

—SENECA

1606. My country, right or wrong; when right, to keep her right; when wrong, to put her right.

—CARL SCHURZ

1607. You can't buy loyalty. You can only get it in an even-steven swap for loyalty of your own.

Luck

1608. Chance favors the prepared mind.

—LOUIS PASTEUR

1609. The harder you work, the luckier you get.

1610. One day fortune actually knocked on a fellow's door. But the fellow didn't hear it. He was over at his neighbor's telling a hard luck story.

1611. Bad luck is a man standing with his hands in his pockets, and a pipe in his mouth, waiting to see how things will turn out. Good luck is a man of pluck, his sleeves rolled up, working to make things come out right.

Luxury

1612. Living in the lap of luxury isn't bad except that you never know when luxury is going to stand up!

1613. Luxury makes a man so soft that it is hard to please him, and easy to trouble him; so that his pleasures at last become his burdens. Luxury is a nice master, hard to be pleased.

—MACKENZIE

Machine–Machinery

1614. One machine can do the work of fifty ordinary men. No machine can do the work of one extraordinary man.

—ELBERT HUBBARD

1615. Civilization requires slaves. Human slavery is wrong, insecure and demoralizing. On mechanical slavery, on the slavery of the machine, the future of the world depends.

—OSCAR WILDE

Magnanimity

1616. Magnanimity despises everything to gain everything.

1617. He who too much fears to be duped can no longer be magnanimous.

—HENRI FRÉDÉRIC AMIEL

Majority

1618. One man with courage makes a majority.

—ANDREW JACKSON

1619. The voice of the majority saves bloodshed, but it is no less the arbitrament of force than is the decree of the most absolute of despots backed by the most powerful armies.

—BENJAMIN R. TUCKER

Majority Rule

1620. In 1747, Mr. John Brown was invited to become the pastor of a church at Hingham. There was but one opponent to his settlement, a man whom Mr. Brown won over by a stroke of good humor. He asked for the grounds of his opposition. "I like your person and your manner," was the reply, "but your preaching, sir, I disapprove." "Then," said Mr. Brown, "we are agreed. I do not like my preaching very well myself, but how great a folly it is for you and me to set up our opinion against that of the whole parish."

—*The Argonaut*

1621. All the great injustices of history have been committed in the name of unchecked and unbridled "majority rule."

The late Senator James A. Reed, of Missouri, in one of the most forceful speeches ever delivered before the Senate, observed with great truth: "The majority crucified Jesus Christ; the majority burned the Christians at the stake; the majority established slavery; the majority jeered when Columbus said the world was round; the majority threw him into a dungeon for having discovered a new world; the majority cut off the ears of John Pym because he dared advocate the liberty of the press."

Man—Woman

1622. A woman without a man is like a garden without a fence.

—*German Proverb*

1623. Men really understand women—they just pretend they don't because it's cheaper like that.

1624. Women are to blame for most of the lying that men do. They insist on asking questions.

1625. The weaker sex is the stronger because of the weakness of the stronger sex for the weaker sex.

1626. One nice thing about being a man is that you don't have to kiss someone who hasn't shaved for two days.

1627. A mother takes twenty years to make a man of her boy, and another woman makes a fool of him in twenty minutes.

—ROBERT FROST

1628. If you flatter a man, you frighten him to death; if you don't, you bore him to death. If you permit him to make love to you, he gets tired of you in the end; and if you don't, he gets tired of you in the beginning. If you believe all he tells you, he thinks you are foolish; if you don't, he thinks you are a cynic.

Management

1629. Management, in the sense of employer, is merely the agent for the public, the stockholders and the employees. It is management's job to preserve the balance fairly between all these interests, that each may have his fair share without imperiling the community of the effort upon which the whole depends.

—JAMES F. BELL

1630. It is the social obligation of management to make certain that its executives are functioning at peak performance, both physically and psychologically. To keep top men from spinning, management must see that executives should: receive periodic medical checkups; receive periodic psychological evaluations; be given an adequate number of assistants of proper ability; have their time pressures reduced through improved selling; be given training in leadership.

—DR. STANLEY G. DUESKY

Mankind

1631. The difference between man and the animals is that man is, or should be, aware that there is more to life than begin, beget and be gone.

—IMOGENE FEY

1632. People are very much like flagstaffs. Some flagstaffs are very tall and prominent and some are small, but the glory of a flagstaff is not its size but the colors that it flies. A very small flagstaff flying the right colors is far more valuable than a very tall one with the wrong flag.

—HARRY EMERSON
FOSDICK

Manners

1633. Children are natural mimics—they act like their parents in spite of every attempt to teach them good manners.

1634. Manners are like the cipher in arithmetic; they may not be of much value in themselves, but they are capable of adding a great deal to the value of everything else.

1635. America can never be called an ill-mannered country. We pay more than ten million dollars every year in toll charges to add the word "please" to our telegrams.

Marriage

1636. Marriage is not a word but a sentence.

—H. L. MENCKEN

1637. To marry a woman for her beauty is like buying a house for its paint.

1638. When a man makes a mistake in his first marriage the victim is his second wife.

1639. If thy daughter marry well, thou hast found a son; if not, thou hast lost a daughter.

—FRANCIS QUARLES

1640. Why are girls so eager to get married and swap an eight-hour day for a fourteen-hour day?

1641. Never marry for money. However, it is well to associate with wealthy women and fall in love.

1642. It doesn't much signify whom one marries, for one is sure to find next morning that it was someone else.

—SAMUEL ROGER

1643. Marriage for beauty is a poor speculation, for any man who sees your wife has got just as much stock in her as you have.

—Josh Billings

1644. At the age of sixty, to marry a beautiful girl of sixteen, is to imitate those ignorant people who buy books to be read by their friends.

—A. Ricard

1645. Marriage is a self-service cafeteria. You pick what you like and then you see what the other chap's got and you wish you had that, too.

Married Life

1646. The best way to keep a husband is in doubt.

1647. Give a husband enough rope—and he'll want to skip.

1648. There are no such things as marriage ties. The wife always wins.

1649. The best way to remember your wife's birthday is to forget it once.

1650. When a man sees eye to eye with his wife, it means that his vision has been corrected.

1651. After a man says "I do," he discovers a long list of things he'd better not do.

1652. Every man who is happily married is a successful man, even if he has failed in everything else.

1653. Wives are people who can't figure out how a husband can spend money during the day when he doesn't play bridge or go to the beauty shop.

1654. Pity the poor women! Before marriage they have to wait up half the night for him to go; after marriage they have to wait up half the night for him to come home.

Martyrdom

1655. A thing is not necessarily true because a man dies for it.

—Oscar Wilde

1656. It is easier to be a martyr to any cause than to spend a life-time living up to its principles.

Maturity

1657. Maturity is the time of life when, if you had the time, you'd have the time of your life.

1658. A mature person is one who does not think only in abso-lutes, who is able to be objective even when deeply stirred emotionally, who has learned that there is both good and bad in all people and in all things, and who walks humbly and deals charitably with the circum-stances of life, knowing that in this world no one is all-knowing and therefore all of us need both love and charity.

—ELEANOR ROOSEVELT

Maxim—Maxims

1659. Maxims mean exactly nothing unless you read them as though each one applied to you.

1660. All maxims have their opposites, and proverbs should be sold in pairs, a single one being half a truth.

1661. Precepts or maxims are of great weight; and a few useful ones at hand do more toward a happy life than whole volumes that we know not where to find.

—SENECA

Medical Profession

1662. He is the best physician who is the most ingenious inspirer of hope.

—SAMUEL TAYLOR
COLERIDGE

1663. If the old-fashioned family doctor has disappeared, perhaps it's because he's out looking for the old-fashioned family.

—BURTON HILLIS in Better
Homes & Gardens

1664. Medical specialization has reached such a state today that patients have to learn to diagnose themselves before they know which specialist to call.

1665. The old doctor never had refused a call from anyone, whether rich or poor, but now he was tired.

"Have you any money?" he asked the midnight caller.

"Certainly!" was the reply.

"Then go to the new doctor. I'm too old to get out of bed for anybody who can pay for it."

1666. When asked by a young interne which medicine he considered the greatest boon, the old doctor looked back thoughtfully over a half century of practice. . . . As memories crowded in upon him, they brought a sharp clear recognition of the one medicine which he believed to be the master medicine of all. To the interne he said: "The most wonderful medicine is not compounded of rare and expensive drugs; it is one of the most commonplace things I know. In fact, it is not a drug at all. You can spell the name of this master medicine with four simple letters, W-O-R-K."

1667. In writing prescriptions physicians usually employ Latin terms. There are several reasons for this.

In the first place, it is a custom which has been followed since the time when medical science was in its infancy and medical men were wont to write what they had to say in Latin.

Secondly, the botanical names of plants are usually in Latin, (1) because scientific men give them their names, and (2) because not infrequently the English name for a plant in one part of the country has an entirely different application in another.

It is often advisable that a patient be kept in ignorance of the character of the drug which he is taking lest he attempt to use it without a physician's advice on another occasion, and thereby do himself injury.

—Dr. M. S. Young

Mediocrity

1668. Only a mediocre person is always at his best.

—W. Somerset Maugham

1669. Mediocrity obtains more with application than superiority without it.

—Baltasar Gracián

1670. The characteristic trait of the mediocre man is his deference to current opinion. He never speaks; he repeats. He judges a man according to social and economic position, his success, his wealth. He has the highest respect for those who are widely known regardless of why they are known; his idols are those currently in the public prints.

He would pay court to his most cruel enemy if this enemy were suddenly to become celebrated; but he does not care much about even his closest friends so long as they remain uneulogized by anyone. It isn't possible for him to believe that a man might very well be a genius and yet be obscure, poor and unknown.

Meeting–Meetings

1671. Too many meetings are held each month for no better reason than that it has been a month since the last one.

—BILL VAUGHN

1672. The trouble with so many club meetings is that they open at 7:30 sharp and close at 10 o'clock dull.

1673. Meetings do not bring out the best in us. They are designed for, and are popular with, the people who would rather do anything except actually go ahead and do it. They are a haven for compulsive talkers, impulsive talkers, and repulsive talkers.

—A. C. CHEVENS

Membership, Club. See Club Membership

Memory

1674. Bad memory has its root in bad attention.

—*Old Proverb*

1675. Don't worry if you start losing your memory. Just forget about it.

1676. A great memory does not make a mind, any more than a dictionary is a piece of literature.

—JOHN HENRY NEWMAN

1677. A good memory is often one of the characteristics of genius, but not always. The British scientist, Faraday, once spent six weeks on a series of experiments, all ending in failure. When they were completed, he sat down to enter the results and details in one of his many notebooks, and discovered he had done the whole series of experiments previously and unsuccessfully, and had entered the results in his notebook—so that he wouldn't forget them!

Mercy

1678. In case of doubt it is best to lean to the side of mercy. (*In dubiis benigniora sunt semper praeferenda.*)

—*Legal Maxim*

1679.
Teach me to feel another's woe,
To hide the fault I see;
That mercy I to others show,
That mercy show to me.

—ALEXANDER POPE

Middle Age

1680. The hardest decision for a woman to make is when to start middle age.

—WARREN HULL

1681. The surest sign of middle age is the sudden discovery that you are contemporary with all the wrong people. Here are a few suggestions that might help.

Avoid class reunions, and so on. When a pop tune from the early '30's is revived, pretend you are hearing it for the first time. In your own circle of friends, select someone who is maybe a year older than you and start calling him "Pop." When a friend mutters: "I don't know what'll ever become of the younger generation," you just tell him: "Don't worry about us!"

Of course, none of this will fool the friends you grew up with, but if you persevere you won't be bothered with those friends much longer, anyway.

Mind

1682. Some minds are like concrete—thoroughly mixed and permanently set.

1683. As tools become rusty, so does the mind; a garden uncared for soon becomes smothered in weeds; a talent neglected withers and dies.

—ETHEL R. PAGE

1684. No fathers or mothers think their children ugly; and this self-deceit is yet stronger with respect to the offspring of the mind.

—MIGUEL DE CERVANTES

Ministry

1685. A minister is God's ambassador.

—MILES SMITH

1686. The Christian ministry is the worst of all trades, but the best of all professions.

—J. NEWTON

1687. When Andrew Jackson was president of the United States, a certain man asked to be appointed to a responsible post. Mr. Jackson asked him about his present occupation. He replied that he was a minister of the Gospel. "Well, sir," said the President, "you will have to come down from that exalted position to accept the highest office I could give you in this government."

Misfortune

1688. Misfortunes test friends, and detect enemies.

—EPICTETUS

1689. The height of misfortune is the roomer who saved his money to spend a night at the Waldorf, went there, and dreamed he was sleeping under a box car.

1690. It is often better to have a great deal of harm happen to one than a little: a great deal may rouse you to remove, what a little will accustom you to endure.

—SIR FULKE GREVILLE
(BARON BROOKE)

Mistake—Mistakes

1691. Do not be ashamed of mistakes—and so make them crimes.

—CONFUCIUS, *The Book
of History*

1692. The only complete mistake is the mistake from which we learn nothing.

1693. The man who never makes mistakes loses a great many chances to learn something.

1694. It's tough to make a mistake, but it's tougher still to find out you're so unimportant nobody noticed it.

1695. You can't get through this world without making mistakes. The fellow who makes no mistakes does nothing, and that is a mistake.

1696. Mistakes are costly and somebody must pay. The time to correct a mistake is before it is made. The causes of mistakes are, first, "I didn't know"; second, "I didn't think"; third, "I didn't care."

—HENRY H. BUCKLEY

1697.   SIX MISTAKES OF MAN

The Roman philosopher and statesman, Cicero, said this some 2,000 years ago, and it is still true. The six mistakes of man:

1. The delusion that personal gain is made by crushing others.
2. The tendency to worry about things that cannot be changed or corrected.
3. Insisting that a thing is impossible because we cannot accomplish it.
4. Refusing to set aside trivial preferences.
5. Neglecting development and refinement of the mind, and not acquiring the habit of reading and study.
6. Attempting to compel others to believe and live as we do.

Moderation

1698.   He will always be a slave who does not know how to live upon a little.

—HORACE

1699.   Moderation in temper is a virtue, but moderation in principle is always a vice.

1700.   It is better to rise from life as from a banquet—neither thirsty nor drunken.

—ARISTOTLE

Modern Age

1701.   Girls used to wear unmentionables, but nowadays they wear nothing to speak of.

1702.   About all that man has learned in the past 25 years is how to go faster, work less, spend more, die quicker.

1703.   If modern architecture is any indication, people who throw stones are practically extinct.

1704.   There's nothing wrong with the younger generation that the older generation didn't outgrow.

Modern Art. See Art, Modern

Modesty

1705.   False modesty is the refinement of vanity. It is a lie.

—JEAN DE LA BRUYÈRE

1706. He who takes his rank lightly raises his own dignity.

—*Hebrew Proverb*

1707. There's a lot to be said for the fellow who doesn't say it himself.

—Maurice Seitter

1708. With people of only moderate ability modesty is mere honesty; but with those who possess great talent it is hypocrisy.

—Arthur Schopenhauer

1709. Through all his illustrious career, Anton Dvorak remained a simple, honest man, with a heart close to the common people of his native Bohemia. One day the admiring people of Prague brought him a wreath marked: "To the Greatest Composer in the World."

The composer was too moved to protest the honor too much, but when visitors came to his house a few days later, they discovered that Dvorak had placed the wreath where he believed it belonged. In a corner of the composer's study stood a bust of Beethoven, and upon its noble brow Dvorak had placed the treasured offering.

Money

1710. When money speaks, the truth is silent.

—*Russian Proverb*

1711. Money talks, and everybody is willing to listen.

1712. Money never made a fool of anybody; it only shows 'em up.

—Frank McKinney
Hubbard

1713. The trouble is, money doesn't talk anymore. It just goes without saying.

1714. Money still talks, but you have to increase the volume if you want to get the message through.

1715. There are many more important things than money. It's just that you need money to buy them.

1716. Love of money is the root of half the evil in the world; lack of money is the root of the other half.

1717. He that is of the opinion money will do everything may well be suspected of doing everything for money.

—Benjamin Franklin

1718. By the time many a man discovers that money doesn't grow on trees, he's already way out on a limb.

Money, Easy. See Wealth

Morality

1719. Morality is simply the attitude we adopt toward people whom we personally dislike.

—Oscar Wilde

1720. Whenever you are to do a thing, though it can never be known but to yourself, ask yourself how you would act were all the world looking at you, and act accordingly.

—Thomas Jefferson

1721. One lesson, and only one, history may be said to repeat with distinctness: that the world is built somehow on moral foundations; that in the long run it is well with the good; in the long run it is ill with the wicked.

But this is no science; it is no more than the old doctrine taught long ago by the Hebrew prophets.

—James A. Froude

Motherhood

1722. The death of a mother is the first sorrow wept without her.

1723. A mother is not a person to lean on but a person to make leaning unnecessary.

—Dorothy Canfield
Fisher

1724. The future of society is in the hands of mothers; if the world was lost through woman, she alone can save it.

—Louis de Beaufort

1725. AN ESSAY ON MOTHERS BY AN
EIGHT-YEAR-OLD

Mothers are the ladies you live with if you're not an orphan. They are very useful, especially at night when you are sick. Mothers rock babies and girls every night, but boys have to pretend that they don't like it; and only do it when there is nobody around. They make you wash your ears every day and they can tell if you do not brush your teeth, even if you wet the toothbrush.

1726.   Before my Mother taught me how to pray,
I trusted her in all things great and small;
My guardian by night, my guide by day,
The constant angel waiting for my call.

Now she is gone, and I must search the sky
For grace and judgment in my anguished
pleas.
O, could I know the heavenly reply
That smiled assurance at my Mother's
knees.

—ROBERT LEE STRAUS

1727. I did not have my mother long, but she cast over me an influence which has lasted all my life. The good effects of her early training I can never lose. If it had not been for her appreciation and her faith in me at a critical time in my experience, I should never likely have become an inventor. I was always a careless boy, and with a mother of different mental calibre, I should have turned out badly. But her firmness, her sweetness, her goodness, were potent powers to keep me in the right path. My mother was the making of me. The memory of her will always be a blessing to me.

—THOMAS A. EDISON

1728. In a New Orleans cemetery there is a monument which has created much interest. It represents a ship in the midst of a storm-tossed sea; a mother and child clinging together on the vessel. On the base is an inscription saying they were drowned on July 4, 1900. They were sole survivors of a large estate, and the question was under whose name should the estate be administered, the name of the mother or the daughter. The Court decided it should be in the name of the child, reckoning she went down last, because the mother would hold her in a place of safety to the end.
A wonderful tribute to mother love!

—*1001 Illustrations for
Pulpit and Platform,*
by AQUILLA WEBB
(Harper)

Mother's Day

1729. On Mother's Day a minister gave this perfect tribute: "My mother practices what I preach."

1730. Mother's Day is appropriately in May because it is the most beautiful month. Father's Day is appropriately in June because about then he usually has recovered from April income tax sufficiently to pay for his own gifts that the children charge to him.

—JAMES J. O'REILLY

1731. Mother's Day brings to mind the beautiful legend of the Roman matron, Cornelia. A widow of modest means but with social position, she associated with people of considerable wealth. Among these was a woman whom we might describe today as "catty." Flaunting an almost vulgar array of her own jewelry, she asked, "And where, Cornelia, are your jewels?"

Cornelia called two of her young sons into the room and affectionately laying her hands on their broad shoulders replied, "These are my jewels."

1732. The mother who can be truly proud of her children is not the indulgent mother. Instead, she is one who is firm, but fair; one whose love and affection for her family commands respect; one who is willing to sacrifice only when the purpose is worthy of the sacrifice. She will not be a mother to give them everything they want, but one who will be ever mindful of what they need. Her children may even think she is a hard mother, until they grow old enough to understand. And when that time comes they will be the kind of children who will always remember her with the deepest affection and the utmost respect, not only on Mother's Day but on every day.

Motive—Motives

1733. Take away the motive and you take away the sin.

—MIGUEL DE CERVANTES

1734. Never judge a man by what he says; try and find out why he said it.

1735. We should often be ashamed of our best actions if the world could see all the motives which produced them.

—FRANÇOIS DE LA
ROCHEFOUCAULD

1736. Better to do right from wrong motives, than wrong from right motives. Whether you lose your own soul is not significant, but how your acts affect others is of vital importance.

—E. W. HELMS

Mourning

1737. The childless couple sleep in weed-covered graves.

—HARRY WILLIAM KING

1738. We do not mourn the absent; why then the dead, who are effectually no other? For they are not gone, but sent before.

—SENECA

1739.
Mourn not death; 'tis but a stair
Built with divinest art,
Up which the deathless footsteps climb,
Of loved ones who depart.

—MINOT J. SAVAGE

Mudslinging

1740. When a man starts throwing dirt, you can be sure he's losing ground.

1741. Never throw mud. You may miss your mark and you are bound to have dirty hands.

Music

1742. Music is harmony, harmony is perfection, perfection is our dream, and our dream is heaven.

—HENRI FRÉDÉRIC AMIEL

1743. If one plays good music people don't listen, and if one plays bad music people don't talk.

—OSCAR WILDE

1744. According to one music critic, the way to write a modern song-hit is to take something that has been written by the masters and decompose it.

1745. Music is much more enjoyable if you listen to it with your eyes shut. It is also more enjoyable if the people sitting near you listen to it with their mouths shut.

1746. What is music? This question occupied my mind for hours last night before I fell asleep. The very existence of music is wonderful, I might even say miraculous. Its domain is between thought and phenomena. Like a twilight mediator, it hovers between spirit and matter, related to both, yet differing from each. It is spirit, but it is spirit subject to the measurement of time. It is matter, but it is matter that can dispense with space.

—HEINRICH HEINE

Name—Names

1747. I agree with you entirely in condemning the mania of giving names to objects of any kind after persons still living. Death alone can seal the title of any man to this honor, by putting it out of his power to forfeit it.

—THOMAS JEFFERSON,
*Letter to Benjamin
Rush,* 1800

1748. It seems the good professors of the Physiology Department at Heidelberg University needed a mirror for their washroom. A request for one was denied because a mirror was classified as a "non-scientific" object.

But the professors got their mirror anyway. How? In the next requisition they used technical-scientific terminology. Their request? One human reflector.

Narrow-mindedness

1749. Have you noticed that a narrow mind and a wide mouth often go together?

1750. When a closed mind re-opens, it's usually under the same old management.

1751. Narrowness of mind is the cause of obstinacy—we do not easily believe what is beyond our sight.

—FRANÇOIS DE LA
ROCHEFOUCAULD

Nationalism

1752. Nationalism is an infantile disease. It is the measles of mankind.

—DR. ALBERT EINSTEIN

1753. The spirit of nationalism springs from the deepest of human emotions. It rises from the yearning of men to be free of foreign domination, to govern themselves. It springs from a thousand rills of race, of history, of sacrifice and pride in national achievement. In our own country, does not the word "America" stir something deeper within us than mere geography? Does not the suffering and the sacrifice of our forebears who fought for our independence flash in our minds with every mention of the word "America"?

—HERBERT HOOVER

Nature

1754. Nature is a revelation of God; art a revelation of man.
—Henry Wadsworth
Longfellow

1755. Nature creates ability; luck provides it with opportunities.
—François de la
Rochefoucauld

1756. To pay homage to beauty is to admire Nature; to admire Nature is to worship God.

1757. Nature must have a sense of humor to let spring fever and housecleaning come at the same time.

1758. Nature never hurries: atom by atom, little by little, she achieves her work. The lesson one learns in fishing, yachting, or planting, is the manners of Nature; patience with the delays of wind and sun, delays of the seasons, bad weather, excess or lack of water.
—Ralph Waldo
Emerson, *Farming*

Necessity

1759. Necessity never made a good bargain.
—Benjamin Franklin

1760. That which necessity compels she excuses.
—*Legal Maxim*

1761. Necessity makes laws, but does not obey them.
—Publilius Syrus

Neglect

1762. Any time a fellow feels neglected he should think of Whistler's father.

1763. We lose our friends, our usefulness and our religion—not by great decisions, but by small neglects.

1764. The best security against revolution is in constant correction of abuses and the introduction of needed improvements. It is the neglect of timely repair that makes rebuilding necessary.
—Richard Whately

Neighbor–Neighbors

1765. It is discouraging to try to be a good neighbor in a bad neighborhood.

—WILLIAM R. CASTLE

1766. Don't expect your neighbor to be better than your neighbor's neighbor.

1767. Behind every successful man can usually be found three people: his wife, and Mr. and Mrs. Jones.

Neutrality

1768. Neutrality is an evidence of weakness.

—FRANCIS KOSSUTH

1769. No nation, wanting to be free or to remain free, can be neutral today. Neutralism means one can stand aside and let others fight out the great issues of modern man. Neutralism is the wife who watches the bear chase her husband and who says impartially, "Go it, husband! Go it, bear!"

—GENERAL CARLOS P. ROMULO, Ambassador of the Republic of the Philippines to the United States, from an address at the University of Richmond

New Year–New Year's Day

1770. The New Year won't do anything for us, except provide the time during which we can do something for ourselves.

1771. While the New Year's wishes of your friends for happiness and prosperity still echo in your ears, roll up your sleeves and start making them come true.

1772. The Chinese New Year is a day of honor and celebration. On this day they have their feasts and festivities, but most significant of all is the fact that the Chinese undertake to pay off all indebtedness and obligations on that day. Friendships, which have been strained and broken, are restored so far as humanly possible. They then bow before Confucius or Buddha, stating their debts have been paid and friendships restored, and ask his New Year blessings.

1773.   RING OUT THE OLD YEAR

Of all sounds of all bells, the most solemn and touching is the peal which rings out the old year. I have never heard it without a gathering up of my mind to a concentration of all the images of the past twelve months, all I have done or suffered, performed or neglected, in that regretted time. But on such occasion it is both more noble and more profitable to take a cheerful and reassuring view of our condition and that of humanity in general, laying aside futile reflections on past imprudence and mismanagement and resolving for the future to do our utmost in fulfilling our duty toward God and our fellow men.

—CHARLES LAMB

Nobility

1774.   Noble by birth, yet nobler by great deeds.

—HENRY WADSWORTH
LONGFELLOW, *Tales
of a Wayside Inn*

1775.   True nobility scorns to trample upon a worm, or to sneak to an emperor.

—SAADI

1776.   Nobility is a dignity based on the presumption that we shall do well because our fathers did well.

—JOSEPH JOUBERT

Nonconformity

1777.   Defiance of social customs has earned many a good woman a bad reputation.

—MINNA THOMAS ANTRIM

1778.   Read every day something no one else is reading. Think every day something no one else is thinking. It is bad for the mind to be always a part of a unanimity.

—CHRISTOPHER MORLEY

1779.   Whoso would be a man must be a nonconformist. He who would gather immortal palms must not be hindered by the name of goodness, but must explore if it be goodness. Nothing is at last sacred but the integrity of your own mind. Absolve you to yourself, and you shall have the suffrage of the world.

—RALPH WALDO EMERSON

Obedience

1780. True obedience is true liberty.

—HENRY WARD BEECHER

1781. When you obey your superior you instruct your inferior.

—*Old Proverb*

Objective—Objectives

1782. Obstacles always show up when you take your eyes off the goal.

1783. In whatever position you find yourself determine first your objective.

—MARSHAL FERDINAND FOCH

Obstacle—Obstacles

1784. Omelettes are not made without breaking eggs.

—MAXIMILIEN FRANÇOIS MARIE ISIDORE DE ROBESPIERRE

1785. Whatever impedes a man but doesn't stop him, aids his progress.

1786. A biologist tells how he watched an ant carrying a piece of straw which seemed a big burden for it. The ant came to a crack in the earth which was too wide for it to cross. It stood for a time as though pondering the situation, then put the straw across the crack and walked over upon it.

Here is a lesson for all mankind! A man's burden can be made a bridge for his progress.

Old Age

1787. The most telling sign of old age is not caring any more.

1788. You are old only if you'd rather win an argument than be right.

1789. Best way to cure a woman of most any illness is to tell her that the symptoms are just a sign of old age.

1790. The records are full of cases of folks who have stayed gingery and productive, even into the 80's and 90's:

George Santayana said at 82, "I have never been happier in my life than right now."

Daniel Auber wrote his *Dream of Love* in his 80's and said, "I'm not 80; I am 4 times 20."

At 88, John Wesley preached every day.

Of Benjamin Franklin, Walter B. Pitkin said: "Men have forgotten the first half of his life. The world will never forget the second." Franklin went to France in the service of his country at 78, and wrote his autobiography at over 80.

Sophocles wrote his *Oedipus* at 90 years of age.

Pope Leo XIII inaugurated most of his enlightened policy after he was 70.

Titian painted his masterpiece, the bronze doors of the sacristy of St. Mark's, at 85.

Elihu Root died in 1937 at over 92 years of age. He was one of the greatest statesmen America ever produced and continued his activities until over 90.

One thinks of Oliver Wendell Holmes, John Dewey, Bernard Baruch, Henry Ford, Arturo Toscanini, John Foster Dulles, Dwight D. Eisenhower, and others who did or are doing their best work since passing 60.

Old-fashioned

1791. Rejecting things because they are old-fashioned would rule out the sun and the moon.

1792. A man behind the times is apt to speak ill of them, on the principle that nothing looks well from behind.

—Dr. Oliver Wendell
Holmes

Open-mindedness

1793. Just because a man is open-minded doesn't mean he has holes in his head.

1794. An open mind is all very well in its way, but it ought to be so open that there is no keeping anything in or out of it. It should be capable of shutting its doors sometimes, or it may be found a little draughty.

—Samuel Butler

Opinion—Opinions

1795. Remember that all things are only opinion and that it is in your power to think as you please.

—Marcus Aurelius

1796. The feeble tremble before opinion, the foolish defy it, the wise judge it, the skillful direct it.

—Mme. Roland

1797. New opinions are always suspected, and usually opposed, without any other reason, but because they are not already common.

—John Locke, *An Essay Concerning Human Understanding*

Opportunism

1798. An opportunist is a man who, finding himself in hot water, decides to take a bath.

1799. Lord Hertford was once asked what he would do if he saw someone cheating at cards.
"What would I do?" he replied. "Bet on him, of course."

Opportunity

1800. Weak men wait for opportunities, strong men make them.

—Marden

1801. There is no security on this earth. Only opportunity.

—General Douglas MacArthur

1802. Most of us never recognize opportunity until it goes to work in our competitor's business.

1803. Even when opportunity knocks a man still has to get up off his seat and open the door.

1804. The trouble with opportunity is that it always comes disguised as hard work.

1805. A very long time ago, in Greece, some politicians thought to play a joke on one of their number and got him appointed Public Scavenger. Instead of being embarrassed he decided to show what a man could do with such a lowly assignment—if he tried. Unsanitary conditions which had encouraged pestilence for decades were eliminated. Habits of cleanliness were promoted. Civic pride was stimulated. In a few years people came to look upon the office of Public Scavenger as one of honor and responsibility and thereafter only men of great ability could aspire to the post.

1806. One night three horsemen were riding across an Eastern desert. As they crossed the dry bed of a river, a voice called "Halt!" They did so and the voice continued, telling them to dismount, pick up some pebbles and put them in their pockets. Then the voice said, "You have done as I commanded. Tomorrow at sunup you will be both glad and sorry."

Mystified, they rode on, as directed. At sunrise, they reached into their pockets, and found that the pebbles were diamonds, rubies and other precious stones. Then they thought of the warning, and they were both glad and sorry—glad they had taken some, sorry they had not taken more.

Opposition

1807. It takes a strong man to swim against the current; any dead fish will float with it.

1808. Men often oppose a thing merely because they have had no agency in planning it, or because it may have been planned by those whom they dislike.

—ALEXANDER HAMILTON,
The Federalist

1809. Ornithologists assure us that the eagle, the condor of the Andes, the albatross of the Pacific, and even the swiftly-flying little dove, like many other birds that are strong on the wing, can fly more swiftly against a wind than in a gentle breeze. It may be that this is because they are stimulated to exert the muscular strength of their pinions. But however this may be, it is a fact that the fires of a steamship burn much more fiercely under the boilers when the vessel is going against a headwind.

1810. You can't make real success without making real enemies. You can't hold a strong position without strong and continued opposition. You can't seem right to any if you don't seem wrong to many.

A useful life can't be entirely peaceful and carefree. You must do your duty as you see it.

The greater you are, the greater the penalty of your progress. The further you go and the wider your range, the more you increase the points of contact with which you must reckon, and therefore you multiply your battles against misconception and slander and envy and malice.

So long as you aspire, others will conspire; so long as you try, others will vie. You'll have hostility to face in every place and at every pace.

Go straight ahead to your goal. As long as your conscience isn't ashamed to acknowledge you as a friend, don't give a rap for your enemies.

Optimism

1811. An optimist counts his blessings—a pessimist discounts his.
—Imogene Fey

1812. Many an optimist has become rich simply by buying out a pessimist.

1813. It's all right to be optimistic, but no cook breaks an egg directly into the pan.

1814. An optimist is a person who sees a green light everywhere, while the pessimist sees only the red stop light. . . . But the truly wise person is color-blind.
—Dr. Albert Schweitzer

1815. In the days of sailing ships, a young and inexperienced seaman was sent aloft in a storm to disentangle a broken rigging from the mainmast. In spite of the raging wind, the youngster climbed up swiftly and did the job. When it was time to descend, he looked down and saw the vessel tossing and rolling in the ugly sea.

Suddenly his courage left him. He felt dizzy and faint. He called to the mate on the deck below, "I'm going to fall!"

The mate, who had spent many years at sea, shouted back above the storm, "Don't look down, boy. Look up!"

The young seaman did as he was told and came down safely. He had regained his courage when he looked up.

If more people would "look up" when everything seems to be going wrong, they would find that their lives would begin to "look up" too.

Oratory

1816. Oratory is the power to talk people out of their natural opinions.
—Paul Chatfield

1817. Trying to settle a problem with oratory is like attempting to unsnarl a traffic jam by blowing horns.

Originality

1818. The most original writers borrow from one another.

1819. To select well among old things is almost equal to inventing new ones.

1820. Many a man fails as an original thinker simply because his memory is too good.

—Friedrich Wilhelm
Nietzsche

1821. It is not at all likely that anyone ever had a totally original idea. He may put together old ideas into a new combination, but the elements which made up the new combination were mostly acquired from other people. Without many borrowed ideas, there would be no invention, no new movements, or anything else that is classed as new.

Ostentation

1822. I know that a man who shows me his wealth is like the beggar who shows me his poverty; they are both looking for alms from me, the rich man for the alms of my envy, the poor man for the alms of my guilt.

—Ben Hecht

1823. Whatever is done without ostentation, and without the people being witnesses of it, is, in my opinion, most praiseworthy; not that the public ever should be entirely avoided, for good actions desire to be placed in the light; but notwithstanding this, the greatest theater for virtue is conscience.

—Cicero

Outer Space

1824. If the moon isn't made of green cheese, how come there's such a rat race to see who gets there first?

1825. With bigger and better bombs in the arsenal, the question is not so much whether there is life on Mars as whether it will continue to be possible to live on Earth.

Overeating

1826. It isn't the hours one spends at the table that put on the avoirdupois; it's the seconds.

1827. Many doctors pay their grocery bill with the money of folks who have eaten too much.

Overweight. See *also* Diet–Dieting

1828. A woman is never overweight until she has run out of places to hide it.

—Franklin P. Jones

1829. About the only thing that'll give you more for your money now than ten years ago is the penny scale at the drugstore.

Parent–Child

1830. Don't wait to make your son a great man—make him a great boy.

1831. The ability to say "no" is perhaps the greatest gift a parent has.

1832. Judge none blessed before his death: for a man shall be known in his children.

—*Ecclesiastes* 2:18

1833. Parents wonder why the streams are bitter when they themselves have poisoned the fountain.

1834. Children who avoid the mistakes their parents made often make the mistakes their parents avoided.

1835. Parents who are afraid to put their foot down usually have children who step on their toes.

—*Chinese Proverb*

1836. It is more important to know where your children are tonight than where your ancestors were when the *Mayflower* sailed.

1837. Parents spend the first part of a child's life getting him to walk and talk, and the rest of his childhood getting him to sit down and shut up.

Parenthood

1838. Very frequently rich parents make poor parents.

1839. Parents should work together as efficiently as two book ends.

1840. Some parents really bring their children up; others let them down.

1841. All women are mothers of great men—it isn't their fault if life disappoints them later.

—From *Doctor Zhivago* by
Boris Pasternak, copy-
right © 1958, Pantheon
Books, Inc.

Parent-Teacher Association

1842. There's this to be said for those who have loved and lost; they don't get drafted to attend P-TA meetings!

1843. In the good old days there was always something back of the one-room country schoolhouse besides the P-TA.

Parting

1844.
They who go
Feel not the pain of parting; it is they
Who stay behind that suffer.

—Henry W. Longfellow,
Michelangelo

1845. Every parting gives a foretaste of death; every coming to-gether again a foretaste of the resurrection. This is why even people who were indifferent to each other rejoice so much if they come together again after twenty or thirty years' separation.

—Arthur Schopenhauer,
*Further Psychological
Observations,* 1851

Past, The

1846. The love of the past is often but the hatred of the present.
—Dorion

1847. To look back to antiquity is one thing, to go back to it is another.

—Charles C. Colton,
Lacon

1848. Sometimes when a man recalls the good old days, he's really thinking of his bad young days.

1849. Your forefathers did without sugar until the 13th century, without coal fires until the 14th century, without buttered bread until the 15th century, without potatoes until the 16th century, without coffee, tea, and soap until the 17th century, without pudding until the 18th century, without gas, matches and electricity until the 19th century and without canned goods until the 20th century.

Patience

1850. Patience is bitter, but its fruit is sweet.
—JEAN JACQUES ROUSSEAU

1851. A man without patience is a lamp without oil.
—ALFRED DE MUSSET

1852. We cannot eat the fruit while the tree is in blossom.
—BENJAMIN DISRAELI

1853. Patience does not mean indifference; it is the art of hoping.
—*Old Proverb*

1854. Patience is good only when it is the shortest way to a good end; otherwise, impatience is better.

1855. A man watches his pear tree day after day, impatient for the ripening of the fruit. Let him attempt to *force* the process, and he may spoil both fruit and tree. But let him patiently *wait*, and the ripe fruit at length falls into his lap.

—ABRAHAM LINCOLN

Patriotism

1856. A man's country is not a certain area of land, of mountains, rivers, and woods, but it is a principle; and patriotism is loyalty to that principle.

—GEORGE WILLIAM CURTIS, American author (1824–1892)

1857. A Japanese mother had given her three sons to the war. The first was reported slain. She smiled and said, "It is well, I am happy." The second lay dead upon the field. She smiled again and said, "I am still happy." The third gave up his life and they said to her, "At last you weep!" "Yes," she said, "but it is because I have no more sons to give to my beloved country!"

—MARSHALL P. WILDER,
*Smiling 'Round the
World*

1858. John Hancock, first signer of the Declaration of Independence, was an earnest worker for the cause of freedom.

During the siege of Boston, General Washington consulted Congress upon the propriety of bombarding the town. His letter was read to Congress, of which Mr. Hancock was president. At first, there was silence. Then a member made a motion that the house should resolve itself into a committee of the whole, in order that Mr. Hancock might give his opinion, since all of his property was located in Boston.

Leaving his chair, John Hancock addressed the chairman of the committee as follows: "It is true, sir, nearly all of the property I have in the world is in houses and other real estate in the town of Boston; but if the liberties of our country require their being burnt to ashes—*issue the order for that purpose immediately!*"

—MABEL RUTH JACKSON

Peace

1859. If peace cannot be maintained with honor, it is no longer peace.

—LORD JOHN RUSSELL,
Speech in Greenoch,
September 14, 1853

1860. What the world needs is the peace that surpasses all misunderstandings.

1861. You may either win your peace or buy it: win it, by resistance to evil; buy it, by compromise with evil.

—JOHN RUSKIN

People

1862. Too many of us are like wheelbarrows—useful only when pushed and too easily upset.

1863. There are three kinds of people in the world, the wills, the won'ts and the can'ts. The first accomplish everything; the second oppose everything; the third fail in everything.

Perfection

1864. No good work whatever can be perfect, and the demand for perfection is always a sign of a misunderstanding of the ends of art.

—JOHN RUSKIN

1865. To arrive at perfection, a man should have very sincere friends or inveterate enemies; because he would be made sensible of his good or ill conduct, either by the censures of the one or the admonitions of the other.

—DIOGENES

1866. To talk about the need for perfection in man is to talk about the need for another species. The essence of man is imperfection. Imperfection and blazing contradictions—between mixed good and evil, altruism and selfishness, cooperativeness and combativeness, optimism and fatalism, affirmation and negation.

—NORMAN COUSINS

1867. Centuries ago there lived in Italy a maker of violins, Antonio Stradivari. When he became able to have a workshop of his own he made it a rule that no violin should ever leave the shop until it was as near perfection as human care and skill could make it. He said, "God needs violins to send his music into the world, and if my violins are defective, God's music will be spoiled."

1868. A New York advertising agency thought up an advertisement for Rolls-Royce which appeared in full pages right across the country. "At 60 m.p.h.," it ran, "the loudest noise in the new Rolls-Royce comes from the electric clock."

The idea was shown with some pride to two visiting Rolls-Royce executives. They did not look overenthusiastic. Said one of them reflectively: "We've got to do something about that clock."

1869. Gibbon worked twenty years writing *The Decline and Fall of the Roman Empire.* Plato wrote the first sentence in his *Republic* nine different ways before he was satisfied with it. Burke wrote the conclusion of his speech at the trial of Hastings sixteen times, and Butler his famous *Analogy* twenty times. Virgil spent seven years on his *Georgics* and twelve on the *Aeneid.* He was so displeased with the latter that he attempted to rise from his deathbed to commit it to flames.

Performance

1870. You are doing your best only when you are trying to improve what you are doing.

1871. 'Tis better that a man's own works than another man's words should praise him.

—Roger L'Estrange

1872. The feeling that you've done a job well is rewarding; the feeling that you've done it perfectly is fatal.

Perseverance

1873. A quitter never wins and a winner never quits.

1874. Any man can see further than he can reach, but that doesn't mean he should quit reaching.

1875. No one ever would have crossed the ocean if he could have gotten off the ship in the storm.

—C. F. Kettering

1876. If Columbus had turned back after sixty-five days of sailing on the uncharted seas, no one could have blamed him. But then, no one would have remembered him, either! Even if you have a good excuse for giving up, remember that all the rewards go to those who stick until they get what they are after.

—*The Speaker's Book of Illustrative Stories*, edited by Maxwell Droke (Droke House)

1877. There is a story told about a sophomore whose grades in mathematics were so poor as to threaten his remaining at the university. To bring up his grades to the required standard he found it necessary to study hard and intensively the subjects he dreaded and disliked. He managed to raise his grades. His dread vanished and with it, of course, his distaste. In what had been his obvious deficiency, a source of real unhappiness, he ultimately found security, achievement and acclaim. He became as a matter of fact, one of the greatest mathematicians and physicists in the world.

That man? None other than the great Charles Steinmetz.

Persistence—Persistency. See *also* Perseverance

1878. The wayside of business is full of brilliant men who started out with a spurt, and lacked the stamina to finish. Their places were taken by patient and unshowy plodders who never knew when to quit.

—J. R. Todd

1879. A government official in Hong Kong tells the Chinese fable about an old man who had to cross a hill every day. Each day he took a stone in each hand from the top of the hill to the bottom. Asked why, he said, "I'm moving this hill. Not in my lifetime or in my son's lifetime, but in time, this hill will be gone."

—Clarence W. Hall,
Copyright by *The
Reader's Digest Asso-
ciation, Inc.* Reprinted
by permission

1880. Eighty-eight letters to Andrew Carnegie, asking him to buy an organ for the Cote Brilliante Presbyterian Church of St. Louis, written within an eight-month period, at last brought a check for $1,125 from the philanthropist.

The check was accompanied only by a printed receipt form, and the church members, while jubilant over getting the price of the organ, wondered whether Mr. Carnegie really wanted to give the money, or if he did so to put an end to the series of letters. The letters had been sent at first at intervals of two weeks by different officials and members of the church, the intervals decreasing to one a day, as the appeals for aid brought no reply.

Perspective

1881. The higher we soar the smaller we look to those who can-not fly.

—Friedrich Wilhelm
Nietzsche

1882. A Dwarf standing on the shoulders of a Giant sees farther than the Giant; but if he stood upon his own basis, he would scarcely see at all. It behooves him to remember that the Giant is a Giant.

—Lewis

Persuasion–Persuasiveness

1883. No one can give faith unless he has faith. It is the persuaded who persuade.

—Joseph Joubert

1884. If you would win a man to your cause, first convince him that you are his sincere friend.

—Abraham Lincoln

1885. Those who have finished by making all others think with them, have usually been those who began by daring to think with them-selves.

—Charles C. Colton

Pessimism

1886. He who foresees calamaties, suffers them twice over.
—B. Porteus

1887. Pessimist: one who sizes himself up and gets sore about it.

Philanthropy

1888. All the other pleasures of life seem to wear out, but the pleasure of helping others in distress never does.
—Julius Rosenwald

1889. When we do good to our fellow sufferers, we invest in a savings-bank from which the heart receives the interest.
—E. Souvestre

Pioneering

1890. The great man is the man who does a thing for the first time.
—Alexander Smith

1891. The "silly question" is the first intimation of some totally new development.
—Alfred North Whitehead

1892. Undertake something that is difficult; it will do you good. Unless you try to do something beyond what you have already mastered, you will never grow.
—Ronald E. Osborn, "Do a Good Job of Living," *The Lookout*, April 26, 1954. Used by permission of the author

Pity

1893. He that pities another remembers himself.
—George Herbert

1894. Most of our misfortunes are more supportable than the comments of our friends upon them.
—Charles C. Colton

Plagiarism

1895. Plagiarists are always suspicious of being stolen from.
—Samuel T. Coleridge

1896. Keep your hands from literary picking and stealing. But if you cannot refrain from this kind of stealth, abstain from murdering what you steal.

—Augustus Toplady

1897. Four commas upside down—two at the beginning of the paragraph, two at the close of the paragraph—will save many a man's integrity and usefulness.

—T. DeWitt Talmage

1898. Take the whole range of imaginative literature, and we are all wholesale borrowers. In every matter that relates to invention, to use, or beauty or form, we are borrowers.

—Wendell Phillips

1899. It was in 1665 that French writer François de La Rochefoucauld said, "In their first passions women love the lover. And in the others they love love." Lord Byron, 140 years later, wrote: "In her first passion a woman loves her lover. In all others all she loves is love." Byron repeatedly is credited with having originated this observation, though it is clearly evident he borrowed it from La Rochefoucauld.

Plan–Plans–Planning

1900. A man who does not think and plan long ahead will find trouble right at his door.

—Confucius

1901. The world turns aside to let any man pass who knows whither he is going.

—David Starr Jordan

1902. Nobody ever pulled a rabbit out of a hat without carefully putting one there in the first place.

—J. H. Kindelberger

1903. He who every morning plans the transactions of the day, and follows that plan, carries a thread that will guide him through the labyrinth of the most busy life. The orderly arrangement of his time is like a ray of light which darts itself through all his occupations. But where no plan is laid, where the disposal of time is surrendered merely to the chance of incidents, all things lie huddled together in one chaos, which admits of neither distribution nor review.

—Victor Hugo

Pleasure

1904. Pleasure must succeed pleasure, else past pleasure turns to pain.

—Robert Browning

1905. Do not bite at the bait of pleasure till you know there is no hook beneath it.

—Thomas Jefferson

1906. The trouble with mixing business with pleasure is that pleasure always comes out on top.

1907. Leonardo da Vinci was in the habit of paying the price demanded by the owners of captive birds, for the pleasure of setting them free.

Poet—Poets—Poetry

1908. A poet is a world enclosed in a man.

—Victor Hugo

1909. Poets crystallize the thoughts that other minds hold in solution.

1910. There is as much difference between good poetry and fine verses as between the smell of a flower garden and a perfumer's shop.

—Augustus Hare

Point of View

1911. What some of us consider failure, others would think of as success.

1912. We have but to change the point of view and the greatest action looks mean.

—William Makepeace Thackeray

1913. Two little children were talking as they watched a man planting seeds. "I don't like to see seeds being planted, it makes me think of digging graves and burying people," said one. "It doesn't make me feel that way a bit," replied the other. "I just look ahead and see them wake up into beautiful flowers."

1914. A man was driving in the country one day, and he saw an old man sitting on a fence rail watching the automobiles go by. Stopping to pass the time of day, the traveler said, "I never could stand living out here. You don't see anything, and I'm sure you don't travel like I do. I'm on the go all the time."

The old man on the fence looked down at the stranger, and drawled, "I can't see much difference in what I'm doing and what you're doing. I set on the fence and watch the autos go by, and you set in your auto and watch the fences go by. It's just the way you look at things."

Politeness

1915. If you bow at all, bow low.
—*Chinese Proverb*

1916. Politeness is good nature regulated by good sense.
—SYDNEY SMITH

1917. Anyone can be polite to a king. It takes a gentleman to be polite to a beggar.

1918. Short skirts have a tendency to make men polite. One never sees a man get on a bus ahead of one.

Politician—Politicians. See also Politics

1919. The politician's promises of yesterday are the taxes of today.
—W. L. MACKENZIE KING

1920. The politician who can be bought sooner or later gives himself away.

1921. Our politicians no longer duel as they often do in other countries, but boy, how they can fence!

1922. Over a long period of time the word "politician" has acquired an odious cast, but where is the American mother who has not praised to her son the achievements of Washington, of Lincoln, of Patrick Henry or Randolph of Roanoke? Politicians all.
—Editorial, *Nation's Business*

Politics

1923. Some go into politics not to do good, but to do well.

1924. He serves his party best who serves his country best.
—RUTHERFORD B. HAYES, Inaugural Address, March 5, 1877

1925. When any issue becomes a political football there are lots of fumbles.

1926. A man's fitness for public office can be judged by the means he uses trying to get it.

1927. Politicians are as good as you are, for the way you vote creates politicians.

1928. There is but one way for a newspaper man to look at a politician, and that is down.

—FRANK H. SIMONDS

1929. The time many political candidates really stump their states is after they are elected.

1930. How badly a Congressman's political fence needs mending depends on how much he has straddled it.

1931. The little lad who went to the store and forgot what his mother sent him after grew up and became a congressman.

1932. Any businessman who says he is not interested in politics is like a drowning man who insists he is not interested in water.

1933. Political problem: If you believe what the opposing candidates say about each other, it will be hard to vote for either of them.

1934. Between elections the politician is in a quandary—what will he promise the next time if he does everything he promised the last time?

1935. We aren't surprised seeing a teacher teach or a lawyer practicing law. Why, then do we express amazement when we witness a politician playing politics?

1936. Years ago an old Roman rebuked a man who had spoken condescendingly about his appointment to a lowly office. "If the office will not lend dignity to me," he said, "I will lend dignity to it."

—BRUCE BARTON

1937. Women are not sufficiently represented in politics or government. If politics is the art of government—and it is—and if government is public housekeeping—and it is—then women's place is quite logically in politics.

—MARY DONLON

1938. One has to admire the candor of the politician in a Tennessee city who announced his candidacy for re-election in these words: "My many friends have *not* prevailed upon me to become a candidate for re-election, and I have *not* been told that the city needs my services. The truth of the matter is simply this: I want the job again."

1939. The nomination of Lincoln in 1860 cost his friends less than seven hundred dollars. Judge David Davis, one of Lincoln's intimates, told Senator John J. Ingalls of Kansas that this covered everything "including headquarters, telegraphing, music, fare of delegates, incidentals." That, of course, was some time ago.

—*Farm Journal*

1940. An eager young lad went to a university professor and said, "Sir, I desire a course of training that will fit me to become the superintendent of a great railroad system. How much will such a course cost, and how long will it take to finish it?"

"Young man," replied the man of letters, "such a course would cost you twenty thousand dollars, and require twenty years of your time. But, on the other hand, by spending five hundred dollars of your money and three months of your time, you may be elected to Congress. Once there, you will feel yourself competent to direct not one, but all the great railroad systems in our country."

Popularity

1941. When Elizabeth II, Queen of England, appeared at a gathering in Birmingham, a friend whispered to her, "Your Majesty, have you seen the mob of people? How wonderful it must be to be so loved!"

"I am sure there were no fewer people in the crowd when Mary Stuart was executed," was Elizabeth's thoughtful response.

1942. There is a difference between being popular and being respected. It is highly desirable to be both, but if a choice must be made, it is far better to be respected. For it is possible to be popular without being respected, and it is equally possible to be respected even though unpopular.

Popularity can come and go quickly. One can be popular by letting others always have their own way regardless of whether or not their way is fair and reasonable. One can be popular by behavior which delights the crowd until the crowd tires of that particular style of behavior. And one can be popular in the best sense of the word through a gracious personality and conduct that is pleasing and admirable.

Respect is hard-earned and consequently more lasting.

Possession—Possessions

1943. Choose rather to want less, than to have more.
—Thomas a Kempis

1944. Our most valuable possessions are those which can be shared without lessening—those which, when shared, multiply. Our least valuable possessions, on the other hand, are those which, when divided, are diminished.
—William H. Danforth

Poverty

1945. Have the courage to own that you are poor, and you disarm poverty of its sharpest sting.
—Stanislaus Leszcynski
(King of Poland),
*Oeuvres du philosophe
bienfaisant,* 1763

1946. One advantage of being poor is that you use all your junk instead of piling it in the attic or closet.

1947. Why do people try so hard to conceal poverty at the time they are experiencing it and then brag about it so in their memoirs?

1948. In a country well governed, poverty is something to be ashamed of. In a country badly governed, wealth is something to be ashamed of.
—Confucius

1949. We have grown literally afraid to be poor. We despise anyone who elects to be poor in order to simplify and save his inner life. We have lost the power of even imagining what the ancient idealization of poverty could have meant; the liberation from material attachments, the unbribed soul, the manlier indifference, the paying our way by what we are or do, and not by what we have, the right to fling away our life at any moment irresponsibly—the more athletic trim; in short, the moral fighting shape. It is certain that the prevalent fear of poverty among the educated classes is the worst moral disease from which our civilization suffers.
—William James

Power

1950. The price of power is responsibility for the public good.
—Winthrop W. Aldrich

1951. "My son," said Themistocles, "you are the most powerful man in all Greece. The Athenians rule the Helenes, I rule the Athenians, your mother rules me, and you rule your mother."

1952. Human nature being what it is, power is always abused. It is to the best interests of society, therefore, to see that no individual or group gets too much power or retains it too long.
—Waldo Lee McAtee

1953. Unlimited power is worse for the average person than unlimited alcohol; and the resulting intoxication is more damaging for others. Very few have not deteriorated when given absolute dominion. It is worse for the governor than for the governed.
—William Lyon Phelps

Praise

1954. Faint praise is disparagement.
—*Old Proverb*

1955. Praise undeserved is scandal in disguise.
—Alexander Pope

1956. They that value not praise will never do anything worthy of praise.
—Thomas Fuller

1957. When a man is being toasted at a banquet, you can bet he is being buttered up, too.

1958. It is the greatest possible praise to be praised by a man who is himself deserving of praise.

1959. Sigmund Freud once refused to attend a festival in his honor, remarking, "When someone abuses me I can defend myself; against praise I am defenseless."
—From *The Life and Work of Sigmund Freud,* Volume III, © 1957 by Ernest Jones, (Basic Books, Inc., Publishers)

Prayer

1960. A good deed is the best prayer.

—Robert G. Ingersoll

1961. If you are too busy to pray, you are too busy.

1962. Don't pray for lighter burdens, but for stronger backs.

1963. Who rises from prayer a better man, his prayer is answered.

—George Meredith

1964. We must remember that "no" can be an answer to prayer.

—Katie Pinson

1965. Prayer doesn't change things. It changes people, and they change things.

1966. The Christian on his knees sees more than the philosopher on his tiptoes.

1967. Those who pray only when in trouble at least know where to turn for help.

1968. It is strange that in our praying we seldom ask for a change of character, but always for a change in circumstances.

1969. The co-ed concluded her prayers with a modest appeal: "I'm not asking for myself, but please send my mother a son-in-law."

1970. A little girl was to undergo an operation. The physician said to her as he was about to place her upon the operating table: "Before we can make you well, we must put you to sleep." The little girl looked up, and smiling, said, "Oh, if you are going to put me to sleep I must say my prayers first." Then she knelt down beside the table and said:

> *"Now I lay me down to sleep,*
> *I pray thee, Lord, my soul to keep,*
> *If I should die before I wake,*
> *I pray thee, Lord, my soul to take."*

The surgeon said afterward that he prayed that night for the first time in thirty years.

Preacher—Preachers

1971. Far too many preachers, when they get into the pulpit, are dealers in dry goods and notions.

—Dr. D. T. Perrine

1972. The best preacher is the heart; the best teacher is time; the best book is the world; the best friend is God.

—*The Talmud*

1973. HOW TO GET RID OF A MINISTER

1. Look him straight in the eye when he is preaching, and say "Amen" once in awhile. He'll preach himself to death in a few weeks.

2. Pat him on the back and brag on his good points. He'll work himself to death.

3. Start paying him a living wage. He's probably been on starvation wages so long he'll eat himself to death.

4. Rededicate your own life to Christ and ask the preacher to give you a job to do. He'll probably die of heart failure.

5. Get the church to unite in prayer for the preacher. He'll become so effective some larger church will take him off your hands.

—Dr. Gerald H. Kennedy, *The Churchman*

1974. A preacher must be full of energy and cheerful hope, never tiring and never despairing of final success. A preacher must be like a man in quest of water who digs a well in an arid tract of land. So long as he sees that the sand is dry and white, he knows that the water is still far off. But let him not be troubled or give up the task as hopeless. The work of removing the dry sand must be done so that he can dig down deeper into the ground. And often the deeper he has to dig, the cooler and purer and more refreshing will the water be. When after some time of digging he sees that the sand becomes moist, he accepts it as a token that the water is near. So long as the people do not listen to the words of truth, the preacher knows that he has to dig deeper into their hearts; but when they begin to heed his words he apprehends that they will soon attain enlightenment.

—Buddha

Preaching

1975. Too many sermons are hung on texts like hats on a hat-tree.

1976. Too few preachers seem to know the difference between a sermon and a lecture.

—Faith Forsyte, *Tit-Bits,*
London

1977. A man usually considers it a good Sunday sermon when he feels that the minister didn't refer directly to him.

1978. Preachers have told us that we should reform in order to be prepared for death. The wise teacher tells men that they should forsake sin to prepare for life.

—Elbert Hubbard

Prejudice

1979. Fortunately for serious minds, a bias recognized is a bias sterilized.

—Benjamin R. Haydon

1980. No prejudice has ever been able to prove its case in the court of reason.

1981. Our early years are spent in learning our elders' prejudices —and our later years in trying to overcome them.

1982. Reasoning against a prejudice is like fighting against a shadow; it exhausts the reasoner, without visibly affecting the prejudice.

—Charles Mildmay

1983. The word *prejudice* originally was neutral. It meant judgment formed beforehand, which might be favorable or unfavorable. Yet so predominantly do men form harsh judgments before knowledge, that *prejudice* came to mean *injurious.*

—Marshall Wingfield

Preparedness

1984. Hope for the best, but be ever ready for the worst.

1985. To be prepared for war is one of the most effectual means of preserving peace.

—George Washington,
Address to Congress,
January 8, 1790

1986. Though a soldier in time of peace is said to be like a chimney in summer, yet what wise man would pull down his chimney because the Almanac tells him it is July?

Present, The

1987. Today is yesterday's plan put into action.
—George Matthew
Adams

1988. The "next year" when you were going to do better is here.

1989. These are "the good old days" you're going to miss in ten years.

1990. Historians tell us the past. Economists tell us the future. Only the present is so confusing.

1991. If all of the jobs to be done tomorrow were done today, what a wonderful place this old world would be . . . tomorrow!

Press, Freedom of

1992. Despotism and freedom of the press cannot exist together.
—Leon Gambetta

1993. Freedom of the press is based on a principle which the whole world must practice if we are to have peace, and that is the principle of tolerance—of being able to stand criticism and of realizing that nobody has the infallible truth.
—Henry Cabot Lodge

Prevention

1994. Prevention is better than knowing who did it.

1995. Hindsight explains the injury that foresight would have prevented.

Pride

1996. Temper gets people into trouble. Pride keeps them there.

1997. A man can fracture his pride in a fall over his own bluff.

1998. In general, pride is at the bottom of all great mistakes. All the other passions do occasional good; but whenever pride puts in *its* word, everything goes wrong, and what it might be desirable to do quietly and innocently, it is morally dangerous to do proudly.
—John Ruskin

Principle–Principles

1999. Men of principle are always bold, but those who are bold are not always men of principle.

—CONFUCIUS

2000. It's no trick to keep one's principles on a high level, but it is hard sometimes to stay up there with them.

Printing

2001. If all printers were determined not to print anything till they were sure that it would offend nobody, there would be very little printed.

—BENJAMIN FRANKLIN

2002. I can out-talk any man on earth but a printer. The man who can sit tight and the next morning talk to a thousand people while I'm talking to one is the man I'm afraid of. I want him for a friend.

—P. T. BARNUM

2003. Benjamin Franklin's prospective mother-in-law hesitated about permitting her daughter to marry a printer. There were already two printing shops in the United States, and she was dubious about the country's being able to support a third.

Private Enterprise

2004. Progress in America has resulted from the freedom of the individual to venture for himself and to assure the gains and take all the losses as they come.

—ROBERT R. WASON

2005. Businessmen who do nothing to heighten public enthusiasm for the voluntary enterprise system are comparable to unscientific farmers who "mine" the soil, always taking something out and not using fertilizers or crop rotation to restore the good earth.

—M. S. RUKEYSER

Problem–Problems

2006. The important thing about a problem is not its solution, but the strength we gain in finding the solution.

2007. If you have ten men and only nine hats, the solution is not to cut off one head; it is, rather, to make another hat.

—G. K. CHESTERTON

Procrastination. *See also* Delay

2008. One of these days is none of these days.

—H. G. BOHN

2009. Don't delay. Today will be yesterday tomorrow.

2010. Don't postpone reading the writing on the wall until you have your back to it.

2011. If you put off until tomorrow what you should do today, somebody may invent a machine to do it.

2012. Procrastination is a fault that most people put off trying to correct.

2013. Putting off an easy thing makes it hard; and putting off a hard thing makes it impossible.

—GEORGE CLAUDE
LORIMER

Professional Fees

2014. The best things in life are fees.

2015. A physician whose services are obtained gratis is worth nothing.

—*The Talmud*

2016. A man may as well open an oyster without a knife as a lawyer's mouth without a fee.

—BARTON HOLYDAY

Progress

2017. Not to go back is somewhat to advance.

—HORACE

2018. Go as far as you can see. When you get there you'll see farther.

2019. The highest point of achievement of yesterday is the starting point of today.

—Motto of Paulist Fathers
in *Thoughts* (Dodge)

2020. I do not believe you can do today's job with yesterday's methods and be in business tomorrow.

—NELSON JACKSON

2021. Much of what we mistakenly call "progress" is merely the substitution of a complicated nuisance for a simple nuisance.

2022. He that is good will infallibly become better, and he that is bad will as certainly become worse; for vice, virtue and time are three things that never stand still.

Promise–Promises

2023. A man apt to promise is apt to forget.

—THOMAS FULLER,
Gnomologia, 1732

2024. We make large promises to avoid making small presents.

—French Proverb

Psychiatry

2025. Confession is good for the soul, but more profitable for the psychiatrist.

2026. I used to be conceited, but since I saw a psychiatrist I'm one of the nicest chaps you'd wish to know.

2027. A psychotic thinks two and two make five. A neurotic is well aware that two and two make four, but it worries the devil out of him.

Public Office

2028. They that buy an office must sell something.

—THOMAS FULLER

2029. No people is wholly civilized where a distinction is drawn between stealing an office and stealing a purse.

—THEODORE ROOSEVELT,
Speech in Chicago,
June 22, 1912

2030. In politics we must choose between the strong man whose real interests are elsewhere and who will leave office the moment bigger opportunity beckons, and the weakling who will cling because he can't hold a job anywhere else. Public office is the last refuge of the incompetent.

—Ascribed to Boise
Penrose

Public Opinion

2031. It is idle to attempt to legislate in advance of public opinion.

2032. It is rare that the public sentiment decides immorally or unwisely, and the individual who differs from it ought to distrust and examine well his own opinion.

—Thomas Jefferson,
*Letter to William
Findley*, March 1801

2033. One should respect public opinion insofar as is necessary to avoid starvation and to keep out of prison, but anything that goes beyond that is voluntary submission to an unnecessary tyranny, and is likely to interfere with happiness in all kinds of ways.

—Bertrand A. Russell

Public Relations

2034. The public relations formula is simple—either do what people like, or make them like what you do.

2035. Good public relations is good performance—publicly appreciated. Business must first do a job that people can think well of, and then intelligently and deftly call attention to it. Most people appraise business not only by the price and quality of its product, but as a neighbor and citizen.

2036. Public relations, in this country, is the art of adapting big business to a democracy so that the people have confidence that they are being well served and at the same time business has freedom to serve them well.

—Arthur W. Page

Public Speaking

2037. I will sit down now, but the time will come when you will hear me.

—Benjamin Disraeli,
Maiden speech in the
House of Commons,
December 7, 1837

2038. Thank you for your wonderful reception which I so richly deserve and so seldom get.

—George Jessel

2039. To be prepared for a speech and not be asked to speak is even worse than being asked when unprepared.

2040. At a dinner meeting, the speaker of the evening was introduced as a live wire. It developed that he was wired mostly for sound.

2041. Many a good dinner has been spoiled by a poor after-dinner speech and many a good after-dinner speech has been spoiled by a poor dinner.

2042. A bartender has invented a convention cocktail. He calls it "The Delegate."

Take two, he explains, and the next thing you know you're speaking from the floor.

2043. The speaker addressing a club meeting began his talk as follows: "My job, this afternoon, as I understand it, is to talk to you. Yours, as I understand it, is to listen. If you finish before I do, just hold up your hand."

2044. One day while lecturing to his Shakespeare class, Harvard's famed George Lyman Kittredge accidentally stepped off the platform and fell to the floor. Scrambling to his feet, he observed: "In 40 years of teaching, this is the first time I have ever descended to the level of my audience."

2045. Mark Twain was once complimented for a brilliant wit that seemed to flash spontaneously from him, but he somewhat dejectedly replied that he deserved no praise. He had spent the whole evening in steering the conversation towards his witticism and he didn't think it was worth the effort. In the same way a speaker sometimes gets a story and builds a speech around it.

Punctuality

2046. Punctuality is the thief of time.

—Oscar Wilde

2047. A woman's promise to be on time carries a lot of wait.

2048. It's a good rule to be early, so that if you're late you'll be on time.

2049. The only meeting that ever started on time was held up for an hour while the chairman explained to people who came in late what had gone on before they got there.

Punishment

2050. Who punishes one threatens a hundred.

—*French Proverb*

2051. Distrust all in whom the impulse to punish is powerful.

—FRIEDRICH WILHELM
NIETZSCHE

2052. It is a cruelty to the innocent not to punish the guilty.

—*Old Proverb*

2053. If punishment reaches not the mind it hardens the offender.

—JOHN LOCKE

2054. Every unpunished murder takes away something from the security of every man's life.

—DANIEL WEBSTER

2055. The worst punishment of all is that in the court of his own conscience, no guilty man is acquitted.

—JUVENAL

Quality

2056. The bitterness of poor quality lingers long after the sweetness of cheap price is forgotten.

2057. There is hardly anything in the world that some man cannot make a little worse and sell a little cheaper.

—JOHN RUSKIN

2058. Bending over his workbench in Cremona, Antonio Stradivari, who died December 18, 1737, issued a vow that, through more than 200 years, has remained valid:

Other men will make other violins, but no man shall make a better one.

Quarrel—Quarrels

2059. Two cannot fall out if one does not choose.
—*Spanish Proverb*

2060. A long dispute means that both parties are wrong.
—Voltaire

2061. A chip on the shoulder indicates there is wood higher up.

2062. If you agree that it's poor judgment to quarrel before company, remember, that two is company.

Question—Questions

2063. A prudent question is one-half of wisdom.
—Francis Bacon

2064. The girl who knows all the answers has very often misunderstood the questions.

2065. A man soon learns how little he knows when a child begins to ask questions.

2066. No question is so difficult to answer as that to which the answer is obvious.
—George Bernard Shaw

2067. Someone has figured out that the peak years of mental activity must be between the ages of four and eighteen . . . at four we know all the questions . . . at eighteen we know all the answers.

Quotation—Quotations

2068. Apt quotations carry convictions.
—William E. Gladstone

2069. An apt quotation is as good as an original remark.
—*Proverb*

2070. Quotations preserve for mankind not only the beauty of literature, but also the wisdom of philosophy, the counsel of experience, and the inspiration of achievement.
—Lewis Copeland

2071. We prefer to think that the absence of inverted commas guarantees the originality of a thought, whereas it may be merely that the utterer has forgotten its source.

—CLIFTON FADIMAN, *The American Treasury, 1455–1955*

Reading

2072. There is no worse robber than a bad book.

—*Italian Proverb*

2073. By reading a man antedates his life and makes himself contemporary with ages past.

—COLLIER

2074. The man who doesn't read good books has no advantage over the man who can't read them.

2075. *Order to bookseller:* You may send me up the complete works of Shakespeare, Goethe and Emerson—also something to read.

2076. When any man tells you that he has no time for reading, you can be sure that he is committing mental suicide. What he says makes no more sense than the man who says, "I do not have the time to eat."

—THOMAS DREIER

2077. Reading is like depositing money in a savings account. The benefits compound themselves like interest. But, unlike a savings account, you can draw on your interest without ever having less remaining.

—E. M. MAGUIRE, *Argonaut*

Reason–Reasons

2078. When a man is drunk, it is no matter upon what he has got drunk.

—WILLIAM MAGINN

2079. He who will not reason, is a bigot; he who cannot, is a fool; and he who dares not, is a slave.

—WILLIAM DRUMMOND

2080. Those who follow the banners of reason are like the well-disciplined battalions which, wearing a more sober uniform and making a less dazzling show than the light troops commanded by imagination, enjoy more safety, and even more honor, in the conflicts of human life.

—SIR WALTER SCOTT

Reconciliation

2081. Beware of a reconciled friend as of a devil.
—*Spanish Proverb*

2082. Reconciliation with our enemies is only a desire of bettering our condition, a weariness of contest, and the fear of some disaster.
—François de la
Rochefoucauld

Recreation

2083. Time you enjoy wasting is not wasted time.

2084. All work and no play makes Jack a dull boy and his wife a wealthy widow.

2085. Make thy recreation servant to thy business, lest thou become a slave to thy recreation.
—Francis Quarles

2086. People who cannot find time for recreation are obliged sooner or later to find time for illness.
—John Wanamaker

2087. The language of play is a universal language. Its activities need no interpreter and cannot be confined by boundaries. . . . Recreation can bring a sense of fulfillment, joy, health, education and an enrichment of life. Shared by the peoples of different nations, it can bring understanding and an attitude of brotherhood.

Reform—Reforms

2088. Every reform needs examples more than advocates.

2089. Reform is sometimes so eager to do good, it tries to right wrongs that do not exist.

2090. Most reformers, like a pair of trousers on a windy clothesline, go through a vast deal of vehement motion, but stay in the same place.

Religion

2091. Religions are many, but Religion is one.

2092. A religion that costs nothing does nothing.

2093. To know but one religion is not to know that one.
—ELBERT HUBBARD

2094. The friend of him who has no friend—Religion!
—JAMES MONTGOMERY,
The Pillow

2095. When your religion gets into the past tense it becomes pretense.

2096. Some folks take up religion as a kind of insurance against hell—and then are not willing to pay the premiums.

2097. Each of the seven days in the week is designated as the Sabbath by various nationalities and religions. *Monday* is the Greek Sabbath, *Tuesday* the Persian, *Wednesday* the Assyrian, *Thursday* the Egyptian, *Friday* the Turkish, *Saturday* the Jewish and *Sunday* the Christian.

Remorse

2098. There is no indigestion worse than that which comes from eating one's own words.

2099. Remorse is the consciousness of doing wrong with no sense of love; penitence the same consciousness with the feeling of sorrow and tenderness added.
—F. W. ROBERTSON

Repentance

2100. He that repents is angry with himself; I need not be angry with him.
—BENJAMIN WHICHCOTE

2101. Don't repent. Put all your energy into doing the right thing next time.

2102. True repentance has a double aspect; it looks upon things past with a weeping eye, and upon the future with a watchful eye.
—ROBERT SOUTH

2103. Life is as a slate where all our sins are written; from time to time we rub the sponge of repentance over it, in order to begin to sin anew.

Reputation

2104. No man is rich enough to buy back his past.

—Oscar Wilde

2105. A has-been is a person who lives on the reputation of his reputation.

2106. The only time you realize you have a reputation is when you're not living up to it.

—Jose Iturbi

2107. My character may be my own, but my reputation belongs to any old body that enjoys gossiping more than telling the truth.

Research

2108. Basic research is what I am doing when I don't know what I am doing.

—Wernher von Braun

2109. Research is an organized method of trying to find out what you are going to do after you cannot do what you are doing now. It may also be said to be the method of keeping a customer reasonably dissatisfied with what he has. That means constant improvement and change so that the customer will be stimulated to desire the new product enough to buy it to replace the one he has.

—Charles F. Kettering

Resourcefulness

2110. When the late Herman Hickman was coaching football at Yale, he began the daily practice sessions at 4 p.m. The players, with heavy scholastic schedules, frequently came late. More often than not, the entire squad would not be assembled until 4:30.

Hickman, a stickler for punctuality, fretted about this loss of precious time. Then he hit on a way to lick the problem. When all the players had arrived, no matter what the time, he would turn the clock back to 4 and practice would begin.

—E. E. Edgar

2111. An elderly lady thought of the following scheme to get rich. She placed an ad in the local newspaper. "Make money answering ads. Information $1." When she was hauled into court on charges of bilking the public, the judge asked her what was this information that was worth a dollar. She replied that when someone answered her ad, she simply put the dollar in the bank, and suggested they put an ad in the paper as she had done.

2112. A merchant wanted to determine which of his two sons was the more worthy of inheriting his property. He gave each a coin and said: "Buy with this money something which will fill this house."

The elder son hurried to the market place where he learned that the cheapest and bulkiest thing he could buy was straw. He spent his coin for that, but had not enough even to cover the floor.

The youngest son, perceiving that his father had entrusted him with a commission which could be executed only by unusual shrewdness, deliberated and finally spent his coin for candles. These he took home and lighted, one in each room, so that the light they gave filled the house.

"To you," said the happy father, "I give over my business. You have shown true wisdom."

Responsibility–Responsibilities

2113. The only way to get rid of responsibilities is to discharge them.

—WALTER S. ROBERTSON

2114. Take the responsibility on your shoulders and it will leave no room for chips.

2115. There are always too many people who reach for the stool when there is a piano to be moved.

Restraint

2116. Hitch your wagon to a star, but hold your horses.

2117. When screams and shouting fill the air, it's often the stage whisper that gets attention.

2118. The most difficult thing in the world is to know how to do a thing and to watch somebody else doing it wrong, without comment.

Result–Results

2119. The world is not interested in the storms you encountered but did you bring the ship in?

—WILLIAM McFEE

2120. It is not the time a man spends in planning—it's the faith and confidence he puts in his planning that really counts.

Retirement

2121. The best time to start thinking about your retirement is before the boss does.

2122. A man is known by the company that keeps him on after retirement age.

2123. A man could retire comfortably in his old age if he only could dispose of his experience for what it cost him.

2124. You are getting close to the age of retirement when you do more and more for the last time, and less and less for the first time.

2125. A sailor about to retire was asked where he was going to live.

"I shall go ashore, put an oar over my shoulder and start walking inland," he said. "When someone stops me and says, 'What's that thing on your shoulder?' that's where I'll settle down."

Revenge

2126. Revenge does not long remain unrevenged.
—*German Proverb*

2127. The most complete revenge is not to imitate the aggressor.
—MARCUS AURELIUS

2128. It is often better not to see an insult than to avenge it.
—SENECA

2129. You will never get ahead of anyone as long as you are trying to get even with him.

2130. By taking revenge, a man becomes the equal of his foe, but in passing over it, he is the superior.

2131. He who injured you was either stronger or weaker. If he was weaker, spare him; if he was stronger, spare yourself.
—SENECA

2132. When the Italian poet, Tasso, attained the zenith of his career, he was told that he was then in a position to take revenge upon a man who had hurt him greatly, relates Thomas Dreier, philosophic writer.

"I do not desire to plunder him," the poet replied, "yet there is one thing I would like to take from him."

"His honor, his wealth, his life?" Tasso was asked.

"No," came the gentle reply. "What I desire to take from him I will try to gain by the exercise of kindness, patience, and forbearance. I will try to take away his ill-will!"

Reward

2133. We all love that for which we work hardest and prize it most when we don't get it.

2134. He that does good for good's sake seeks neither praise nor reward, but he is sure of both in the end.

—WILLIAM PENN

Risk

2135. Who rides a tiger cannot dismount.

2136. Without danger we cannot get beyond danger.

—GEORGE HERBERT

Romance

2137. Old flames seem to burn forever.

2138. The progress of romance: First, an engagement ring; then a wedding ring; then the suffering.

2139. This is the sequel to many an expedition down Lover's Lane: He swept her off her feet—now he has her on his hands.

Rudeness

2140. Rudeness is a weak man's imitation of strength.

2141. Three of the rudest people in the world, according to an Irish proverb, are: a young fellow making fun of an old man, a strong person jeering at an invalid, a wise man mocking a fool.

2142. Then there was the time the late General George C. Marshall met a British military boor at a reception in London during World War II.

"By George," remarked the boor, "I'm surprised we haven't run into each other long before this."

General Marshall smiled icily. Then, crisply, "I suppose I've always been lucky."

—ANDREW TULLY, *Scripps-Howard Newspapers*

Sacrifice–Sacrifices

2143. They never fail who die in a great cause.

—LORD BYRON

2144. The wise man does not expose himself needlessly to danger, since there are few things for which he cares sufficiently; but he is willing, in great crises, to give even his life—knowing that under certain conditions it is not worthwhile to live.

—ARISTOTLE

2145. A woodman came into a forest to ask the trees to give him a handle for his axe. It seemed so modest a request that the principal trees at once agreed to it, and it was settled among them that the plain, homely ash should furnish what was wanted.

No sooner had the woodman fitted the staff to his purpose, than he began laying about him on all sides, felling the noblest trees in the forest. The oak whispered to the cedar, "The first concession has lost all. If we had not sacrificed our humblest neighbor, we might have yet stood for ages ourselves."

—*The Midrash*

Salesmanship

2146. A salesman is known by the customers he keeps.

2147. Selling is easy if you work hard enough at it.

2148. The difference between "out selling" and "out-selling" is just a little dash!

—S. S. BIDDLE

2149. Salesmen are frequently employed to say things their employers would not dare to put on paper.

2150. The first job in an interview is not to sell the prospect on the idea of buying but to sell him on the idea of listening.

2151. Salesmen should remember customers are interested in the results and benefits they derive from your goods, rather than the goods itself. Millions of drills are sold—not because folks want drills, but because they want holes!

2152. He who works with his *hands* is a laborer.
He who works with his *hands* and his *head* is a craftsman.
He who works with his *hands*, his *head* and his *heart* is an artist.
He who works with his *hands*, his *head*, his *heart* and his *feet* is a salesman.

2153. An old salesman said that whenever a man told him he was not interested in his proposition, he would smile and say:
"I know you are not. That is the very reason I have come to see you. Had you been interested in my proposition you would have come to see me."
Never apologize for calling by saying, "I was just passing and thought I would drop in." It is better that you should tell him you have come quite a bit out of your way to see him.

Santa Claus

2154. They err who think Santa Claus enters through the chimney. *He enters through the heart.*

2155. One of our present troubles seems to be that too many adults, and not enough children, believe in Santa Claus.

Science

2156. Science that jumps to measurement too soon is as unsound as science that ignores measurement too long.
—JOHN RODGERS, *Science Digest*

2157. Nearly every great discovery in science has come as the result of providing a new question rather than a new answer.
—PAUL M. MEGLITSCH, *Forbes*

2158. Although this may seem a paradox, all exact science is dominated by the idea of approximation. When a man tells you that he knows the exact truth about anything, you are safe in inferring that he is an inexact man.

—BERTRAND RUSSELL

2159. Few of us realize how short the career of what we know as "science" has been. Three hundred and fifty years ago hardly any one believed in the Copernican planetary theory. Optical combinations were not discovered. The circulation of the blood, the weight of air, the conduction of heat, the laws of motion were unknown; the common pump was inexplicable; there were no clocks; no thermometers; no general gravitation; the world was five thousand years old; spirits moved the planets; alchemy, magic, astrology imposed on every one's belief.

—*Some Problems of Philosophy* (R. Reynolds & Sons) 1911

Science–Religion

2160. Science and religion no more contradict each other than light and electricity.

—WILLIAM HIRAM FAULKES

2161. It is good for man to open his mind to wonder and awe. Without science we are helpless children. But without a deep religion, we are blundering fools, reeling in our new and terrible cocksureness into one disaster after another.

—J. B. PRIESTLEY

2162. After close to two centuries of passionate struggles, neither science nor faith has succeeded in discrediting its adversary. On the contrary, it becomes obvious that neither can develop normally without the other. And the reason is simple: The same life animates both. Neither in its impetus nor its achievements can science go to its limits without becoming tinged with mysticism and charged with faith.

—PÈRE TEILHARD DE CHARDIN

Secret–Secrets–Secrecy

2163. Where secrecy or mystery begins, vice or roguery is not far off.

—DR. SAMUEL JOHNSON

2164. If you would wish another to keep your secret, first keep it yourself.

—SENECA

2165. He who gives up the smallest part of a secret has the rest no longer in his power.

—JEAN PAUL RICHTER

2166. Try your friend with a falsehood, and if he keeps it a secret tell him the truth.

Security

2167. The best example of perfect security is a man serving a life term in a federal prison.

2168. Too many people are thinking of security instead of opportunity. They seem more afraid of life than death.

—James F. Byrnes

2169. It's an old adage that the way to be safe is never to be secure. . . . Each one of us requires the spur of insecurity to force us to do our best.

—Harold W. Dodds

2170. Security is the priceless product of freedom. Only the strong can be secure, and only in freedom can men produce those material resources which can secure them from want at home and against aggression abroad.

—B. E. Hutchinson

Self-admiration

2171. A man who feels no self-admiration insults his Maker and has no right to live.

—St. John Ervine

Self-analysis

2172. What lies behind us and what lies before us are tiny matters compared to what lies within us.

—William Morrow

2173. Analyzing what you haven't got as well as what you have is a necessary ingredient of a career.

2174. Lotte Lehmann, who retired from the opera years ago, was celebrating her 69th birthday when a young soprano said to her: "It must be awful for a great singer like you to realize that you've lost your voice."

"No," said the great diva of her day, "what would be awful is if I *didn't* realize it."

Self-appraisal

2175. If you feel you have no faults, that makes another one.

2176. There is hope for any man who can look in a mirror and laugh at what he sees.

2177. If you were in business for yourself, would you give yourself a job?

Self-betrayal

2178. When you tell a dirty story, you are snitching on yourself.
—HARRY WILLIAM KING

2179. People always say that they are not themselves when tempted by anger into betraying what they really are.
—EDGAR WATSON HOWE

Self-blame

2180. When everything seems to be going dead wrong, take a good look and see if you are not headed in the wrong direction.

2181. If you could kick the person responsible for most of your troubles, you wouldn't be able to sit down for six months.

Self-confidence

2182. He who thinks himself good for everything is often good for nothing.
—PICARD

2183. Calm self-confidence is as far from conceit as the desire to earn a decent living is remote from greed.
—CHANNING POLLOCK

2184. The world turns aside to let any man pass who knows where he is going. The ability to make up your mind inspires self-confidence, it gives you inner power, and it commands the respect of your fellow men.
—DAVID STARR JORDAN

Self-control

2185. When a man loses his self-control it means his steering apparatus is broken.

2186. I think the first virtue is to restrain the tongue: he approaches nearest to the Gods, who knows how to be silent, even though he is in the right.
—CATO

2187. Prove that you can control yourself and you are an educated man; without this, all other education is good for nothing.

Self-denial

2188. A man is rich in proportion to the number of things which he can afford to let alone.

—HENRY DAVID THOREAU

2189. To have what we want is riches; but to be able to do without is power.

—GEORGE McDONALD

Self-depreciation

2190. By despising himself too much a man comes to be worthy of his own contempt.

—HENRI FRÉDÉRIC AMIEL

2191. A man should be careful never to tell tales of himself to his own disadvantage; people may be amused, and laugh at the time, but they will be remembered, and brought up against him upon some subsequent occasion.

—DR. SAMUEL JOHNSON

2192. Modesty is the lowest of the virtues, and is a confession of the deficiency it indicates. He who undervalues himself, is justly undervalued by others.

—WILLIAM HAZLITT

Self-discipline

2193. If we don't discipline ourselves the world will do it for us.

—WILLIAM FEATHER

2194. The greatest freedom man has is the freedom to discipline himself.

—BERNARD M. BARUCH

2195. To demand more of yourself than most people demand of you is what pays the ultimate dividends.

—CLAUDIA CASSIDY

Self-importance

2196. If you are all wrapped up in yourself, you are overdressed.

2197. It is well to remember that the whole sense of one's importance is merely an evaluation of self by self.

2198. Socrates was once asked by one of his disciples: "Why is it, sir, that you tell everybody who wants to become your disciple to look into this pond here and tell you what he sees?"

"That is very simple, my friend," answered the sage. "I am ready to accept all those who tell me they see the fish swimming around. But those who see only their own image mirrored in the water are in love with their ego. I have no use for them."

Self-improvement

2199. No one objects to a man being himself if he's trying to do better.

—G. NORMAN COLLIE

2200. Be what you are. This is the first step toward becoming better than you are.

—JULIUS AND AUGUSTUS HARE

2201. Sweep first before your own door, before you sweep the doorsteps of your neighbors.

—Swedish Proverb

Selfishness

2202. No one has less to live for than one who lives only for himself.

2203. One who cares only for himself when young will be stingy in middle age, and a wretched miser in old age.

2204. A farmer whose barns were full of corn was accustomed to praying that the needy be supplied; but when anyone in needy circumstances asked for a little of his corn, he invariably said he had none to spare. One day after hearing his father pray for the poor and needy, his little son said to him, "Father, I wish I had your corn."

"What would you do with it?" asked the father.

"I would answer your prayer," replied the child.

2205. A farmer imported some especially fine seed-corn and produced a crop that was the envy of his neighbors. When they sought some of the seed, he refused, fearing to lose the competitive advantage he had gained.

The second year, his crop was not so good; the third year, results were even worse. Suddenly, it dawned upon him that the poor grade corn of his neighbors was pollinating his prize corn. His selfishness had caught up with him.

Self-praise

2206. The man who sings his own praises always gets the wrong pitch.

2207. It is a sign that your reputation is small and sinking, if your own tongue must praise you.

—SIR MATTHEW HALE

2208. Nature knows best; she hasn't arranged your anatomy so as to make it easy for you to pat yourself on the back.

Self-respect

2209. Self-respect is the secure feeling that no one, as yet, is suspicious.

2210. The great victory is preservation of self-respect—but the world so little values self-respect that the man who wins that victory is denied any other.

—WALDO LEE MCATEE

Sense of Humor. See Humor, Sense of

Serendipity

2211. I find that a great part of the information I have was acquired by looking up something and finding something else on the way.

—FRANKLIN P. ADAMS

2212.   HOW IT HAPPENED

The history of science shows that many valuable discoveries were made by accident, observes Rudolf Flesch in *The Art of Clear Thinking.* For example:

In 1786, Luigi Galvani noticed the accidental twitching of a frog's leg, and thereby discovered the principle of the electric battery.

In 1822, the Danish physicist Oersted, at the end of a lecture, happened to put a wire conducting an electric current near a magnet, which led to Faraday's invention of the dynamo.

In 1858, a 17-year-old boy named William Henry Perkin, trying to make artificial quinine, cooked up a black-looking mass, which led to his discovery of aniline dyes.

In 1895, Roentgen noticed that cathode rays penetrated black pepper and thereby discovered X-rays, which have been priceless boons to the fields of medicine and industry.

In 1929, Sir Alexander Fleming noticed that a culture of bacteria had been accidentally contaminated by a mold. He said to himself, "My, that's a funny thing!" He had, through accident, discovered penicillin.

But these accidents would have been meaningless if they had not happened to Galvani, Perkin, Roentgen, and the others, or to such men possessing equal powers of perception and insight. As Pasteur once said, "Chance favors the prepared mind."

Service

2213. Service is the rent we pay for our room on earth and I'd like to be a good tenant.

> —*Take My Life,* by EDDIE
> CANTOR, Copyright
> Doubleday & Company,
> 1957

2214. Real wealth comes to the man who has learned he is paid best for the things he does for nothing.

2215. The bee is more honored than other animals, not because she labors, but because she labors for others.

> —ST. JOHN CHRYSOSTOM

2216. The man who holds the ladder at the bottom is frequently of more service than the man at the top.

2217.
If I can stop one heart from breaking,
I shall not live in vain.
If I can ease one life the aching,
Or cool one pain,
Or help one fainting robin
Unto his nest again,
I shall not live in vain.

> —EMILY DICKINSON

Sharing

2218. Keep your fears to yourself, but share your courage with others.

> —ROBERT LOUIS
> STEVENSON

2219. By sharing the joy of another, we increase it. By sharing the woe of another, we diminish it.

2220. A man would have no pleasures in discovering all the beauties of the universe, even in heaven itself, unless he had a partner to whom he might communicate his joys.

—CICERO

Silence

2221. Sometimes silence is not golden—just yellow.

2222. One thing about silence—it can't be repeated.

2223. Silence is the most perfect expression of scorn.

—GEORGE BERNARD SHAW

2224. Silence is a wonderful substitute for brains.

2225. Weak nature must always tell. It takes will-power to be silent.

2226. By silence, I hear other men's imperfections and conceal my own.

—ZENO

2227. One way to keep people from jumping down your throat is to keep your mouth shut.

2228. To speak wisely may not always be easy, but not to speak ill requires only silence.

—*Thoughts* (Dodge)

Simplicity

2229. Affected simplicity is refined imposture.

—FRANÇOIS DE LA
ROCHEFOUCAULD

2230. The greatest truths are the simplest; and so are the greatest men.

—AUGUSTUS HARE

2231. SIMPLICITY IS THE KEY TO READABILITY as witness the following:

𝕾𝕴𝕸𝕻𝕷𝕴𝕮𝕴𝕿𝖄 𝕴𝕾 𝕿𝕳𝕰 𝕶𝕰𝖄 𝕿𝕺 𝕽𝕰𝕬𝕯𝕬𝕭𝕴𝕷𝕴𝕿𝖄

Sin–Sins

2232. We are not punished for our sins, but by them.
—ELBERT HUBBARD

2233. Only the wages of sin have no deductions.

2234. A preacher recently announced there are 726 sins. He is now being besieged by requests for the list by people who think they're missing something.

Sincerity

2235. Sincerity is the face of the soul, as simulation is its mask.

2236. It's much better to be known by the company you keep than by the friends you give away.

2237. Be resolutely and faithfully what you are; be humbly what you aspire to be. Man's noblest gift to man is his sincerity, for it embraces his integrity also.
—HENRY DAVID THOREAU

Small Things. See Little Things

Smile–Smiles

2238. The smile that lights the face will also warm the heart.

2239. Keep smiling. It makes everyone wonder what you've been up to.

2240. A smile costs nothing but creates much. It enriches those who receive without impoverishing those who give. It happens in a flash and the memory of it sometimes lasts forever. None are so rich they can get along without it and none so poor but are richer for its benefits. It creates happiness in the home, fosters good will in a business, and is the countersign of friends. It is rest to the weary, daylight to the discouraged, sunshine to the sad, and Nature's best antidote for trouble. Yet it cannot be bought, begged, borrowed or stolen, for it is something that is no earthly good to anybody until it is given away. Nobody needs a smile so much as those who have none left to give.

Smoking

2241. The best way to stop smoking is to carry wet matches.

2242. One thing you get out of giving up cigarettes is confidence that you can do it again.

2243. An Army doctor has suggested a method for losing the tobacco habit. Each day the smoker postpones for one hour longer that first cigarette.

On the first day, as many cigarettes as desired may be smoked. On the second day, the first cigarette is put off for one hour, but after that the smoker consumes as many as he wishes. On the third day, no cigarettes are smoked until two hours after rising, but, again, as many thereafter as are craved. Smoking will cease in about two weeks.

The theory is that if a smoker can consume an unlimited number of cigarettes after his period of abstinence, he loses his fear of the program.

—Peter Briggs in *Ladies' Home Journal,* © 1959 Curtis Publishing Company

Solitude

2244. If you can't stand solitude, perhaps you bore others too!

—*Duxbury's Notebook for Speakers* (University of London Press, Ltd.)

2245. All men's misfortunes proceed from their aversion to being alone; hence gambling, extravagance, dissipation, wine, women, ignorance, slander, envy and forgetfulness of what we owe to God and ourselves.

—Jean de la Bruyère

2246. Without a den or place of refuge, a man can achieve neither tranquility nor greatness. Jefferson wrote the Declaration of Independence in a quiet rooming house in Philadelphia. The soaring ideas that went into it evolved during hours of reading and contemplation in a secluded library. Had it been a study-TV-guest-family room, the United States might still be a colony.

Sorrow

2247. One can bear grief, but it takes two to be glad.

—Elbert Hubbard

2248. While grief is fresh, any attempt to divert it only irritates.

—Dr. Samuel Johnson

2249. It is good that affliction is good for us all. Take all the sorrow out of life, and you take from it its tenderness, riches and depth.

Soul

2250. The soul, like the body, lives by what it feeds on.

—J. G. Holland

2251. It is much more necessary to cure the soul than the body, for death is better than a bad life.

—Epictetus

Space Age. See *also* Outer Space

2252. We are getting to the point where we know more about outer space than about inner peace.

2253. If a train had started out from the earth toward the planet Neptune at the time of the birth of Christ and traveled 60 miles an hour, day and night, ever since, it would not yet be halfway there.

2254. You may think all this nonsense, but I tell you these are great times. Man has mounted science, and is now run away with. I firmly believe that before many centuries more, science will be the master of man. The engines he will have invented will be beyond his strength to control. Some day science may have the existence of mankind in its power and the human race commit suicide by blowing up the world. Not only shall we be able to cruise in space, but I see no reason why some future generation wouldn't give it another rotary motion so that every zone would receive in turn its due portion of heat and light.

—Henry Adams, 1862

Speaker, Introduction of. See Public Speaking

Speculation

2255. When speculation has done its worst, two and two still make four.

—Dr. Samuel Johnson

2256. Speculation is a word that sometimes begins with its second letter.

2257. The way to stop financial "joy-riding" is to arrest the chauffeur, not the automobile.

—Woodrow Wilson

Speech. *See also* Public Speaking

2258. Speaking without thinking is shooting without taking aim.
—*Ancient Proverb*

2259. The imprudent man reflects on what he has said; the wise man, on what he is going to say.

Speech, Freedom of

2260. It is by the goodness of God that in our country we have these three unspeakably precious things: freedom of speech, freedom of conscience and the prudence never to practice either of them.
—MARK TWAIN

2261. Free speech is to a great people what winds are to oceans and malarial regions, which waft away the elements of disease and bring new elements of health; and where free speech is stopped, miasma is bred, and death comes fast.
—HENRY WARD BEECHER

2262. I have always been among those who believe that the greatest freedom of speech was the greatest safety, because if a man is a fool the best thing to do is to encourage him to advertise the fact by speaking. It cannot be so easily discovered if you allow him to remain silent and look wise, but if you let him speak the secret is out and the world knows that he is a fool.
—WOODROW WILSON

Sports

2263. When a man wants to murder a tiger he calls it sport; when the tiger wants to murder him he calls it ferocity.
—GEORGE BERNARD SHAW

2264. Wild animals never kill for sport. Man is the only one to whom the torture and death of his fellow creatures is amusing in itself.
—JAMES ANTHONY FROUDE

Sportsmanship

2265. Everybody likes a good loser—provided it is the other team.

2266. It's harder to be a good winner than a good loser—one has less practice.

2267. The manner in which a man wins life's battles shows something of his character. The manner in which he loses shows all.

—ARTEMUS CALLOWAY

Statesmanship

2268. The statesman shears the sheep, the politician skins them.

—*Keystones of Thought,* by AUSTIN O'MALLEY (The Devin-Adair Company)

2269. A disposition to preserve, and an ability to improve, taken together, would be my standard of a statesman.

—EDMUND BURKE

2270. Statesmen who want peace in the world must contend with those who want a piece of the world.

Statistics

2271. Nothing can be more hurtful to creative thinking than the dogmatic assumption that statistics are the final answer to everything.

—WALTER O'MEARA

2272. The population of this country is 180 million, but there are 70 million over sixty-two years of age, leaving 110 million to do the work. People under twenty-one total 60 million, which leaves 50 million to do the work. Then there are 25 million who are employed by the government, and that leaves 25 million to do the work. Ten million are in the Armed Forces, leaving 15 million to do the work. Deduct 14,800,000 housewives, who actually do nothing but housework, and that leaves 200,000 to do the work. There are 126,000 hospitals, institutions, and the like with the sick and invalided, and that leaves 74,000 people.

But 62,000 of these are derelicts or others who will not work, so that leaves 12,000 to do the work.

However, it may interest you to know that there are 11,998 people in jail, so that leaves just 2 people to do the work. And that is you and I, and, brother, *I'm* getting tired of doing everything myself.

Steadfastness

2273. The greatest firmness is the greatest mercy.

—HENRY WADSWORTH LONGFELLOW

2274. Steadfastness is a noble quality, but unguided by knowledge or humility it becomes rashness or obstinacy.

—J. SWARTZ

Stubbornness

2275. A stubborn man doesn't hold opinions—they hold him.

2276. To cling stubbornly to old opinions just because we once cherished them is as stupid as to cling to them because they once belonged to our grandfather.

Success

2277. Success has many friends.

—*Greek Proverb*

2278. Deserve success, and you shall command it.

2279. Success is relative. The more success the more relatives.

2280. If at first you don't succeed, try a little ardor.

2281. The secret of success: Never let down! Never let up!

2282. Any success which leaves a bad after-taste is failure.

2283. Behind most successful men today there is a publicity department.

2284. If at first you don't succeed, that makes you just about average.

—WARREN HULL

2285. It is always well to remember that success is a ladder not an escalator.

2286. If success comes too late in life, it causes more regrets than comforts.

2287. Have success, and there will always be fools to say that you have talent.

—EDOUARD PAILLERON

2288. You're on the road to success when you realize that failure is merely a detour.

2289. Success depends upon a person's getting along with some people and ahead of others.

2290. Sometimes the people who succeed have neither gold nor silver, but lots of brass.

2291. Before a man climbs the ladder of success he usually finds the right woman to needle him up.

2292. One of the biggest troubles with success these days is that its recipe is about the same as that for a nervous breakdown.

2293. When you can think of yesterday without a regret and of tomorrow without a fear, you are on the road to success.

2294. The amount of money in your bank account is not the true measure of your success. If you are honest, fair, tolerant, kindly, charitable of others and well behaved, you are a success, no matter how small your bank account.

2295. We grow up believing that you have to work hard in order to be a success and then we read where some "authority" on the subject states that a successful executive won't do anything himself that he can get someone to do for him.

2296. He who would succeed must arm himself with three vital and most necessary weapons. First, he must have ceaseless industry; second, he must have limitless ambition of purpose; third, he must possess unquenchable enthusiasm, coupled with a determination to succeed. Given these three, and something else beside—the gift of imagination— and it matters not, I believe, whether the life of a man begins in a cobbler's shop or a grocery store, or whether it begins in such an illuminating joyfulness in beautiful things as that which brightened my early childhood. With any beginning, success will, of a surety, be his who makes himself truly deserving of it.

—HOWARD PYLE

2297.   WHAT IS SUCCESS?

Success is speaking words of praise
    In cheering other people's ways,
In doing just the best you can
    With every task and every plan.

It's silence when your speech would hurt,
    Politeness when your neighbor's curt.
It's deafness when the scandal flows,
    And sympathy with others' woes.

It's loyalty when duty calls;
   It's courage when disaster falls,
It's patience when the hours are long;
   It's found in laughter and in song.

It's in the silent time of prayer,
   In happiness and in despair.
In all of life and nothing less,
   We find the thing we call success.

—Anonymous

2298. Andrew Carnegie, the great industrialist and philanthropist, once addressed a graduating class in New York as follows:

"There are several classes of young men. There are those who do not do all their duty, there are those who profess to do their duty, and there is a third class, far better than the other two, that do their duty and a little more.

"There are many great pianists, but Paderewski is at the head because he does a little more than the others. There are hundreds of race horses, but it is those who go a few seconds faster than the others that acquire renown. So it is in the sailing of yachts. It is the little more that wins. So it is with the young and old men who do a little more than their duty. Do your duty and a little more, and the future will take care of itself."

Suffering

2299. It requires more courage to suffer than to die.

—Napoleon I, to Gaspard
Gourgaud at St. Helena,
April 16, 1816

2300. Most people are quite happy to suffer in silence, if they are sure everybody knows they are doing it.

Superiority

2301. Be wiser than other people if you can; but do not tell them so.

—Lord Chesterfield,
Letters to his Son

2302. A man should live with his superiors as he does with his fire, not too near, lest he burn; nor too far off, lest he freeze.

—Diogenes

2303. It is the mark of a superior man that, left to himself, he is able endlessly to amuse, interest and entertain himself out of his personal stock of meditations, ideas, criticisms, memories, philosophy, humor, and what not.

—George Jean Nathan

Superstition

2304. Few of us acknowledge our superstitions, but we would prefer room No. 12 to room No. 13.

2305. Have you ever noticed that most beds in hotels are placed so that their left sides are against the wall? This is done because of an ancient superstition, so that patrons will not be able to "get up on the wrong side of the bed." Ancient people believed that the gods and forces of good lived within the right side of the body, while the devil and all the forces of evil dwelt within the left side of the body. With this belief, according to the *Journal of the American Medical Association,* if a person got out of bed on the left side, he would be giving the advantage to the forces of evil for that day, and could expect misfortune and bad luck!

Suspicion

2306. A man suspected is half condemned.

2307. Suspicion is a mental picture seen through an imaginary keyhole.

2308. When a man tells me he's going to put all his cards on the table, I always look up his sleeve.

—Leslie Hore-Belisha

Tact

2309. Never *help* an old lady across the street—*escort* her.

2310. A foolish man tells a woman to stop talking, but a wise man tells her that her mouth is extremely beautiful when her lips are closed.

Talent

2311. To encourage talent is to create it.

2312. The real tragedy of life is not in being limited to one talent, but in the failure to use the one talent.

—Edgar W. Work

2313. Talent is power, tact is skill. Talent is weight, tact is momentum. Talent knows what to do, tact knows how to do it. Talent makes a man respectable, tact will make him respected. Talent is wealth, tact is ready money. Talent is pleased that it ought to have succeeded, tact is delighted that it has succeeded. Talent toils for posterity which will never repay it, tact throws away no pains, but catches the passions of the passing hour. Talent builds for eternity, tact for a short lease, and gets good interest.

2314. Benjamin Haydon, a 19th century British artist, spent a lifetime trying to convince the world he was a great epic painter. His career was a succession of debts, humiliations, and grandiose schemes that invariably ended in disaster. At sixty he committed suicide.

But while painting his huge, worthless canvases, Haydon was also jotting down the memoirs later published as his autobiography. Today, the book is recognized as a work of genius. Had he followed his natural bent for writing, he might have achieved immortality.

Tardiness

2315. People count up the faults of those who keep them waiting.
—*French Proverb*

2316. He that always thinks it is too soon is sure to come too late.
—*German Proverb*

Taxation. *See also* Taxes

2317. The power to tax involves the power to destroy.
—CHIEF JUSTICE JOHN
MARSHALL in *Mc-
Culloch* v. *Mary-
land,* 1819

2318. Today, after you make money, you have to hire an accountant to explain how you did it.

2319. The individual who serves the state through taxation and military duty has the right to demand that the state shall also serve him.

2320. In 17th century England and America, the government taxed fresh air and sunlight! A levy was made against all householders with eight or more windows.

2321. The power to tax is the one great power on which the whole national fabric is based. . . . It is not only the power to destroy, but also the power to keep alive.

—UNITED STATES SUPREME
COURT

Taxes. See *also* Taxation

2322. The government should be glad that the American people have what it takes.

2323. Any politician will tell you—the trick is to hit the taxpayer without hitting the voter!

2324. The word "tax" comes from the Latin word "taxare," which means "to touch sharply."

2325. The reward for saving your money is being able to pay your taxes without borrowing.

2326. A citizen is a man who demands better roads, bigger schools, a new post office—and lower taxes.

2327. It seems that every time that Congress sets out to trim the budget, the knife slips and trims the taxpayers.

2328. Taxes are not burdens; they are the price of liberty, the assurance of freedom of religion, the protection of our homes, the education of our children, the right to vote, and the guarantee that we may speak from our hearts without fear. Taxes are not assessments, they are the small down payments on life's most priceless commodities: faith, hope, and the dignity to live in the image of God.

—DAVID GUY POWERS,
*How to Say a Few
Words* (Doubleday &
Company, 1956)

Teacher—Teachers. See *also* Teaching

2329. Experience is an expensive teacher. All others are underpaid.

2330. A schoolmaster is like a hone; he sharpens a number of blades, but he wears himself out in doing it.

2331. The test of a good teacher is not how many questions he can ask his pupils that they will answer readily, but how many questions he inspires them to ask him which he finds it hard to answer.
—ALICE WELLINGTON
ROLLINS

2332. The teacher is literally the keystone of any organized society. His product, always hard to visualize, is the disciplined intelligence which fills the ranks of the professions and of business and industrial management. . . . In no capacity have "best minds" made a more valuable contribution to American life and progress than on college and university faculties.

2333. Teachers of today just go on repeating things in a rigmarole fashion, annoy the students with questions, and say the same things over and over again. They do not try to find out what the student's natural inclinations are, nor do they try to bring out the best in their talents. Only through education does one come to be dissatisfied with his own knowledge, and only through teaching does one come to realize the uncomfortable inadequacy of his own knowledge.
—Attributed to CONFUCIUS
and written over 2400
years ago

Teaching

2334. Who teaches me for a day is my father for a lifetime.
—*Chinese Proverb*

2335. To be good is noble, but to teach others how to be good is nobler—and less trouble.
—MARK TWAIN

2336. The secret of teaching is to appear to have known all your life what you learned this afternoon.

2337. The perfect teacher has the education of a college president, executive ability of a financier, humility of a deacon, discipline of a demon, adaptability of a chameleon, hope of an optimist, courage of a hero, wisdom of a serpent, gentleness of a dove, patience of Job, and persistence of the devil.

Technique

2338. The sting of a bee is a convincing argument that Spring has arrived, but the brush of a butterfly's wing tells the same story in a more pleasant manner.

2339. Mrs. Eleanor Roosevelt used to tell how to shake thousands of hands a day painlessly:

My cousin Teddy Roosevelt told my husband and me that the secret was never to let anyone else shake your hand. You shake theirs first. It works. I can shake 2,000 hands a day without strain.

Teen-age

2340. Perhaps the reason why teen-agers know all the answers is that they haven't heard all the questions yet.

2341. The nice thing about being a teen-ager these days is that you can pick up any magazine and have your suspicions about your parents confirmed.

2342. There is no teen-age problem, just a middle-age problem of how to stop middle-aged people from thinking there is a teen-age problem.

—Dr. Richard Asher

Television

2343. This world could use more vision and less television.

2344. Television should be kept in its proper place—beside us, before us, but never between us and the larger life.

—Sir Robert Fraser, Director General, Independent Television Authority, Britain

2345. One trouble with TV seems to be that the program directors do not know the difference between a beautiful singer and one who sings beautifully.

Temper

2346. He who loses his head is usually the last one to miss it.

2347. Too many people work up a head of steam before they find out what's cooking.

2348. The worst-tempered people I've ever met were people who knew they were wrong.

—Wilson Mizner

2349. A good thing to remember is that you can't save face if you lose your head!

Temperance

2350. Choose rather to punish your appetites than to be punished by them.

—TYRIUS MAXIMUS

2351. There is no difference between knowledge and temperance; for he who knows what is good and embraces it, who knows what is bad and avoids it, is learned and temperate. But they who know very well what ought to be done, and yet do quite otherwise, are ignorant and stupid.

—SOCRATES

Temptation

2352. When Satan knocks, I just send Christ to the door.

—BILLY GRAHAM, "Why I Believe in the Devil," *This Week*

2353. Take away the motive and you take away the sin.

—DON QUIXOTE

2354. When you meet temptation, turn to the right.

2355. Most people who fly from temptation usually leave a forwarding address.

2356. Don't worry about avoiding temptation—as you grow older it starts avoiding you.

2357. The man who is suddenly overpowered by temptation has probably been dreaming about it for a long time.

2358. William James, the psychologist and writer, believed that every person ought to do an unpleasant duty every day just to keep himself in moral trim. The moral "muscles" grow with exercise and use. If we want them to be strong for the times of great temptation, we must make them strong by using them to resist the ever recurring small temptations.

It is like the youth of mythology who picked up the newborn calf in the field. Every day he went out and lifted it in his arms. Since the calf's weight increased only a little each day, the youth did not notice the increase. By continuing to lift the calf day after day, his strength grew with the calf's weight so that he could still lift it after it had grown into a full-sized bull.

Thanksgiving Day

2359. Thanksgiving, to be truly Thanksgiving, is first thanks, then giving.

2360. I do recommend and assign Thursday the Twenty-Sixth Day of November next, to be devoted by the people of these States, to the Service of that great and glorious Being, who is the beneficent Author of all the good that was, that is, or that will be.

—GEORGE WASHINGTON, first national Thanksgiving Day Proclamation, November 26, 1789

2361. There is urgent need of the recovery of a more meaningful observance of Thanksgiving Day. Feasting, fellowship, and other social activities are not substitutes for thanksgiving to God. In these days, when many people forget God, and when there is a growing totalitarian control, which rules God out and seeks to enforce a pagan philosophy of life, we as a nation need to remind ourselves of our national heritage.

—BISHOP JOHN S. STAMM

2362. Don't fill your heart with bitterness over the things that go wrong in life. Fill your heart with gratitude for the things that are right. Forget those you may think have hurt you; remember those you know have helped you. And repay any good you receive with all the good you can give. And then you can be truly thankful on every Thanksgiving Day.

2363. In 1827, Sarah J. Hale, a magazine editor in Boston, Massachusetts, began a campaign urging the adoption of a uniform day for the observance of Thanksgiving throughout the country. She wrote editorials and personal letters to the governors of all the states and also wrote to the President.

Her campaign was eventually successful. On October 3, 1863, President Lincoln issued his first national Thanksgiving Proclamation, setting apart the last Thursday in November as Thanksgiving Day.

Today, it is a legal holiday in all states, the District of Columbia, Canal Zone, Guam, Puerto Rico and the Virgin Islands.

2364.   LET US GIVE THANKS

> Dear Father, as we bow our heads in thanks
> For these Thy gifts so bountifully bestowed:
> Our daily bread, and work that satisfies,
> And love that lights the way and shares the load—
> Help us to look beyond the feast for ways
> To bring all men the blessings that we know—
> Thy peace, and freedom to enjoy its boons;
> To move, unchallenged, safely to and fro,
> Freely without fear to speak and teach,
> To worship Thee as conscience points the way.
> Lord, give us grace to know how blest we are
> And make our lives one long Thanksgiving Day.
>
> —MAUREEN MURDOCH

Theory—Theories

2365.   Theory may raise a man's hopes but practice raises his income.

2366.   When I was research head of General Motors and wanted a problem solved, I'd place a table outside the meeting room with a sign: "Leave slide-rules here." If I didn't do that, I'd find some engineer reaching for his slide-rule. Then he'd be on his feet saying, "Boss, you can't do it."

> —CHARLES F. KETTERING,
> laying cornerstone of
> new Cleveland Engineer-
> ing & Scientific Center

Thinking. See also Thought—Thoughts

2367.   The true standard of quality is seated in the mind; those who think nobly are noble.

> —ISAAC BICKERSTAFFE

2368.   The trouble with most people is that they think with their hopes or fears or wishes rather than with their minds.

> —WALTER DURANTY

Thought—Thoughts

2369.   As a man thinketh in his heart, so is he.

> —KING SOLOMON

2370. There are no such things as idle thoughts. All your thinking works either for good or bad. Positive thinking can make you stronger. Negative thinking is exhausting.

—Arnold H. Glasow

Thrift

2371. What a married couple should save for their old age is each other.

2372. Many people have a hard time saving money because they never start until they run out.

2373. Saving money is still a pretty good idea. Who knows—it may be valuable again some day.

2374. A man who both spends and saves money is the happiest man, because he has both enjoyments.

—Dr. Samuel Johnson,
Boswell's Life, April 25,
1778

2375. WHAT SOME OF OUR PRESIDENTS
HAVE HAD TO SAY ABOUT THRIFT

By saving nickels and dimes thrifty persons lay the foundations of fortunes.

—James A. Garfield

Save your money and thrive or pay the price in poverty and disgrace.

—Andrew Jackson

While still young learn to save. When you're old no one will have to pass the hat for your benefit.

—Grover Cleveland

Prosperity is the fruit of labor. It begins with saving money.

—Abraham Lincoln

The men and women who pay attention to small savings become independent.

—James K. Polk

Wealth can be accumulated only in the earnings of industry and the savings of frugality.

—John Tyler

The habit of saving will prove a resource which cannot fail.

—Franklin Pierce

"Dear Harry— . . . Keep on gaining and put the reward in your little savings bank."

—Franklin Delano
Roosevelt

Save! You will find the little treasure a faithful servant.

—Ulysses S. Grant

The man who saves is the man who wins.

—Calvin Coolidge

No boy will ever succeed as a man who does not in his youth begin to save.

—Theodore Roosevelt

A man can protect his loved ones no better than by a savings account.

—William Howard Taft

Time

2376. Time misspent is not lived but lost.

—Thomas Fuller

2377. Counting time is not so important as making time count.

2378. One thing you can learn by watching the clock is that it passes the time by keeping its hands busy.

2379. There are two kinds of key men. When the work day begins and ends is of great importance to the first kind . . . and of no importance to the second.

2380. Distance is no longer a serious obstacle due to modern means of travel. But time remains unconquerable. It cannot be expanded, accumulated, mortgaged, hastened or retarded. It is the one thing completely beyond man's control.

2381. Have you ever stopped to figure the cost of the phrase, "Wait a minute"? If you're making $5,000 a year, every minute you have to wait costs nearly 5 cents. At $10,000 a year this figure doubles to nearly 10 cents a minute. And, if you should reach the $100,000-a-year category, your minutes will each be worth $1.

2382. While we usually think of dawn as the beginning of a new day, it is not actually the case, except in certain countries. The day begins at sunset with the Jews, Athenians, Chinese, Mohammedans, Italians, and Bohemians; at sunrise with the Babylonians, Syrians, Persians, and modern Greeks; at noon with ancient Egyptians and modern astronomers; at midnight with the English, French, Dutch, German, Portuguese, and Americans.

Tit for Tat

2383. If you get something for nothing, someone else gets nothing for something.

2384. Many irate citizens complained to the Better Business Bureaus about having merchandise mailed to them that they had not ordered and did not want—and then being billed for it. A Chicago physician received such a package with the following letter: "We are taking the liberty of sending you three exceptionally fine ties. Because these ties have the approval of thousands of discriminating dressers, we know you will like them. Please send $2."

The indignant doctor replied: "I am taking the liberty of sending you $2 worth of extra fine pills. These pills have helped thousands and I am sure you will appreciate my thoughtfulness in sending them. Please accept them in payment of the ties which you sent me recently."

Tolerance

2385. Tolerance is the oil which takes the friction out of life.
—WILBERT E. SCHEER

2386. Tolerance: that uncomfortable feeling that the other fellow may be right after all.

2387. It isn't necessary to blow out the other person's light to let your own shine.

2388. We all have weaknesses. But I have figured that others have put up with mine so tolerably that I would be much less than fair not to make a reasonable discount for theirs.
—WILLIAM ALLEN WHITE

2389. It is not tolerance that one is entitled to in America. It is the right of every citizen in America to be treated by other citizens as an equal.
—WENDELL L. WILLKIE

Tradition

2390. There is greatness in tradition—when it is kept alive and not worshipped in its tomb.

—Lord Wakefield

2391. Many traditions are not only absurd but tend to become evil, since they eventually burden men with an unchanging dogma that attempts to defy the ever-moving forces of time and nature.

—Lumir Victor Mika

2392. Tradition is not a tomb in which to hide from progress. It is rich ground well-tilled and warm with the sunshine of hope for an even greater future. Into it we drop the seeds of our aspirations for a better world and from it they grow strong and well-nourished and bear fruit and become new traditions to nourish others as time passes.

—Philip Ogilvie

Traffic, Automobile

2393. Drive safely and avoid the mourning after.

2394. The race to the crossing often ends in a dead heat.

2395. Many tombstones are carved by chiseling in traffic.

2396. Better to cross on the *green* than to be buried under it.

2397. Don't gamble in traffic—the cars may be stacked against you.

2398. Any automobile will last you a lifetime if you're not careful.

2399. If you think driving recklessly is funny, you may die laughing.

2400. One of life's mysteries is how the other half lives the way the other half drives.

2401. The place to stop drunken drivers is at the bend of the elbow, not at the curve on the highway.

2402. *Mathematics equation:* The number of blasts that come from auto horns in a traffic jam is equal to the sum of the squares at the wheels.

2403.   ON THE TOMBSTONE OF A PEDESTRIAN

This is the grave of Mike O'Day
Who died maintaining his right of way.
His right was clear, his will was strong,
But he's just as dead as if he'd been wrong.

Travel

2404. The best way to travel is to go well-heeled.

2405. Traveling in the company of those we love is home in motion.

—LEIGH HUNT

2406. Travel only with thy equals or thy betters; if there are none, travel alone.

—*A New Dictionary of Quotations on Historical Principles from Ancient and Modern Sources*, by H. L. MENCKEN (Alfred Knopf)

2407. Too often travel, instead of broadening the mind, merely lengthens the conversation.

—ELIZABETH DREW

2408. A good traveler is one who does not know where he is going and a perfect traveler does not know where he came from.

—LIN YUTANG

2409. No matter how widely you have traveled, you haven't seen the world if you have failed to look into the human hearts that inhabit it.

2410. When you travel, remember that a foreign country is not designed to make you comfortable. It is designed to make its own people comfortable.

—CLIFTON FADIMAN in *Holiday*

2411. Every now and then go away, have a little relaxation, for when you come back to your work your judgment will be surer since to remain constantly at work will cause you to lose power of judgment. . . . Go some distance away because then the work appears smaller, and more of it can be taken in at a glance, and a lack of harmony or proportion is more readily seen.

—LEONARDO DA VINCI

Trifle–Trifles. See *also* Little Things

2412. Little strokes fell great oaks.

—BENJAMIN FRANKLIN

2413. Trifles make perfection—and perfection is no trifle.

—Ascribed to MICHEL-
ANGELO BUONARROTI

2414.   Small ills are the fountains
             Of most of our groans.
             Men trip not on mountains,
             They stumble on stones.

—*From the Chinese*

2415. Only the little man sees no great possibilities in trifles. "The creation of a thousand forests is in one acorn," said Emerson. He but echoed the thought of Lao-tse, the ancient Chinese philosopher, who said that "the journey of a thousand miles begins with one pace."

The jerking of a pan full of dressed frogs' legs when touched by a knife led to the discovery of dynamic electricity.

The trembling lid of a teakettle boiling over the fire was the beginning of the steam engine.

A wet shirt hanging on a clothesline, inflated by the wind, suggested the balloon.

A spider's web strung across the corner of a garden inspired the idea of a suspension bridge.

A lantern swinging from the dome of a cathedral revealed the principle of the pendulum, by which for many centuries time has been accurately measured.

An apple falling from a tree led to the discovery and formulation of the laws of gravitation.

Wise old Doctor Johnson truly said: "There is nothing too little for so little a creature as man. It is by studying little things that we attain the great art of having as little misery and as much happiness as possible."

Trouble–Troubles

2416. Trouble hunters are not always trouble shooters.

2417. Borrowed trouble soon becomes a real possession.

2418. One trouble with trouble is that it usually starts out like fun.

2419. If a man could have half his wishes he would double his troubles.

—BENJAMIN FRANKLIN

2420. If you are big enough, your troubles will be smaller than you are.

2421. Trouble, like the hill ahead, straightens out when you advance upon it.

2422. In the presence of trouble, some people grow wings; others buy crutches.

—Harold W. Ruopp

2423. One way for a man to keep his head above water is to keep out of expensive dives.

2424. The best reason for holding your chin up when in trouble is that it keeps the mouth closed.

—Ivern Boyett

2425. Queer thing the way trouble acts on different people. Like hot weather it sours milk but sweetens apples.

2426. When it comes to trouble, the real problem is how to get out of the hole without making the hole any bigger.

2427. Trouble is the next best thing to enjoyment. There is no fate in the world so horrible as to have no share in either its joy or sorrow.

2428. If you will call your troubles "experiences," and remember that every experience develops some latent force within you, you will grow vigorous and happy, however adverse your circumstances may seem to be.

2429. A small trouble is like a pebble. Hold it too close to your eye, and it fills the whole world and puts everything out of focus. Hold it at proper viewing distance, and it can be examined and properly classified. Throw it at your feet, and it can be seen in its true setting, just one more tiny bump on the pathway to eternity.

—Celia Luce

Trust

2430. Confidence, like the soul, never returns whence it has once departed.

—Publilius Syrus

2431. It is better to suffer wrong than to do it, and happier to be sometimes cheated than not to trust.

—Dr. Samuel Johnson

Truth. See *also* Veracity

2432. Truth ill-timed is as bad as a lie.

—*German Proverb*

2433. Truth angers those whom it does not convince.

2434. Beware of a half-truth; it may be the wrong half.

2435. He that speaks truth must have one foot in the stirrup.

—*Turkish Proverb*

2436. The surest way to be lonesome is always to tell the truth.

2437. When truth stands in your way it's time to change directions.

2438. Truth is not only stranger than fiction, but nowadays it is a lot more decent.

2439. Truth always originates in a minority of one, and every custom begins as a broken precedent.

—Will Durant

2440. The highest compact two people can make is that there shall be Truth between them for evermore.

—Ralph Waldo Emerson

2441. Truth often suffers more by the heat of its defenders, than from the arguments of its opposers.

—William Penn, *Fruits of Solitude* (1693)

2442. Truth crushed to earth will rise again—another point of resemblance between it and a robust lie.

2443. It is one thing to wish to have truth on our side, and another thing to wish to be on the side of truth.

—Richard Whately

2444. Some disguised falsehoods represent the truth so well, that it would be bad judgment not to be deceived by them.

—François de la Rochefoucauld

2445. Such is the irresistible nature of truth that all it asks, and all that it wants, is the liberty of appearing. The sun needs no inscription to distinguish it from darkness.

—THOMAS PAINE

2446. All truth is safe and nothing else is safe; and he who keeps back the truth, or withholds it from men, from motives of expediency, is either a coward or a criminal, or both.

—MAX MULLER

2447. The truth is the truth, whether it is believed or not. It doesn't hurt the truth not to be believed, but it hurts you and me if we don't believe it.

—GEORGE H. HEPWORTH

2448. I believe I never knew any one who was not ashamed of the truth. Did you ever notice that a railroad company numbers its cars from 1,000, instead of from 1?

—E. W. HOWE

2449. Speaking the truth may be a very good thing, or it may be a very bad thing. Its merit depends on the spirit which prompts it, or which is shown in its utterance. Speaking the truth in love is always well; but speaking the truth in unkindness, or with a purpose of giving pain, or even in thoughtlessness when it may do harm to others, is never well. The question which we should ponder before we speak is, "Why should I say this?" "Because it is true," is not a sufficient answer to this question. Unless we can honestly say, "Because love prompts the utterance," or "Because I think God would have me say this as a means of good," we had better keep silence. It is many a time mean and cruel to speak the truth unnecessarily.

Tyranny

2450. There is a secret pride in every human heart that revolts at tyranny. You may order and drive an individual, but you cannot make him respect you.

—WILLIAM HAZLITT

2451. Tyrants commonly cut off the stairs by which they climb up unto their thrones . . . for fear that, if they still be left standing, others will come up the same way.

—THOMAS FULLER

2452. There is no week nor day nor hour when tyranny may not enter upon this country, if the people lose their roughness and spirit of defiance. Tyranny may always enter—there is no charm, no bar against it—the only bar against it is a large, resolute breed of men.

—WALT WHITMAN

Uncertainty

2453. When we are not sure, we are alive.

—GRAHAM GREENE

2454. Ancaeus, King of the Leleges in Samos, planted a vineyard; and so heavily did he oppress his slaves that one of them, it is said, prophesied to him that he would never live to taste the wine from the grapes. When the wine was made, the King sent for his slave, and said, "What do you think of your prophecy now?" The slave made answer, "There's many a slip 'twixt the cup and the lip." The words were scarcely uttered when Ancaeus was informed that a wild boar had broken into his vineyard, and was destroying it. Ancaeus, setting down the cup untasted, hastened to attack and drive out the boar; but he was killed in the encounter.

Understanding

2455. He who does not understand your silence will probably not understand your words.

—ELBERT HUBBARD

2456. Be not disturbed at being misunderstood; be disturbed rather at not being understanding.

—*Chinese Proverb*

2457. If you can keep your head when others all about you are losing theirs *then* maybe you don't understand the problem.

2458. The improvement of the understanding is for two ends: first, our own increase of knowledge; secondly, to enable us to deliver that knowledge to others.

—JOHN LOCKE

2459. We must always remember that knowledge of understanding is not the same thing as the understanding, which is the raw material of that knowledge. It is as different from understanding as the doctor's prescription for penicillin is different from penicillin.

—ALDOUS HUXLEY, *Tomorrow and Tomorrow and Tomorrow* (Harper)

2460. Nobody is fully understood by anybody. The best friends are not so well known to each other that the veil of personality does not come between them. A husband and wife live together half a century, yet, at the death of one, the other may discover that, after all, there were depths of character, thought, and feeling, never sounded in all those fifty years. We can never hope to understand our dearest comrade perfectly until we "know fully." That knowledge God has reserved for himself, in order that he may be a more perfect friend to man than any other.

Unhappiness

2461. Unhappiness is in not knowing what we want and killing ourselves to get it.

2462. Unhappiness indicates wrong thinking; just as ill health indicates a bad regimen.

—PAUL BOURGET

Uniformity

2463. Where all think alike, no one thinks very much.

—WALTER LIPPMANN

2464. That which is to be most desired in America is oneness and not sameness. Sameness is the worst thing that could happen to the people of this country. To make all people the same would lower their quality, but oneness would raise it.

—RABBI STEPHEN S. WISE

United Nations

2465. A new invention has hit the market—a United Nations pen which writes under protest.

2466. The United Nations was founded on the principle of world cooperation. It was assumed at San Francisco that the nations were prepared to live together and work together as good neighbors. They agreed that this was their purpose. We can only achieve full success in creating a decent world for all of mankind if the nations work together in that direction. There is no other way.

—TRYGVE LIE

United States Flag. See Flag, U. S.

Unselfishness

2467. Lord, keep me big enough to work with other people and let them get the credit.

2468. We cannot live only for ourselves. A thousand fibers connect us with our fellow men; and along those fibers, as sympathetic threads, our actions run as causes, and they come back to us as effects.
—HERMAN MELVILLE

2469. Do not be selfish. If you have something you do not want, and know someone who has no use for it, give it to that person. In this way you can be generous without expenditure of self-denial and also help another to be the same.
—ELBERT HUBBARD

2470. Be unselfish. That is the first and final commandment for those who would be useful, and happy in their usefulness. If you think of yourself only, you cannot develop because you are choking the sources of development, which is spiritual expansion through thought for others.
—DR. CHARLES W. ELIOT

Usefulness

2471. No life is pleasing to God that is not useful to man.

2472. Some men are like a clock on a roof; they are useful only to the neighbors.
—AUSTIN O'MALLEY

2473. In the humblest mortal there is a throne room. Its door unfolds silently, magically, whenever one dares to be creatively useful; to benefit his kind by breaking new paths, building new structures, awakening new deeds and restoring new ideals.
—JOHANN WOLFGANG VON GOETHE

Vacation

2474. The bigger the summer vacation the harder the fall.

2475. If you come home as happy as you leave, you have had a good vacation.

2476. The rainy days a man saves for usually seem to arrive during his vacation.

2477. Then there's this final observation about vacation hotels. Everything usually averages out about fifty-fifty. The weather, 50 percent rain, 50 percent sunshine. Half the meals are good, the other half only so-so. You usually like about half the people you meet and loathe the other half. And about half the women there are looking for husbands. And about half the husbands are looking for women.

Value–Values

2478. You may be overcharged for something good, but you never get a poor thing cheap.

2479. What we obtain too cheap, we esteem too lightly; it is dearness only that gives everything its value. Heaven knows how to put a proper price upon its goods; and it would be strange indeed if so celestial an article as Freedom should not be highly rated.

—Thomas Paine, *The Crisis,* 1776

2480. It is said that about 200 years ago, the tomb of the great conquerer Charlemagne was opened. The sight the workmen saw was startling. There was his body in a sitting position, clothed in the most elaborate of kingly garments, with a scepter in his bony hand. On his knee there lay a New Testament, with a cold lifeless finger pointing to *Mark 8:36;* "For what shall it profit a man, if he shall gain the whole world, and lose his own soul?"

2481. When you buy for price you can never be sure. It's unwise to pay too much, but it's worse to pay too little. When you pay too much, you lose a little money, that is all. But when you pay too little, you sometimes lose everything, because the thing you bought was incapable of doing the thing it was bought to do. If you deal with the lowest bidder, it is well to add something for the risk you run. And if you do that, you will have enough to pay for something better.

Vanity

2482. What renders the vanity of others insupportable is that it wounds our own.

—François de La Rochefoucauld, *Maxims,* 1665

2483. It may easily come to pass that a vain man may become proud and imagine himself pleasing to all when he is in reality a universal nuisance.

—BENEDICT SPINOZA

Veracity. See also Truth

2484. A lie, like a note, must be met at last.

2485. Show me a liar and I will show you a thief.

—Ancient Saying

2486. Liars begin by imposing upon others, but end by deceiving themselves.

—Ancient Proverb

2487. Persistently telling little white lies soon makes one color-blind.

2488. A man who says he is boss in his own home will lie about other things also.

2489. Telling white lies may be all right; but most fools can't tell black from white.

Verbosity

2490. The more ideas a man has the fewer words he takes to express them. Wise men never talk to make time, they talk to save it.

2491. In composing, as a rule, run your pen through every other word you have written; you have no idea what vigor it will give your style.

—SYDNEY SMITH

Vice

2492. One big vice in a man is apt to keep out a great many smaller ones.

—BRET HARTE

2493. Virtues are learned at mother's knee; vices are picked up at some other joint.

Victory

2494. The next dreadful thing to a battle lost is a battle won.

—DUKE OF WELLINGTON

2495. One may know how to gain a victory, and know not how to use it.

—BARCA THE
CARTHAGINIAN

2496. The greatest conqueror is he who overcomes the enemy without a blow.

—*Chinese Proverb*

2497. College alumni who take such a fierce pride in the prowess of their Alma Mater's football team could well heed the words of one of polo's great players, Devereux Milburn, who said: "It is nonsense to say that the 'will to win' is all that matters. It is the battle—the contest—that counts, not the score. If two meet, one must win and one must lose. But they can both have a great afternoon."

Violence

2498. Violence does even justice unjustly.

—THOMAS CARLYLE

2499. Power will accomplish more by gentle than by violent means, and calmness will best enforce the imperial mandates.

—CLAUDIAN

Virtue

2500. Woman's virtue is man's greatest invention.

—CORNELIA OTIS SKINNER

2501. Virtue, with some women, is but the precaution of locking doors.

—LEMONLEY

2502. While virtue is its own reward, most people are looking for a better offer.

2503. Virtue is not to be considered in the light of mere innocence, or abstaining from doing harm; but as the exertion of our faculties in doing good.

—SAMUEL BUTLER

Vision

2504. Only eyes washed by tears can see clearly.

—DR. LOUIS L. MANN

2505. It is never safe to look into the future with eyes of fear.

—Edward H. Harriman

2506. We cry loudly for a man of vision and when we get one we call him a visionary.

2507. We do not see things *with* our eyes—we see them *through* our eyes and *with* our minds.

2508. A vision without a task is a dream;
A task without vision is drudgery;
A vision and a task is the hope of the world.

Vote—Votes—Voting

2509. Always vote for a principle, though you vote alone, and you may cherish the sweet reflection that your vote is never lost.

—John Quincy Adams

2510. In this Republic a voter who stays away from the polls at an election cannot be classified as a non-voter. Such an absentee type of voter votes "for" what he would vote against, were he interested sufficiently to go to the polls and declare his intentions.

Wages

2511. Our rocket experts could learn a lot by studying the wage-price spiral.

2512. Of course, it is not the employer who pays wages. He only handles the money. It is the product that pays wages and it is the management that arranges the production so that the product may pay the wages.

—Henry Ford

2513. After all, what the worker does is buy back from those who finance him the goods that he himself produces. Pay him a wage that enables him to buy, and you will fill your market with ready consumers.

—James J. Davis

War

2514. War is not an act of God but a crime of man.

—Cordell Hull

2515. There are no warlike peoples—just warlike leaders.

—Ralph J. Bunche

2516. War is not merely the willingness to endure suffering but to inflict it.

2517. Since wars begin in the minds of men, it is in the minds of men that the defense of peace must be constructed.

—CLEMENT ATTLEE

2518. If there must be warfare in the world, let it be between good and evil and not between nations.

2519. It makes little difference how magnificent are our new buildings or how impressive are our private kingdoms. If no answer is found to war, all men will die poor.

—NORMAN COUSINS

2520. Justice is as strictly due between neighbor nations as between neighbor citizens. A highwayman is as much a robber when he plunders in a gang, as when single; and a nation that makes an unjust war is only a great gang.

—BENJAMIN FRANKLIN

2521.   THE LITANY OF THE "POILU"

The French soldiers are said to find both amusement and consolation in the following set of aphorisms:

Of two things one is certain: Either you're mobilized or you're not mobilized.

If you're not mobilized there is no need to worry; if you are mobilized, of two things one is certain: Either you're behind the lines or you're on the front.

If you're behind the lines there is no need to worry; if you're on the front, of two things one is certain: Either you're resting in a safe place or you're exposed to danger.

If you're resting in a safe place, there is no need to worry; if you're exposed to danger, of two things one is certain: Either you're wounded or you're not wounded.

If you're not wounded there is no need to worry; if you are wounded, of two things one is certain: Either you're wounded seriously or you're wounded slightly.

If you're wounded slightly there is no need to worry; if you're wounded seriously, of two things one is certain: Either you recover or you die.

If you recover there is no need to worry; if you die you can't worry.

Waste

2522. Short as life is, we make it still shorter by the careless waste of time.

—Victor Hugo

2523. A man who dares to waste one hour of life has not discovered the value of life.

—Charles Darwin

2524. Waste is worse than loss. The time is coming when every person who lays claim to ability will keep the question of waste before him constantly. The scope of thrift is limitless.

—Thomas A. Edison

Weakness

2525. A weak mind is like a microscope, which magnifies trifling things but cannot receive great ones.

—Lord Chesterfield

2526. You cannot run away from a weakness; you must some time fight it out or perish; and if that be so, why not now, and where you stand?

—Robert Louis Stevenson

2527. The more weakness, the more falsehood; strength goes straight; every cannonball that has in it hollows or holes, goes crooked. Weaklings must lie.

—Jean Paul Richter

2528. For fifteen hundred years the great wall of China stood unconquered. One day, by the gate, a guard was drunk, and a simple, harmless-looking shepherd came along and engaged him in conversation, corrupted and bribed him. The guard left the gate a moment, it was thrown back and hordes of barbarians poured in. They could not overcome China by bringing force against the wall, but they gained entrance through one man who was weak.

—Dr. Norman Vincent Peale

Wealth

2529. He is rich who owes nothing

2530. He does not possess wealth that allows it to possess him.
—BENJAMIN FRANKLIN

2531. The prosperous man does not know whether he is loved.
—LUCAN

2532. It is not wealth but the arrogance of wealth that offends the poor.

2533. The use of money is all the advantage there is in having money.
—BENJAMIN FRANKLIN

2534. It is only when the rich are sick that they fully feel the impotence of wealth.
—CHARLES C. COLTON

2535. The sole secret of being well-heeled is to get on your feet and keep on your toes.

2536. God shows His contempt for wealth by the kind of persons He selects to receive it.

2537. Some people think they are worth a lot of money just because they happen to have it.

2538. Count your assets. If you have a clear conscience, a good liver, three good friends and a happy home; if your heart has kept its youth and your soul its honesty—cheer up!—you are still one of life's richest millionaires.

2539. The man who makes it the habit of his life to go to bed at nine o'clock, usually gets rich and is always reliable. Of course, going to bed does not make him rich—I merely mean that such a man will in all probability be up early in the morning and do a big day's work, so his weary bones put him to bed early. Rogues do their work at night. Honest men work by day. It's all a matter of habit, and good habits in America make any man rich. Wealth is largely a result of habit.
—JOHN JACOB ASTOR

Wickedness

2540. It is bad enough to be bad, but to be bad in bad taste is unpardonable.
—AGNES REPPLIER

2541. Wickedness is a myth invented by good people to account for the curious attractiveness of others.

—OSCAR WILDE

Widowhood

2542. The tears of a young widow lose their bitterness when wiped by the hands of a new love.

2543. It is not easy to be a widow: one must resume all the modesty of girlhood, without being allowed to even feign its ignorance.

—MME. DE GIRARDIN

2544. Big empty houses lived in by widows are often pitiful monuments to tired men who worked themselves to death so their widows some day could have big empty houses.

Wife—Wives

2545. All married women are not wives.

—*Japanese Proverb*

2546. A wife is a gift bestowed upon man to reconcile him to the loss of Paradise.

—JOHANN WOLFGANG VON GOETHE

2547. One of the chief reasons that widowers get married so quickly is because they find out that it bankrupts them to pay for the work that a wife has done for her board and clothes.

—DOROTHY DIX

Willingness

2548. If you're too big to willingly do little things, you are probably too little to be trusted with big things.

2549. Never shrink from anything which your business calls you to do. The man who is above his business may one day find his business above him.

Will Power

2550. People do not lack strength; they lack will.

—VICTOR HUGO

2551. Some folks' will power becomes stagnant from lack of exercise.

2552. When our vices quit us we flatter ourselves with the belief that it is we who quit them.

—François de la
Rochefoucauld

Wisdom

2553. Wisdom comes by disillusionment.

—George Santayana

2554. Be wiser than other people if you can; but do not tell them so.

—Lord Chesterfield

2555. A man doesn't attain wisdom until he recognizes that he is no longer indispensable.

—Richard E. Byrd

2556. A man remains wise so long as he seeks wisdom. The moment he thinks he has found it, he becomes a fool.

2557. It seems to me we can never give up longing and wishing while we are thoroughly alive. There are certain things we feel to be beautiful and good, and we must hunger after them.

—George Eliot

Wit and Humor

2558. No mind is thoroughly well organized that is deficient in a sense of humor.

—Samuel Taylor
Coleridge

2559. Humor is the lubricating oil of business. It prevents friction and wins good will.

2560. Wit is a zero added to our moral qualities; but which, standing alone, represents nothing.

—C. Jordan

2561. The fellow who tries to be the life of the party by telling jokes, really needs more effective gags—right across the mouth.

2562. A companion once reminded Henry Erskine that "the pun is the lowest form of wit."

"Truly," replied Erskine, "for it is the foundation of all wit!"

Woman—Women

2563. Women rouge that they may not blush.

—Italian Proverb

2564. Man has his will; but woman has her way.

—Oliver Wendell Holmes

2565. Woman once made equal to man becomes his superior.

—Socrates

2566. A woman may suffer in many ways. But never in silence.

2567. If you don't think women are explosive, try dropping one.

2568. Friendship between women is only a suspension of hostilities.

—French Proverb

2569. Women may not be much, but they are the best other sex we have.

2570. Women like a strong silent man because they think he is listening.

2571. All women think they're different. That's why they're so much alike.

2572. A psychologist reports that out of every five women-haters, only one is a man. The other four are women.

2573. There are two kinds of women—one who wants to correct a man's mistakes and the other who wants to be one.

2574. The difference between a model woman and a woman model is that one is a bare possibility and the other is a naked fact.

2575. Women, collectively, are divided into four classes: the mental, the temperamental, accidental, and experimental.

2576. A wise woman puts a grain of sugar into everything she says to a man, and takes everything he says to her with a grain of salt.

2577. The trouble with women in business is that if you treat 'em like men, they cry. If you treat 'em like women, darned if they don't get the best of you.

2578. Dante adored woman; Wordsworth commended her; Shakespeare loved her; Tolstoi planted her in sunshine and watered her with his tears, only to tear her up by the roots at last; Burns smiled at her; Moore succumbed to her; Henry James studied her; de Maupassant thought her wicked, but interesting; Bourget dissected her; Balzac understood her.

Women's Clubs

2579. Most women have dropped their rolling pins and taken up clubs.

—RAYMOND DUNCAN

2580. *Woman's club member at meeting:* "If I had known the crowd was going to be this small I wouldn't have worn my girdle."

Word—Words

2581. Without knowing the force of words, it is impossible to know men.

—CONFUCIUS

2582. It is with words as with sunbeams—the more they are condensed, the deeper they burn.

—ROBERT SOUTHEY

2583. The power of words is immense. A well-chosen word has often sufficed to stop a flying army, to change defeat into victory, and to save an empire.

—ÉMILE DE GIRARDIN

2584. There is a great difference between the right word and one that is similar but all wrong. For instance, you can call a woman a kitten, but not a cat; a mouse, but not a rat; a chicken, but not a hen; a duck, but not a goose; a vision, but not a sight.

2585. Never fear big, long words. Big, long words name little things. All big things have little names such as life and death, peace and war, or dawn, day, night, hope, love, home. Learn to use little words in a big way. It is hard to do, but they say what you mean. When you don't know what they mean, use big words—that often fools little people.

2586. THE POWER OF WORDS

A careless word may kindle strife.
A cruel word may wreck a life,
A bitter word may hate instill;
A brutal word may smite and kill,
A gracious word may smooth the way;
A joyous word may light the day.
A timely word may lessen stress;
A loving word may heal and bless.

—*Author Unknown*

Work

2587. The victory of success is half won when one gains the habit of work.

—SARAH A. BOLTON

2588. Some folks are like blisters. They show up after the work is done.

2589. It is the biggest mistake to think you are working for someone else.

—NASHUA CAVALIER

2590. The hardest work in the world to do is that which should have been done yesterday.

2591. Work as if you were to live 100 years. Pray as if you were to die tomorrow.

—BENJAMIN FRANKLIN

2592. I never did anything worth doing by accident, nor did any of my inventions come by accident.

—THOMAS A. EDISON

2593. Nature seems determined to make us work. The less hair we have to comb, the more face we have to wash.

2594. We work day after day, not to finish things; but to make the future better . . . because we will spend the rest of our lives there.

—CHARLES F. KETTERING

2595. Often we hear the expression, "a fair day's work for a fair day's pay." 'Twould be better if we talked about a good day's work for a good day's pay.

2596. Work is all important because that is the only visible and intelligible excuse for our existence. Man expresses the forces with which he is endowed. Work is the most satisfying experience of the day.

—DAVID SARNOFF

2597. Man must work. That is certain as the sun. But he may work grudgingly or he may work gracefully; he may work as a man, or he may work as a machine. There is no work so rude, that he may not exalt it; no work so impassive, that he may not breathe a soul into it; no work so dull that he may not enliven it.

—HENRY GILES

2598. "Work does more to dignify the individual than high office or public praise!" declared John Ruskin, the English critic. "Young men and women who learn to respect work, and who enter into it with eagerness and abandon, will reach maturity with a solid foundation for happy and useful living."

Work is a tonic that tones the system for play.

Work is not only a way to make a living, it is the way to make a life.

If "all work and no play makes Jack a dull boy," then all play and no work makes Jack a dangerous boy.

Work with the hands can only result from work with the brain, for the brain is the master of the hands.

Work is not merely a means to an end, it is an end itself. Blessed is he who loves his work, for he shall know great joy from day to day.

World, The

2599. We can only change the world by changing men.

—CHARLES WELLS

2600. This may be a man's world, but women are partly to blame.

2601. If it's such a small world, why does it take so much of our money to run it?

World Relations

2602. Friendship is the only cement that will ever hold the world together.

—WOODROW WILSON

2603. There should be no inferiors and no superiors for true world friendship.

—CARLOS P. ROMULO

2604. There never has been, there isn't now and there never will be, any race of people on the earth fit to serve as masters over their fellow men.

—FRANKLIN D. ROOSEVELT

2605. It is permissible for a man to be an American first; it is inexcusable for him to be an American first and last. We are citizens of the world. No longer can we dismiss poverty, injustice, or exploitation anywhere in the world by saying, "That's their funeral." It's liable to be ours, too.

—CHARLES B. TEMPLETON

Worry

2606. Worry often gives a small thing a big shadow.
—*Swedish Proverb*

2607. To take a great weight off your mind, discard your halo.

2608. Don't upset yourself more than a quarter's worth over a lost quarter.

2609. If you are standing upright, don't worry if your shadow is crooked.

—*Chinese Proverb*

2610. Worry never robs tomorrow of its sorrows; it only saps today of its strength.

—A. J. CRONIN

2611. If you really want to test your memory, just try to think of the things that were worrying you last week at this time.

2612. There is no reason to worry about your station in life because somebody will always tell you where to get off.

2613. Worry affects the circulation, the heart, the glands, the whole nervous system, and profoundly affects the health. I have never known a man who died from overwork, but many who died from doubt.

—DR. CHARLES H. MAYO

2614. The word "worry" is derived from an old Anglo-Saxon word meaning to strangle or to choke. How well-named the emotion is has been demonstrated again and again in persons who have lost their effectiveness due to the stultifying effect of anxiety and apprehension. A certain well-controlled carefreeness may well be an asset. Normal sensible concern is an important attribute of the mature person. But worry frustrates one's best functioning.

—Dr. Norman Vincent
Peale

2615.   It is not the work, but the worry,
That drives all sleep away,
As we toss and turn and wonder
About the cares of the day.
Do we think of the hands' hard labour,
Or the steps of the tired feet?
Ah, no! but we plan and wonder
How to make both ends meet.

It is not the work, but the worry,
That makes us troubled and sad,
That makes us narrow and sordid
When we should be cheery and glad.
There's a shadow before the sunlight,
And ever a cloud in the blue,
The scent of the rose is tainted,
The notes of the song are untrue.

It is not the work, but the worry,
That makes the world grow old,
That numbers the years of its children
Ere half their story is told;
That weakens their faith in heaven
And the wisdom of God's great plan.
Ah! 'tis not the work, but the worry
That breaks the heart of man.

—Anonymous

Writing. See Authorship

Youth

2616.   If youth only knew; if age only could.

2617.   You are young at any age if you are planning for tomorrow.

2618.   Impatience and not inexperience is the greatest handicap of youth.

—Arnold H. Glasow

2619.   It must be wonderful to be young enough to know *every-thing!*

2620. All of us must be drunk once, youth is drunkenness without wine.

—JOHANN WOLFGANG VON
GOETHE

2621. A man that is young in years may be old in hours, if he has lost no time.

—FRANCIS BACON

2622. A boy has two jobs. One is just being a boy. The other is growing up to be a man.

—HERBERT HOOVER

2623. Men and nations can only be reformed in their youth; they become incorrigible as they grow old.

—JEAN JACQUES ROUSSEAU

2624. A boy becomes a young man when he stops asking his father for money and requests a loan.

2625. There is nothing wrong with the younger generation that the older generation didn't outgrow.

2626. If the younger generation doesn't know where it is going, it must be following in its father's footsteps.

2627. Yes, the young people of today are tomorrow's leaders, no doubt. But sometimes I wonder whether they are going to be followed or chased.

2628. A boy is a bank where you may deposit your most precious treasures—the hard-won wisdom, the dreams for a better world. A boy can guard and protect these, and perhaps invest them wisely and win a profit—a larger one than you ever dreamed.

2629. For as I like a young man in whom there is something of the old, so I like an old man in whom there is something of the young; and he who follows this maxim, in body will possibly be an old man, but he will never be an old man in mind.

—CICERO

2630. I leave everything to the young men. You've got to give youthful men authority and responsibility if you are going to build up an organization. Otherwise you'll be the boss yourself and you won't leave anything behind you.

—A. P. GIANNINI (at the
age of 70)

2631. A boy is the person who is going to carry on what you have started . . .

He is going to sit at your desk in Congress and occupy your place on the Supreme Court bench . . .

All your work is for him, and the fate of the nations and humanity is in his hands.

So, it might be well to pay him some attention.

2632. It has been truly said that youth is not entirely a time of life. It is a state of mind, a temper of the will, a quality of the imagination. We do not grow old by living a number of years. We grow old by deserting our ideals and usefulness, by losing the will and the faith to accomplish. Years may wrinkle the skin and grey the hair, but to give up interest and work wrinkles the soul. We are as young as our faith and hope, and as old as our fears and despairs. If you want to stay young, keep an unbounded faith in the future. Remember that America was built by people who work, not by those who quit working.

2633. ANOTHER TRY AT DEFINING BOYS

After a male baby has grown out of long clothes and triangles and has acquired pants, and freckles, and so much dirt that relatives do not dare to kiss it between meals, it becomes a *boy*.

A boy can swim like a fish, run like a deer, climb like a squirrel, balk like a mule, bellow like a bull, eat like a pig or act like a jackass, according to climatic conditions.

He is a piece of skin stretched over an appetite. A noise, covered with smudges.

He is called a tornado because he comes at the most unexpected times, hits the most unexpected places, and leaves everything a wreck behind him.

He is a growing animal of superlative promise, to be fed and watered, and kept warm.

He is a joy forever, a periodic nuisance, the problem of our times, and hope of a nation. Every boy is evidence that God is not discouraged by man.

Were it not for boys, the newspapers would go unread, and a thousand picture shows would go bankrupt.

Boys are useful in running errands. A boy can easily do the family errands with the aid of five or six adults. The zest with which a boy does an errand is equalled only by the speed of a turtle on a July day.

A boy is a natural spectator. He watches parades, fires, fights, ball games, automobiles, boats, and airplanes with equal fervor, but not the clock.

Boys faithfully imitate their dads in spite of all efforts to teach them good manners.

A boy, if not washed too often and if kept in a cool quiet place after each accident, will survive broken bones, hornets, swimming holes, fights and nine helpings of pie.

—*The Rotarian*

Zeal

2634. Zeal is fit only for wise men but is found mostly in fools.
—*Ancient Proverb*

2635. Too much zeal is a bad soldier who fires before the word of command.

2636. There is no zeal so intemperate and cruel as that which is backed by ignorance.
—STILSON HUTCHINS

2637. A zealous soul without meekness is like a ship in a storm, in danger of wrecks. A meek soul without zeal is like a ship in a calm, that moves not so fast as it ought.
—JAMES M. MASON

2638. The heights by great men reached and kept
Were not attained by sudden flight,
But they while their companions slept
Were toiling upward in the night.
—HENRY WADSWORTH
LONGFELLOW

2639. Zeal without knowledge is like fire without a grate to contain it; like a sword without a hilt to wield it by; like a high-bred horse without a bridle to guide him. It speaks without thinking, acts without planning, seeks to accomplish a good end without the adoption of becoming mean.
—JULIUS BATE

Subject Index

(Numbers in the index refer to **selections** in the text, *not to page numbers*.)

Interpreter–Interpreters, 2087
Interview, Sales, 2150
Intimidation, 1298
Intolerance, 146, *1459, 1460*
Intoxication, 334, 1130, 1700, 1953, 2078, 2401, 2528, 2620
Introduction of speaker, 623
Invalid–Invalids, 1286
Invalidism, 1302, 2141
Invention–Inventions, 293, *1461–1463,* 1475, 1819, 1821, 1898, 2011, 2042, 2254, 2465, 2500, 2592
Inventor–Inventors, 297, 1461, 1727
Investment–Investments, 376, 1116, *1464–1466,* 1570, 1888, 2628
Irish, 173
Iron, 1395
Iron bars, 1156
Irreparability, 796
Irresponsibility, 262
Irritation, 9
Islamism, 1237
Isolation, 1419
Israel (Ancient), 375
Israelites, 231
Israel, Redemption of, 1258
Israel, State of, 1258
Italy, 1867
Ivory tiles, 481
Ivory Towers, 1366

J

Jackass, 94, 401, 2633
Jade, 51
Jail–Jails, 37, 358, 601, 975, 980, 1492, 2033, 2167, 2272
Japan, 881
Japanese, 1857
Jealousy, 229, 1146, 1168, *1467–1470,* 1810, 2287
Jew–Jews, 2382
Jewel–Jewels, 744
Jewelry, 1731
Jewish people, The, 1258
Jewish Sabbath, 2097
Job application, 1007
Job–Jobs, 1543
Joint bank account, 327, 328
Joint effort, 247, 447, *1471, 1472,* 1839
Joint ownership, 1643
Joke–Jokes, 1321, 2561
Journalism, 278, 427, *1473–1476,* 1928, 2002
Journey–Journeys, 2415
Joy, 25, 557, 1434, 2087, 2218, 2220, 2247, 2427, 2586, 2598

Joy-riding, Financial, 2257
Judaism, 1237
Judge–Judges, 508, 567, 740, 807, 1389, *1477–1479,* 1519–1521
Judgment, 107, 454, 461, 829, 938, *1480–1482,* 1726, 1734, 1832, 1983, 2062, 2411
Judiciary. See *Judge–Judges*
July, Fourth of. See *Fourth of July*
Jungle–Jungles, 560
Junk, 1946
Jury, 1484
Justice, 319, 638, 737, 868, 1124, 1136, 1229, 1258, 1389, 1477, *1483–1485,* 1512, 1514, 1520, 2520
Justice, Miscarriage of, 810
Justification, 926, 1057, 1223, 1671, 1896
Juvenile delinquency, 355, *1486–1489*
Juxtaposition, 123, 817, 922

K

"Kentucky Cardinal," 412
Kenyon College, 463
Key–Keys, 64
Keyhole–Keyholes, 2307
Key personnel, 2379
Kill–Killing, 847
Kindergarten, 1059
Kindliness, 2294
Kindness, 361, 411, 480, 533, 737, 799, 1307, *1490–1492,* 1501, 2132
Kindness, Human, 426
Kind words, 1492
King–Kings, 1267, 1917
Kiss–Kisses–Kissing, 1321, *1493–1495,* 1565, 1626
Kite–Kites, 1073
Kitten–Kittens, 2584
Kiwanis Club, 644
Knave–Knavery, 1127
Knee joint, 2493
Knee–Knees, 789, 940, 1265, 1966
Kneeling, 789, 1966
Knife–Knives, 258, 2016, 2327
Know-how, *1496–1498,* 2313
Know-it-all, 711
Knowledge, 23, 262, 358, 394, 589, 708, 734, 863, 1065, 1345, *1499–1502,* 1696, 1983, 2065, 2274, 2333, 2351, 2458, 2459, 2616, 2639

L

Label–Labels–Labelling, 413, 439
Labor. See also *Capital-Labor,* 295, 475, *1503–1505,* 2513

Author and Source Index

(Numbers in the index refer to **selections** in the text, *not to page numbers.*)

$\mathcal{N}$ ames and Personalities

(Numbers in the index refer to **selections** in the text, *not to page numbers*.)